YANKEE® Magazine's

Get More
THAN YOUR
MONEY'S
WORTH
EVERY TIME

1,501
SECRET BARGAINS,
MONEY-SAVERS,
AND FREEBIES

This book has previously been published as *Yankee Magazine's Living Well on a Shoestring* (© 2000 by Yankee Publishing Inc.)

© 2001 by Yankee Publishing Inc.

Illustrations © 2000 by Yankee Publishing Inc.

Printed in the United States of America on acid-free ∞, recycled paper ♺

ISBN 0–89909–386–8 hardcover

Distributed to the book trade by St. Martin's Press

2   4   6   8   10   9   7   5   3   1   hardcover

YANKEE. **Magazine's**

Get More Than Your Money's Worth Every Time

YANKEE BOOKS STAFF

EDITOR: Christian Millman
COVER DESIGNER: Tara Long

YANKEE PUBLISHING STAFF

PUBLISHING DIRECTOR: Jamie Trowbridge

BOOK EDITOR: Lori L. Baird

CONTRIBUTING WRITERS: Linda Buchanan Allen, Larry Bean, Anne Cahill, Tom Cavalieri, Tom Donnelly, Susan Gagnon, Mary Johnson, Rose Kennedy, Lynn Naliboff, Chris Peterson, Michelle Seaton

EDITORIAL CONSULTANTS: Amesbury Quilting Group, Elissa Barr, Chris Bean, Ellen Bean, James Bean, Julie Bean, Diane Bleu, Lea Bohrer, Elizabeth B. Buchanan, Karen B. Buchanan, Ann-Marie Cunniff, Mary Daly, Jack Falla, Carol Frost, Madelyn Gray, Geoff Harlan, Jill Heath, Paula Hoyt, Ed Jensen, Mildred Jensen, Margaret Monto, Carolyn Muller, Nancy Musil, Carol O'Keefe, Kathleen O'Rourke, Carol Peterson, Cindy Roach, Becky Schulz, Janet Schwalm, Don Seaton, Nancy Seaton, Stephen Sickles, Catherine Smith, Dexter Van Zile, Debi Wheeler-Bean, Carole Wilson, TJ Wilson, Lauri Zack, Laurie Zwaan

BOOK DESIGNER: Eugenie S. Delaney

ILLUSTRATOR: Michael Gellatly

INDEXER: Nanette Bendyna

FACT CHECKER: Tom Cavalieri

COPY EDITOR: Barbara Jatkola

PROOFREADERS: Barbara Jatkola, Mary Johnson, Lynn Naliboff

CONTENTS

PART I

The Frugal Philosophy

THE ART OF LIVING (WELL) ON LESS

*A*s YOU READ through these pages of clever ideas for saving money, take a few seconds to contemplate an amazing concept: Somebody, somewhere, came up with each of these ideas, and somebody had to try each one—storing magazines in empty cereal boxes, decorating a light switch plate with wrapping paper for a low-cost Christmas look, or starting a local babysitting cooperative.

So the way we see it, that means there is an ingenious, frugal Yankee behind every single idea contained in this book. Whether it be travel, cooking, gardening, or finances, someone knows (or knew) what it means to live well on the proverbial shoestring.

Throughout the book, we share tips, quips, and anecdotes in the "It Worked for Me" boxes. These folks use their own words to describe their ideas, giving each one an individual perspective. Kathleen O'Rourke of Long Valley, New Jersey, for example, tells how to make an Easter egg with real grass hair, while Amy Witsil of Chapel Hill, North Carolina, remembers her father's Sunday morning treat of ice cream in orange juice.

We acknowledge our indebtedness to various editorial consultants on the credits page. But in these opening chapters of *Get More Than Your Money's Worth Every Time,* we take the first-person approach even further. Here you'll meet a few folks who we think embody the spirit and the passion of Yankee frugality. Elizabeth Eulinger, for example, represents the importance of consistent and mindful savings. A retired schoolteacher, she was able to save enough money to buy a dream mansion. Bob Grimac shows the importance of striving to live well with what you have. He's happy to scavenge a discarded garden hose in working order on a neighborhood sidewalk.

Each of these role models demonstrates that there are many paths to living well on a shoestring. Like them, you can adopt the strategies that suit you best—or think of a new one.

CHAPTER 1

LIVING AND ACTING FRUGALLY

WHAT FRUGALITY ISN'T

*W*e've long suspected that Yankee frugality can get in your blood and stay there long after you, or your family, has moved to another area of the country. But now we have proof.

Oh, it's not empirical evidence. But we do have Bob Kennedy, contributing writer Rose Kennedy's father. When it comes to living well on less, Bob is the quintessential Yankee. About 20 years ago, when he found some navy hatch covers at a salvage yard, for example, he bought them up for a few bucks apiece, refinished them, and used them to top "arty" coffee tables his adult children still cherish. For years, he was known as "the watch man," because he bought a machine that would wash watch parts and used it to fix hundreds of broken watches people sold or gave to him—all at a fraction of the cost of buying new ones. When his seven daughters wanted to have their ears pierced in the 1970s, Bob found out how much the jeweler was charging, then went out and purchased his own piercing gun. He did the job himself—seven for the price of two. After a Big Lots discount department store came to his area, he never purchased cereal, bread, light bulbs, or wrapping paper at retail prices again—which allowed him to buy extra to give to the local food pantry.

Most of Bob's strategies never made it into this book because they aren't things just anyone can do, but interestingly enough, his name and ideas kept coming up in our conversations as we worked to define Yankee frugality.

Interesting because Bob has lived his entire life in Maryland, New Jersey, Pennsylvania, and Virginia. It was his father's family that was from Massachusetts. Bob could say he inherited his Yankee frugality, but his example also proves an important point: Yankee-style frugality is about living well on less, not about where you live.

And there are so many other things that frugality is not. It is not cheapness—we're not talking about buying shoddy goods or inflicting twice-used tea bags on your guests. Nor do we suggest cheating and calling it frugality—no taking from other people so you can have more, no lifting of saltshakers from restaurants, towels from hotels, or heirlooms from unsuspecting relatives. No, Yankee frugality means that you ferret out the best deals, the offers that are there for the taking, or the loopholes that work in your favor without slighting anyone else.

There are other habits that the word *frugal* does not embrace. Try to forget all those great stories about wealthy old friends trying to outmaneuver each other when the tab arrives or the man down the street who'd do anything to avoid tipping the paperboy—they don't have a place in the frugal attitude. Frugality has nothing to do with meanness. In fact, the true spirit of frugality often allows you to be more generous. Whipping up your own batch of sun-dried tomatoes, for example, might allow you to share a jar with several friends—for the price of one tiny package at the gourmet food store. Using cast-off materials for the garden might mean that you can plant twice as much to share.

Sometimes frugality even means planning these "surprise" windfalls. In fact, frugality always has a method behind the madness—going to a free horse show instead of a movie so that you can spend more money on art supplies, for example. There's always a reason for being frugal—even if it's just that the cheaper way is every bit as good as, or even superior to, the more expensive one. But *frugality* is not synonymous with odd undertakings or bizarre behaviors. Of course, there are probably a few so-called frugal people who have millions of dollars salted away but choose to live on canned beans and wear mismatched shoes and moth-eaten cardigans. But that's not what Yankee frugality aspires to—some penny-pinching ideal regardless of your income. Far from it. The frugal Yankee's goal is to live within your means so you'll have the resources to accomplish what you want to achieve.

Which isn't to say frugality can't be a bit, shall we say, quirky. A few tips we give in later chapters spring to mind—displaying long-stemmed flowers in a rubber boot, for example, or supporting tomatoes with a bra. But these quirks will help you get good results while spending less money—and to show off your resourcefulness and imagination while you're at it.

Unique expressions of frugality remind us that different people are *supposed* to do the frugality thing differently. Nowhere is it written that to be frugal, you must melt slivers of soap into a new bar or save aluminum foil scraps in a ball. You need not save money at every single opportunity just because you can. If you can afford gourmet coffee from the shop down the street every morning, cable television, or a $300 outfit and that's what you don't want to live without, purchase it with pleasure, and never look back. You won't lose your frugal credentials! Frugality means deciding what you, with your unique values, likes, and dislikes, want most of all. By the same token, when you decide what you must do without to have what you want, do it without complaining. Once you've pinpointed where you can best save or spend, you're well on your way to thinking and acting like a frugal Yankee.

WHAT FRUGALITY IS

Now that you know what frugality isn't, you can spend your time reading the next few hundred pages to find out what frugality *is*. Essentially, it's just what you might think: finding clever ways to save money. And there's no dollar limit. Frugality is for everyone, from the people who use silver saltshakers for holiday candleholders to those who save $5,000 on an automobile by writing letters to clean up their credit rating. Some of us have longer shoestrings than others.

But frugality always involves mindfulness—paying attention to how and where your money goes and making conscious decisions about how to spend it. These tactics can be as simple as keeping a small rock in your car ashtray to weight down that collection of receipts you accumulate riding around town buying gas, fast food, and the like. Or maybe you'll work up to canceling the "automatic payment by credit card" clause on your health club membership, so that when you pay the invoice each month, you can evaluate whether you're getting your money's worth. Or perhaps you'll take the time to call around and make sure that mail-order "bargain" doesn't cost less at a local department store. Whatever the tactics you use, keep in mind that you can't pursue your heart's desire until you know where your money is going—and whether you approve of its destination.

Like Bob Kennedy and his ear-piercing gun, frugality is definitely a matter of doing what you can for yourself rather than paying someone else to do it. Lots of times we overlook the possibilities here—springing for a store-bought housewarming gift, for example, when your friends would appreciate your coming over and breaking down their cardboard moving boxes far more. Or maybe you could forgo the spa and give yourself a foot massage using glass marbles warmed in the microwave.

The other half of the "saving by doing for yourself" equation is knowing what you can't do, or can't do well, and what you don't want to do. Frugality means staying in touch with your emotions, expectations, and shortcomings, so that you know when it's actually frugal to pay a plumber $600 to fix the sink or to pay someone else $50 to clean the house so that you can maintain your sanity.

Although it sounds odd to talk about $600 plumbing bills and frugality in the same sentence, even a top-dollar purchase can fit in with frugality when you are buying, not being sold. What's the difference? *Being sold* means making purchases that don't make sense for you, buying by habit, or failing to analyze a deal that seems to be too good to be true. *Frugality* means doing your research, asking questions, and finding less expensive alternatives, even on so-called frivolous purchases such as perfume or a dozen red roses. And this approach definitely applies to everyday expenses, whether you are deciding whether to invest in a Gold Card (which may offer benefits you already have on other policies or cards) or where to buy a small bookshelf (try the lumberyard, not the yuppie home store).

Even after you've made your purchases, you're not off the hook. Frugality also means taking care of what you have so that it lasts longer. When you stretch the life of your possessions, you not only postpone buying new ones but you can frequently avoid paying interest or obnoxious credit card charges. Sometimes making things last is simplicity itself: keeping your hand off the gearshift when cruising, for example, to reduce your chances of having to rebuild the transmission at a cost of several hundred dollars. Other times making things last is a matter of buying high-quality items in the first place. A well-made unlined jacket, for example, should have finished seams. Note, however, that no one is saying that well-made objects have to be new.

One of the most eye-opening aspects of frugality is realizing that small steps can cumulatively make a big difference. See what happens when you start carrying muffins and coffee from home instead of buying them at the cafeteria at work. Or try driving with the windows closed during your commute (and at other times, too), and see if you don't save around 10 percent on your fuel bill. Of course, part of accumulating small savings is keeping track of those savings by turning them into tangible cash or putting them in a piggy bank or individual savings account. If your small efforts are simply absorbed into a mass of spending and saving, it's much more difficult to stay motivated to be frugal.

Last, and most important, frugality doesn't mean you

can't live well. In fact, it should mean exactly the opposite. Food is one obvious example. Home-cooked meals, with unprocessed, simple ingredients, are usually far tastier than their fast-food or convenience-food counterparts, at a fraction of the cost. In addition, you can occasionally buy "luxury" ingredients such as fresh basil or scallops to prepare meals at home because these ingredients still cost less than ordering out.

The list of "frugal is better" items is exhaustive. Just about any well-made piece of furniture or clothing that you buy secondhand is going to be more valuable (and maybe more stylish and comfortable) than one you can buy new with the same amount of money. Frugally scrutinizing your taxes to make sure you save every penny you have coming to you and not making any costly mistakes will save you money, maybe enough so that you won't have to work as hard at making more money. If you decorate your home creatively by using thrifty materials, you can probably afford to redecorate more often. The list goes on and on.

Tommy and Dorothy McClure of Saltville, Virginia, will be the first to tell you about the superiority of frugally tended gardens. The two are part of a circle of friends who provide each other with cuttings and seeds for free, and they have flowers framing their porch most of the year.

Dorothy says that tying Popsicle sticks to young squash and melon sprouts works far better than using expensive store-bought chemicals to combat cutworms, and she has a bumper crop to share with friends and family to prove it. (The sticks make the plants too thick for the worms to wrap themselves around.) She also makes pickles from home-grown cucumbers, peppers, and onions that outshine any store-bought variety—and cost about $3 less per quart. The two, along with any relatives or "church family" members that happen by, feast on vegetables canned from their own garden. They also can beans from a plot they pay an acquaintance to grow for them, at a lower cost than they would pay for off-brand canned vegetables. Their other advertisement for "better eating through frugality" is their home's wood-burning stove, which costs virtually nothing to run but helps Dorothy bake peerless pies, cakes, and biscuits.

The McClures live in a small but structurally sound colonial-style house in the mountains that they inherited. Moving somewhere else would mean easier access to jobs, but by avoiding a house payment, they are able to purchase a new vehicle when they want one. Plus, with the mountains in clear view, their church nearby, and a porch swing to sit in when the weather is nice, they can't think of anywhere better to live—or to live well for less. And isn't that what frugality is all about?

CHAPTER 2

THE FOUR KEYS
TO FRUGAL LIVING

*T*here are two sides to the art of living well on less. There's the minute-by-minute aspect, where you take advantage of the many opportunities to spend wisely, to give up the things that don't add to your life, and to save money on the things you do want and will use. This book furnishes you with hundreds of innovative, tried-and-true, "real people" tips for handling everything from a children's clothing lending library to funeral arrangements. These ingenious, sometimes zany, neighbor-to-neighbor tips are unbeatable.

But while you're trying some of these tips, keep in mind the other half of the frugal formula: establishing some basic attitudes and approaches so that you can maximize the impact of your frugal ways. In a nutshell, the four keys to frugal living are (1) knowing budget basics, (2) getting out of and avoiding debt, (3) increasing your savings, and (4) living well within your means. Each of these tactics relies on setting some overarching goals and thinking things through.

Throughout the process, remember that you are an individual (or an individual family or couple) and you're the only one who knows what's right for you, what you can live with, and what you can live without. Who cares if you decide to drive an old clunker and put your money into a beautiful carpet for the living room? Or buy gourmet dinners for your cats and frozen pot pies for yourself? Or keep all your receipts in a coffee can and balance your checkbook once a year? That's for you to say. You may find that you're not willing or able to follow every one of these basics. But examine each one to see whether it holds the key to your living well on less—as defined by you and you alone.

KEY NUMBER 1:
KNOW YOUR BUDGET BASICS

The key to the household budget is to stop thinking of it as drudgery and to start thinking of it as a puzzle—something that you can figure out and put together, and might even have fun doing. Preparing a budget is nothing more than figuring out what you spend and whether that's how you want to spend your money—which is what makes it a building block of Yankee-style frugality.

There are dozens of ways to get motivated to keep track of your expenses and then to stay motivated to make the necessary changes in spending. You can toss all your food receipts in an empty cereal box, for example, then sketch out spending patterns on a piece of scrap paper taped to the back. Or put a child in charge of the soda and snack budget. Ideally, you should tackle the budget a little at a time—no sweeping reformations here. But do get the record-keeping and goal-setting habits established, because the rewards can be enormous.

Consider the case of Janet Paré, a homemaker from Nashua, New Hampshire. For almost a decade, she has carefully monitored which foods her family eats and how much she spends on groceries each week. She clips coupons and cash-back offers and has even joined an online chat group to discuss offers her family can take advantage of. She never takes a trip to the store without saving at least a few dollars on everything from doughnuts to an oil change. And after months of checking deals and cross-referencing the file cabinets and record books she keeps, she was able to obtain $469.07 worth of groceries for 3 cents! Naturally, not everyone's talents run to clipping coupons, nor do we all have somewhere to redeem them.

But Janet's research methods—calling, reading, tracking—may work just as well to save you money on expenses such as transportation and entertainment.

KEY NUMBER 2:
GET OUT OF AND AVOID DEBT

We'd be the last to say that all credit is bad. Few of us have cash at the ready to purchase homes, for example, and sometimes borrowing a bit of money lets you take advantage of a now-or-never deal that will pay back more than the interest you incur. The trick with credit is to determine what is necessary in assisting you with your life's goals and what is—or will be—dragging you down. It is essential to compute how much credit purchases will cost you over the long run and then keep those facts and figures in plain view. That way, you'll make informed decisions about what to buy on credit and which credit purchases to pay off first if you're trying to get out of debt.

One key to avoiding debt is avoiding temptation. High-risk times include holidays, vacations, clothes and home entertainment shopping sprees, and even trips to the convenience store when you gas up. In this book, you'll find tips for handling all these temptations.

Steve Mangum has hit on a way to avoid running up his credit cards on vacation. He works for a company in Durham, North Carolina, that has a flexible spending program that allows employees to take pretax money out of their paychecks for day care. They must pay day care directly, then file the canceled checks to get their money back. Steve pays day care out of pocket and then tries to live within his budget without filing for the reimbursement. If he can make it, he waits and files for the entire reimbursement at the end of the year, then uses it to increase his savings or pay for a family vacation. As you'll discover in later chapters, there are many ways to "hide" money from yourself until you amass enough for a vacation or another splurge item, but it's important not to save funds in that manner while high-interest loans or credit card balances go unpaid.

KEY NUMBER 3: INCREASE YOUR SAVINGS

Retired Missouri schoolteacher Elizabeth Eulinger demonstrates perfectly the merits of a lifelong savings plan—not just for savings' sake but so that you'll have the money you need for security and maybe to spend when a once-in-a-lifetime opportunity presents itself. "When you save, you must have a goal," Elizabeth says. In the pages ahead, you'll find ways to save for college, retirement, vacations, homes—you name it. Or perhaps, like Elizabeth, you'll save for peace of mind.

Elizabeth was married with young children when she watched her father-in-law die young. From that time on, she asked herself, "What would I do if something happened to my husband?" The solution the couple hit on was for Elizabeth to work toward a teaching degree, which she did while having several more children. It took her 16 years to earn her master's degree, but "that degree was our insurance policy," she says.

In the meantime, the couple lived mostly on her husband's salary and saved Elizabeth's earnings. (Before earning her degree, she held a teacher's certificate, which allowed her to teach based on experience.) When her husband died, Elizabeth still had two school-age children. She supported them with her savings and by continuing to teach. She also continued to save what she could. "I was even more frugal after he died, putting so much away each week for savings," she says. "When I got a raise, I'd put part of it directly into savings, so I wouldn't have a chance to get used to it." Later, Elizabeth remarried and always felt "lucky and fortunate" to have a comfortable lifestyle.

When Elizabeth was in her late sixties and a widow once again, she had a chance to make a big difference. You see, Elizabeth's hometown is Independence, Missouri, the place where President Harry Truman was born and lived. Although Truman's home had been lovingly preserved, another home in his neighborhood, the Choplin house, was slated for demolition in 1994. "(Demolishing) it was a disgrace to Harry Truman's memory," Elizabeth says.

Some people in town received a grant to do basic repairs on the home, but it still needed a sponsor. "I fretted and stewed and asked the kids what they thought," Elizabeth says. "They said, 'Mom, it's your money. Do what you think is right.'" Elizabeth bought the house with money she'd earmarked to build a small home for herself, and paid to have the house restored.

"If you save here and there and don't blow it all in one wad, and if your kids aren't looking for an inheritance, you can do this sort of thing," Elizabeth says. "I do love the home, but it would be foolish for me to live there because I need a one-story place. When I find the right people, I will sell it." Until then, because she's been frugal—and fortunate—she can wait.

KEY NUMBER 4:
LIVING (WELL) WITHIN YOUR MEANS

This is perhaps the key to the keys: to live well with the resources you have and to be happy with the choices you make. For Bob Grimac, a frugal lifestyle is the very thing that enables him to live well. That's because his definition of living well is "doing what you love." He loves being a freelance teacher—folk dance, crafts, sign language, and conservation. Based in Knoxville, Tennessee, he is able to go to New York and Maine for "working holidays" at children's camps. To no one's surprise, this kind of work doesn't pay a whole lot. But Bob has gotten his expenses down so low that he can afford to pick up and take off on a whim, seeing the world and teaching kids about foreign cultures and earth-friendly crafts.

"I've got good food, a little house, and a car that runs," Bob says. What he doesn't have is an air-conditioning bill, a dishwasher, or a car payment. "I've gotten my utility bill down to about $17 a month," he says. "That really helps me take off when I want to."

Bob quickly points out that many of the "frugal" steps he takes are also part of living well. Riding his bike to the store saves on fuel bills, but it also keeps his weight down and helps him stay energetic. His vegetarian diet is cheap, but it also helps him stay healthy. He loves to buy hats, but he can support that habit for next to nothing by buying at flea markets and garage sales.

Bob is amazed at the things he gets for free, just because someone else didn't want them. "I've found books, envelopes, and paper just there for the taking," he says. "I've got skylights made from free sliding glass door panels. I've picked up furniture off the curb, along with a lot of good pots and pans and even a perfectly good garden hose."

Bob has so much that he's able to share his goods with his students. He turns in books he's scavenged to a local secondhand bookstore, in exchange for gift certificates and foreign language dictionaries. At one of the inner-city schools where he teaches, he hosts folk dance parties with door prizes from his stock of finds. He underwrites after-school-activity snacks with discounts he earns volunteering at a local food co-op.

Bob will tell you that he has the luxury few people think they can afford. "I work independently; I set my own schedule," he says. "I have the freedom to take all the jobs that I like, and I don't take the jobs that I don't like."

This is just one example of how you can live well on less. All over the nation, folks are putting their own stamps on Yankee frugality, making their own choices and applying the strategies that work for them. In the following pages, you'll read about them, and you'll learn thousands of ways that you can join their ranks. Go on, get out that shoe-string, and let's see how far you can go.

PART II

Frugal Finances

BUILDING A FOUNDATION FOR THE GOOD LIFE

So ARE YOU one of those people who constantly covets someone else's tools? You know, you say, "Sure, my lawn would be mowed at 9:00 A.M. every Saturday morning, too, if I had a $4,000 walk-behind mower," or "Of course she sews all her own clothes! She's got a computer-ized machine with all the attachments."

Well, rest assured. In this section, we'll give you all the financial tools you'll ever need—and they're downright cheap: an empty cereal box and a sharp pencil, old jar lids, or envelopes that became obsolete when your local congressman lost the election.

And you know what? The homemade stuff will work better than any expensive software or highfalutin seminar, because it's powered by your philosophies, your goals, your savings techniques, and the methods you'll learn in this section. First, we'll walk you through the process of creating a budget. Once you know where the money goes, read on for downright homey ways to redirect it if you decide you need to. Let's see, how does a series of savings accounts sound? Or how about paying yourself a dividend from the money you save?

Right at the top of the tip parade are ways to get out of debt and to avoid that fiery pit in the future. We're also big on the idea of saving for special events—retirement, college, once-in-a-lifetime vacations. And we don't think anyone should work hard to save money and then end up giving it back to the bank in fees and charges, so we'll steer you clear of that.

Need help getting started on new spending and savings habits? Try some of our quirky, "real people" techniques, such as shopping with cash for a few weeks or paying yourself the market rate for jobs you do around the house. We can also recommend some places you've probably never thought of to keep credit cards out of sight and some ways to find frequently overlooked tax deductions.

But no matter how many of our techniques you borrow, you'll be making up the rules yourself. You have the best tools money can buy right in your own hands—and head.

CHAPTER 3

BUDGET BASICS

*E*ver hear the expression "If you keep on doing what you're doing, you'll keep on getting what you've got"?

That, in a nutshell, is the reason you should prepare a household budget.

If you keep going along in your life without identifying where your money goes, you'll miss the opportunity to find better ways to handle your financial resources. With a household budget in hand, you can see whether your spending is in line with your priorities and if it isn't, you can make some adjustments.

Preparing a budget requires three basic steps: (1) keeping a written record of your current spending, (2) evaluating it and designating how you would like to shift your spending patterns, and (3) tracking your spending to see if you've been able to alter your spending habits.

Remember, you shouldn't concern yourself with how other people spend their money. This is your life, after all. You must compare your expenditures to your goals and to your other expenditures to see whether you are doing the best you can with what you have.

The most important aspect of budgeting (and quite frankly, the most difficult) is working through your inertia to start finding out how you currently spend—even if you just save gasoline receipts for a week. Until you know exactly where you are, you can't work toward getting to where you want to be.

TRACKING AND PLANNING YOUR SPENDING

Act for High Impact

❖ Before you try sweeping changes, experiment with managing one portion of your budget. Select an area over which you have direct, immediate control—entertainment expenses, for example—not something you can't control, such as cold-weather heating and electric bills. Make meticulous notes about current expenditures, evaluate them, and then decide how and if you can make changes.

Get a Clue with Blue

❖ Those leather-bound accounting ledgers can be intimidating—and expensive. Instead, ask around at a local high school, college, or university to see if the students use blue books—inexpensive booklets of notebook paper with blue covers—for exams. If they do, ask if you can get a stash of those that have been written in but still have pages left in the back. Use them to write down expenses and tally receipts. They're small enough that you can use a separate book for each week or month or for each expenditure category you track.

Mark Your Calendar

❖ Use outdated calendars to total monthly expenses. Cross out the days of the week, then write your flexible expense categories at the top of the columns: food, entertainment, utilities, transportation, clothing, household, and debt, for example. This gives you a place to compare month to month, and even this April to next April.

Envision No Means of Support

❖ Try going about your daily rounds for an entire week without cash, credit cards, or a checkbook. Bring a notepad to record all the times you find yourself reaching for money, and ask yourself, "Is this something I need or want, or is it something I buy out of habit?"

Does Pay-as-You-Go Pay Off?

❖ Make sure you're getting top value for the money you spend on bulk purchases, whether you're buying 3 pounds of luncheon meat at a wholesale club or an unlimited membership at a health club. For each such expense, figure out how much it costs for what you use, not what you buy. If you pay $3 a pound for the meat but use only half of it before it goes bad, you'd be better off paying $2 for a half a pound. In the same fashion, the unlimited membership isn't worth the expenditure if you make only a few visits.

I Worked a Week for This?

❖ To gain control of your current and future spending, it's important to be able to link the money you earn to the money you spend. Try compiling your monthly expenses, from soup to nuts, for 3 months, then average each category over the months. Now figure your daily after-tax earnings, using a 5-day workweek. Take out next month's calendar and mark how long it will take you to earn the money to pay for each expense. Start with your top priority and work your way down the list, using a different-colored marker for each category. Seeing that you're still working for your auto payment on the 15th of the month or that you work six times longer for fast-food meals than you do to have someone mow the lawn might motivate you to make some positive changes.

IT WORKED FOR ME
We've Gotta Get Outta This Place

During the course of a single year, my wife and I both became self-employed—she for the second time and I for the first. We were really having a tough time figuring out who would have a check coming in when and which bills we needed to keep track of for our taxes. What we decided to do was have a short meeting every Sunday. We'd take the newspaper and the coupons we wanted to clip and "meet" at a neighborhood deli, where we could spread out our work. We'd each bring an agenda, and we'd work out a weekly budget: "You have this check coming in; that will cover the electric bill. I need to invoice so-and-so, or I won't be able to handle the car insurance next month." Sure, it cost a few extra dollars to eat out (although we used two-for-one coupons that the deli offered through the schools), but leaving the house made us feel official, and we could concentrate without distractions. And because we didn't get out a whole lot that first year, doing the budget was actually something we looked forward to.

—Wade Slate
Williamsburg, Virginia

Let's Make a List

❖ No doubt you and your mate negotiate often about how you'll spend your money. But do you really know what your mate thinks about long-term goals, financial security, or borrowing? If you establish the ground rules early on, you can avoid a lot of frivolous debates later. Set aside an hour for this simple drill. Take 10 minutes to each fill out a sheet of paper titled "Five Things We Could Do Without If I Lost My Job." Take turns discussing your answers, starting with each person's number 5 and working your way up the list. Agree on a mutual list, then ask yourselves, "Can we do without any of these things right now?"

And Where Do You Think You're Going?

❖ Before you think about cashing a paycheck, sit down with your spouse and determine where the money will go. If you don't plan for every penny ahead of time, a trip to the mall on payday or a yard sale find can derail your best intentions.

Meet Our Junior Accountant

❖ Once a child is 9 or 10, consider turning over some small portion of your household budget to him to handle. This tactic should yield some savings, and it will definitely give your child a close-up view of the joys and challenges of budgeting, earning, and spending. Snack food is a good area to start with. Have your child track current expenditures, evaluate their worth (with input from other family members), and make suggestions for getting the budget in line with family goals and priorities. Then cut him loose to purchase snacks, dole them out, and so forth—as long as he can stick to the budget.

CHECKS AND BALANCES

Our Budget Is Grrrreat!

❖ Count on constantly revising your budget, based on how well it works in your life. To keep track, glue a piece of notebook paper on the outside of a large, empty cereal box. Draw two columns. On the left, write your projected budget for a week or a month (or for a particular category of expenditures). On the right, record your actual expenses for the same period of time or category. Why the cereal box? So you can keep the relevant check stubs, receipts, and bills inside until you're ready to do the paperwork.

RECEIPT STORAGE IDEAS

Mobile Receipt Storage

❖ If you spend a lot of time on the road—even just running errands around town—you probably have a lot of

HOW TO MAKE A RECEIPT STICK

You know those snazzy metal spindles receptionists use to impale messages and other office paperwork? Make your own, and you'll have an easy and oddly satisfying way to save receipts.

1. Find two jar lids, both at least ⅓ inch deep (deeper is better, but they should be the same depth) and at least 3 inches across. The diameter of one lid should be at least ¼ inch greater than the other.

2. Invert the smaller lid (as you would screw it on a jar), and rest it inside the larger lid. Now flip the whole thing over so that the larger lid is on top.

3. Drive a 4- to 6-inch nail through the centers of the two lids so that the

head of the nail ends up on the outside of the larger lid.

4. Flip the whole thing over again and slip the smaller lid off the nail. (If you have small children, you may want to dull the end of the nail with a metal file.)

5. Fill the larger lid with sand, gravel, or modeling clay to give it some weight.

6. Slip the smaller lid back on, covering the weighting material.

Use jar lids, a nail, and sand to make a receipt spindle.

small expenditures that add up. So that you don't discard or lose the receipts, outfit your car ashtray to become a minifile (assuming you don't use it for its original purpose). Simply cut a piece of cardboard that will fit over the top of the ashtray when the drawer is open but still allows you to close the ashtray easily. Slip receipts under the cardboard, then weight it down with a small, flat rock and slide the drawer shut. No more flyaway receipts.

Keep receipts in your car ashtray under a small rock and a piece of cardboard.

Canisters, Cups, and Clothespins—Oh, My!

❖ To track receipts, you need containers that you can access easily, and enough of them so that you can separate your record keeping however you need to—one for each month or week, for each type of expenditure, or for each person who makes purchases.

❖ Label potato chip or snack canisters (the cylindrical kind) with a marker. Use them as is or cut a slot in the plastic cover.

❖ Pour about ½ inch of sand, pebbles, or marbles into a stadium cup to weight it down. If you have strong team loyalty in the house, designate a different team's cup for each person or budget.

❖ Hang a fabric clothespin holder from the wall or doorknob and use it to store receipts.

❖ Use the clothespins, too. Glue them to the top of a bulletin board, with the clamps pointing down, 3 to 4 inches apart. Then just clip your receipts to the board.

❖ Mark the separate compartments of a hanging shoe bag with paper labels or a washable marker. Store your receipts in the pockets.

CHAPTER 4

GETTING OUT OF DEBT

People have a tendency to invest the word *debt* with great power. Debt is not evil, inevitable, or mysterious. In fact, as any dyed-in-the-wool Yankee will tell you, the power is in your hands. Just as with all the financial tools at your disposal, you can manage debt to give yourself the maximum benefit. If you know how, you can control your debt so that it helps you extend your spending power in areas where you need a boost to achieve "the good life"—and so that it doesn't sap your financial security, drain your resources, or make you feel guilty.

Most people think they have too much debt. Evaluating your situation realistically is the first step on the road to recovery. After you know exactly what you're paying out and what you're getting in return, you can decide how much debt you need and how much is too much. Reducing your debt requires only two steps: (1) renegotiating current obligations to pay less interest and (2) saving cash on other expenses and using that cash to pay down high-interest debts. But the same debt-reduction plan doesn't work for everyone. In fact, some debt-reduction ideas contradict each other. That's because some folks need to make sweeping changes, while others have to change gradually, chipping away at old habits so as not to get so frustrated that they give up. Some people respond well to a psychological approach, while others want to know only whether the plan will save them money. The right plan for you is the plan that best suits your wants and needs. So consider things carefully. All you have to lose is some bills.

ASSESSING YOUR DEBT STATUS

Home In on Your Mortgage Rate

❖ If you haven't reviewed your mortgage in the past 4 or 5 months, haul it out. Most lenders consider you able to repay your loan if your annual payments are around 28 percent of your annual net income. If you've recently been divorced or had a drop in your income, you may now be outside the acceptable limit. That doesn't mean you won't be able to repay your loan, but it does mean that you might have too much money tied up in mortgage payments. If so, take some time to consider the big picture: Would you consider purchasing less house, renting out a portion of your home, or getting a roommate? Or are you willing to give up other things to accommodate a higher debt ratio on your house?

Become a Statistic

❖ Most lenders consider 36 percent an acceptable debt-to-income ratio. Compare your total annual debt to your total annual income and see where you rate. Each lender should include an annual breakdown of how much you've spent on that year's debt in a yearly report. Save all these reports to tally at the end of the year.

Just How Close Is the Brink?

❖ To get a feel for how manageable your current debt load is, use the same formula financial advisors recommend for those considering bankruptcy. Write down a realistic summary of your monthly expenditures, including mortgage and car payments but leaving out all other debt. Include everything, even cat food, cosmetics, and Christmas presents. Deduct this amount from your current monthly income. Compare the remainder to your other existing debt. With the money you have left after paying your monthly expenses, can you pay off your other debt (with accumulated interest) in three years? If so, you can likely solve any debt woes with your own resources. If possible, strive for a budget that will allow you to pay off all your debt (except mortgage and auto debt) in a shorter period of time so that you're not flirting with bankruptcy.

GETTING CREDIT CARDS UNDER CONTROL

Switch without Taking the Bait

❖ Lots of credit card companies offer a substantially lower interest rate for an introductory period of 6 months to 1 year. If you qualify, consider transferring your higher-interest balance. But put a memory tickler in place so that you'll have a substantial amount of the balance paid off by the time the rate goes up, or at least a month to shop around for another teaser rate.

❖ To remind yourself of that expiration date, write it on a piece of adhesive tape and apply it to the card. If you

THE YANKEE MISER RECOMMENDS . . .
Getting a Cost-Free Credit Report

I wouldn't dream of paying anywhere from $3 to $20 for a copy of my credit report. Instead, I apply for a credit card I don't have a prayer of qualifying for (such as a $50,000-limit Platinum card). I get the application at my bank or from a credit card company, and when my application is turned down, I'm eligible to receive a free copy of my credit report from the agency that the bank or credit card company used to qualify my credit. If you're interested in doing the same

thing, keep two things in mind. First, apply for a card only if you don't frequently apply for cards. Too many credit card applications will show up on your credit report and make potential lenders put you in a high-risk category. Second, if you're actually approved, make certain that you turn down the card and ask to have all records stricken from your credit report. Cards you don't even access may show up on your report and make creditors think you're overextended.

haven't paid off the debt by a month before the date, you can transfer your balance again.

Make a Cold, Calculating Move

❖ To prevent impulse trips to the mall (or even just charging gasoline so you can spend your petty cash on Girl Scout cookies), freeze your credit card in a block of ice. You will have to wait for it to defrost before you can use it, and since microwaving will melt the card, you'll have to let it thaw at room temperature. That ought to give you a good long time to think twice about charging. Place your credit card in the bottom of an empty ice cream box and fill it with ice cubes (which will keep the card from floating to the top). Then fill the box with water and freeze it.

Put the freeze on impulse purchases.

Cut Out the False Emergencies

❖ It's so easy to tell yourself that you're going to keep one credit card current for "emergencies," but the emergency turns out to be buying a pizza for dinner on a nonpayday Friday. Try a different tactic: Keep the card current but don't keep the card. Cut it up. That way, if you have a real financial emergency—you need a plane ticket for a distant funeral, or you incur some major medical expense—you can either use the number or send for a replacement card. Once the emergency has passed, take out the scissors again.

Cut the Credit Line, Then Cut the Check

❖ Do you have a credit card that has gotten out of hand, and you have to struggle to pay even the minimum balance every month? Do yourself a favor: Cancel the card immediately. That way, you can't make new charges while you're getting the balance under control. If you get back on solid ground, you can always apply for a new card. Don't cancel more than two cards in one month, however. Potential lenders may think you're having money problems.

Sweat the Small Stuff First

❖ It's good practice to find out which credit card is costing you the most in interest and fees and attempt to pay it off first. If that's too daunting, consider paying off the card with the lowest balance, be it a department store card, gas card, or major credit card. Then cancel the card and have fun cutting it to bits. Sometimes just proving to yourself that you can pay off an entire balance will inspire you to tackle the bigger jobs.

Beware the Kinder, Gentler Bill

❖ Sometimes when you continually pay a card late or let several months go by without a payment, the credit card company will offer to work out a lower payment plan for you for a few months, usually with revoked charging privileges. Before you accept those terms, do the math. Because you're paying less, you're probably not even keeping up with the interest charges, much less the balance. At the same time, the charges on the card will keep accruing interest. All told, you may be adding hundreds of dollars to your bill at the very time that you need to reduce it. So instead of breathing a sigh of relief at the more manageable payments, stick with the standard minimum payment if you can.

FREEING UP CASH, PAYING DOWN DEBTS

More Isn't Always Better

❖ Conventional wisdom says that you should always try to pay more than the minimum payment due on your credit card; otherwise, you'll never make a

---

WORLD-CLASS FRUGALITY

But I Still Have Checks Left!

My wife doesn't like to keep track of her money, so I generally do it for her by calling the bank regularly to check on her balance and then adding money to her account when she needs it. Once I was slow in doing this, and Nancy stopped by the bank to withdraw some money. The clerk informed her that not only did she not have any money in her account but she was overdrawn by $90 and would have to pay an overdraft fee of $15. Without even pausing, Nancy reached for her purse and said, "Oh, I'm sorry. Let me write you a check."

—Don Seaton
Hastings, Nebraska

dent in the debt. Although that's almost always true, ask yourself this question: "Is that money I pay over the minimum money I could use to pay cash on necessities instead of making more charges?" In other words, are you paying $50 over and then falling $50 short at the end of the month—and using your credit card to charge that $50 and some more besides? Studies show that people spend more when they charge than they do when they pay cash. To make your way back to the "cash only" habit, consider paying only the minimum on your accounts for a month or two and using the extra cash to reduce credit card charges.

IT WORKED FOR ME
Take This Card and Cut It

One year I got a bonus and used it to pay off a bothersome credit card. I then cut up the card and mailed it in with my check, which said "Cancel card" on the memo line. Imagine my surprise when I received a bill from the same company the next month. It turned out that the company had ignored my note and was so happy with my large payment that it mailed me two new copies of the card. My husband thought it was the card we were still using and made purchases with it.

Now when I pay off a credit card, I call the toll-free number before I mail my final check. I inform the company that I'm going to pay off my charges and cancel the card, then ask where I should send my final payment and in what amount. Often it's a different address than usual. I include a signed note, stating that I am canceling my account, along with a memo requesting that the company confirm, in writing, that I am no longer a cardholder. This takes away any temptation to reactivate the account, and it helps my credit rating. My credit report rarely says that I still have an active card after I've paid it off. If it does, I have a record that shows I canceled the card.

Caution: Never cancel more than two cards in one month. Doing so may raise a red flag in your credit report indicating that you might be having money problems.

—Rose Kennedy
Knoxville, Tennessee

Designate an "I Did It!" Fund

❖ Reducing debt and conserving cash is hard work, and you should expect to be rewarded for your effort. To keep from going overboard, plan appropriate rewards for designated goals—cutting up the gasoline card, paying off a visit to the emergency room, refinancing the house. Work your "reward" budget into your payment plan. For example, earmark $30 a week for the doctor's bill and $3 for the concert fund to celebrate the day you pay off the bill. For accomplishments that require less than around $500 of payments over time, pay an additional 10 percent of the amount to a "reward fund" for dinner out, movie tickets, a new compact disc, or the like. If you're saving yourself thousands of dollars, a reward that costs around $100 is reasonable—just make sure you save the reward money before you make the final payment so that you don't incur additional debt.

Home Loans? Not in This Neighborhood!

❖ Avoid home equity loans if the housing values in your neighborhood are going down or if the resale market is flat. Otherwise, you risk borrowing money on the current value of your house, only to have the value plunge or not to be able to sell your house for its full value. Then if you must sell, you'll have to use most or all of the money you get for the house to repay the loan, and you may not have anything left over for a down payment on a new home.

Take 10 (Percent Off)

❖ You might qualify to have the 10 percent IRA early-withdrawal penalty waived for things such as qualified college expenses, medical bills, and the purchase of your first house. If you're paying those bills, with cash, consider getting a disbursement from your IRA to pay qualified expenses, then using the cash you free up to pay off high-interest credit cards. Ask your IRA provider for information on qualified programs, then talk things through with your tax preparer or financial advisor.

GETTING MORE HELP

Ask the Experts

❖ Tap into your local Consumer Credit Counseling Service if you need outside assistance to settle old debts, reorganize your current debt load, or prepare a household budget. You can find the local telephone number in the White Pages or Yellow Pages of your phone book. Another source of credit counseling is the Cooperative Extension Service. Look for the number of your local extension office

FOUR WAYS TO DIVIDE AND CONQUER CREDIT CARD BILLS

When a huge balance is looming over you, it's mighty tempting to pay just the minimum amount. Instead, divide the total into an amount you can handle.

1. Interest-ing. Determine what your balance should be to halve your current annual interest charges. Work on paying down your balance to the desired level—say, within 6 to 12 months—and still pay the minimum charge on the statement.

2. Annual improvement. Calculate this year's new charges— without the interest—and strive to pay off that amount in the next 4 to 6 months (in addition to the minimum). Then pay last year's charges, and so forth. This will remind you just how long you pay for some purchases.

3. Use it, lose it. Sift through the past 6 months' worth of statements and total charges for things you've already consumed—meals, entertainment, and the like. Create a payment schedule to pay for those items in the next 4 months, in addition to the minimum amount due. Then tackle the previous 6 months' worth.

4. Not me. Calculate the cost of all the things you purchased with the card that benefited others in the past 6 months—or benefited no one (like that makeup kit still in its box in the cabinet). Plan to pay those charges in a few months' or a year's time (along with keeping your other payment current), and you'll get a dual benefit: lower interest and reinforcement not to charge things unless they'll have a long-term benefit.

in the government listings of the White Pages. Here's how these services ordinarily work: You pay a $10 to $15 application fee (or other income-based nominal fee) to show that you are truly interested in resolving your debt woes. They'll walk you through a budget and help you establish ways to free up cash. At the same time, if you qualify, they can intervene with your creditors to help you set up a suitable repayment plan.

Accept No Imitators

❖ Lots of firms advertise "consumer credit counseling services" or include some or all of those words in their names. But don't assume that they're part of the national nonprofit Consumer Credit Counseling Service or that they'll give you free or low-cost counseling. Before you sign on with any company or give out personal information over the Web, find out whether it's a nonprofit and whether it's a member of the National Foundation for Consumer Credit. If not, keep looking for a company that is.

Consider the Source

❖ Be leery of financial advisors who sell the same services they are recommending (consolidation loans, for instance) or are paid for referrals to people who do. Ask up front whether the firm has a financial interest in the options it recommends. One tip-off is when the company recommends a service and gives only one resource for you to evaluate. Before you sign for a loan, refinancing, or a credit card, always compare at least three options.

Don't Get Tangled in Web Offers

❖ When you search on keywords such as "credit counseling" or "financial advice," lots of Web sites will pop up promising free stuff. But if a Web site won't allow you to access information without your giving out personal data, skip it. There are plenty of sites that will allow you to access all types of advice and information for free—their fees come from advertising on the site.

Hassle, Not Help

❖ Some unscrupulous companies tantalize those suffering from heavy debt loads with unrealistic promises. Although they may seem to be offering a magical formula to reduce debt, they might be suggesting unwarranted bankruptcy proceedings, which could cost you more than resolving your debts in a less drastic way. Bankruptcy proceedings involve lawyers and rules about what you can keep and spend, among other restrictions. Here are some marketing phrases that might indicate that bankruptcy proceedings are part of the hidden agenda: "Consolidate your bills into one monthly payment without borrowing." "Stop creditors from hassling you! Leave behind foreclosures, repossessions, tax levies, and garnishments! Keep your property!" "Wipe out your debts! Consolidate your bills! How? Let the federal law work for you this time."

Take an Online Test Drive

❖ When you're crunching numbers to determine how basic debt-reducing measures will affect your situation, use one of the many free online calculators. You fill in your numbers, and the calculator computes the data. Most free calculations are offered by companies that want to loan you money or give you financial advice, but you can access many of them without giving out any personal information. Search under "consumer credit counseling," "refinancing," or "borrowing" to find some worthy home pages. Many have separate links to calculators, while others include calculators within their text. Here are some of the questions you can answer using an online calculator: How much will I pay if I extend my student loan from 10 years to 30? What is my break-even point if I refinance my home? How much can I save by reducing my spending? How much will I save by paying off my loan sooner? What is my debt-to-income ratio?

CHAPTER 5

SECRETS OF A DEBT-FREE LIFE

*E*ver notice that some people just don't go into unnecessary debt? They pay cash for everything except homes and maybe cars and seem blissfully immune to the advertisements, salespeople, friends, and neighbors luring them to "enjoy now, pay later."

Want to become one of them? You can avoid the kind of debt that will drag you down and still manage to charge an outfit or a week at the beach every now and then. You won't be depriving yourself—you'll be establishing which debts you consider worthy, once you've evaluated precisely what you're getting in exchange for your interest payment.

And that's half the work of avoiding debt: stripping away the cheery language that masks high-interest propositions and weighing the long-term advantages and disadvantages before you plunk down a credit card or sign on for an installment plan.

So what's the other half of the job? Getting to know your spending habits so that you can make it inconvenient for yourself to make impulse purchases.

In this chapter, you'll find ways to keep from taking on debt you don't need or want. For instance, consider how much you'd save by avoiding convenience stores and mail-order catalogs. Adopt a few of these strategies, and you may become the one who inspires other people to pay cash and maximize their spending power.

CURB IMPULSE BUYING

Pay Outside, Stay Outside

❖ It's amazingly easy to run up a major credit card or gas card bill at gas stations that have coffee shops or convenience stores attached—particularly if you're with coffee drinkers or kids who want snacks and drinks. To avoid the temptation, patronize stations that allow you to charge gasoline outside without having to go into the store.

❖ If your area doesn't have such a gas station, or if you have a different company's credit card, look for a station that accepts credit only for gasoline, not for other purchases. Or make it a hard-and-fast rule that you'll charge only gas.

THE YANKEE MISER RECOMMENDS . . .
Christmas in July, and February, and September . . .

I know that a lot of people plan to make their own crafts to give as Christmas presents, and I heartily support the idea. But I have friends who every year rush out and buy expensive supplies for woodworking, sewing, or needlework projects, then never quite get around to finishing the projects, at least not in time for Christmas. There they are at the last minute with nothing to give, so they rush out and charge replacement gifts and end up spending more than they wanted or paying lots of interest.

I don't let that happen to me. I plan precisely what I am going to make for each person on my list, and I start in January. I use a calendar, posted in my workroom, to schedule when I am going to make each gift and about how much the material will cost. For more complicated gifts, such as a sweater, I schedule when each portion of the project will be done. And I buy material for only one gift at a time. Until it's done, I don't buy more material. If I never get around to buying material for a certain gift, I see how much I planned to spend to make the gift, then buy a present that's within that price range.

Will You Take My Name (Off)?

❖ If you don't receive new mail-order catalogs and mailings, you won't be tempted to try their wares at the expense of your debt load. So sort through the order forms in catalogs and through the standard subscriber information at the back of the magazines you subscribe to. You should find some pleasant language saying that this company or publication sometimes shares its mailing list but won't share your name if you tell it not to. If you don't see a postage-paid card for your request, call any toll-free number listed for customers or subscribers and politely insist that the representative steer you to the right place, free of charge.

Send Me the Bill

❖ Having regular charges—such as newspaper delivery, health club memberships, and magazine subscriptions—automatically billed to your credit card is certainly convenient, but it can be too convenient. Often you're paying charges and interest on a service that's outlived its usefulness, but you don't notice because it's automatic. Reclaim some of those charges by calling the billing department at each service provider and requesting that the company bill you at home. Then pay by check.

Review before You Renew

❖ For charges that must be paid by credit card (such as some online fees), at least reject automatic renewal of your membership, subscription, or service contract. That way, you'll have a chance to reevaluate the arrangement each time it comes up for renewal. Contact each company you deal with and specify that you don't want automatic renewal. If the company is not cooperative and you don't want to cancel your service, contact your credit card company and see what arrangements it can make on its end.

Wait It Out

❖ Impose a mandatory 3-day waiting period for the purchases that create the most trouble for your budget. To

Making Memories, Not Bills

I have a large, loving family, and most of us have kids. We're fairly spread out around the country, and we don't all get to see each other every Christmas. Exchanging presents was getting expensive, so we hit on a compromise: Each family draws the name of one other family and sends them a Christmas ornament or a collection of ornaments. This works well for us because we all decorate big trees. My immediate family travels a lot, so we always get ornaments from a place we've visited, like the wonderful miniature Nativity set we bought in the Southwest and sent my sister. Every year, as we unpack the ornaments, we remember who sent us what and when, and which ornaments of ours are just like some we gave someone else. It's fun and encourages closeness, but it's not expensive.

—Caroline Kirschner
Jackson, Tennessee

determine which charges are wreaking havoc, review your credit card and overdraft protection charges for the past 3 months. Put a check mark next to any charge you consider unnecessary. Write down the dollar amounts of all these charges, highest to lowest. Pinpoint the amount in the middle of the list, known as your *impulse indicator*. In the future, any purchase that's not on the household necessities list and is higher than the impulse indicator will require a waiting period of 3 business days between spotting the item and purchasing it.

Shop at One Stop

❖ Whenever you can do so frugally, shop at a freestanding establishment rather than at a mall, where the businesses are close together. If you have to walk 50 yards or make another stop with the car, you're much less likely go into a store to see what you need.

That's $50 per Swim

❖ Gotta have that article of clothing? Before you run up your credit card balance, get out your calculator. Estimate exactly how many times you'll wear it this season and with what. Then calculate exactly how much it will cost you each time you wear it. This is a particularly profitable exercise with short-season items, such as parkas or dress-up clothing. But for this to work, you must be tough on yourself: If you have only one pair of pants that matches the sweater in question, for example, don't estimate that you'll wear the sweater three times a week.

❖ Getting ready to buy a "dry-clean only" item? Do the same drill but add in the dry-cleaning cost for each use.

CONTROL CREDIT
Pay Like the Old Days

❖ Credit card companies don't increase your credit limit because they're trying to help you reduce your debt load. They increase your limit because you've proven that you can pay increased amounts of very profitable interest on your card. So stick with your old limit. Or, better yet, sift through your bills and impose a limit similar to one you had 5 years ago or when you were starting your first job. If you can't find the records, call the credit card company and ask it. Make it a goal to steadily decrease your self-imposed credit limit until it reaches zero and you can cut the card in two.

Give Me a Little Credit

❖ Haul out all your credit cards and add up the credit limits. If, combined with your home loan, auto loan, and any other debt, the limits add up to more than 36 percent of your net income, you have access to more credit than you can easily assume. And that's just the highest acceptable limit; less than 36 percent is preferable.

❖ If you have more credit than you need, cancel the credit cards with the highest interest rates (or highest annual fees, if you haven't made any charges on them) until your combined available credit is at an acceptable level. Of course, you should deduct only the portion of the credit limit that you haven't used yet when you cancel the card. Never cancel more than two cards a month; that can cause red flags in your credit report.

Don't Buy a Bigger Bill

❖ You've probably noticed that a lot of credit cards send advertisements with the bill or in separate mailings

describing items you can finance with your credit card. Examine each deal critically: Is this a good deal, something you really need at a good price? Or is it appealing only because you can purchase it conveniently, without a credit hassle, and you'll never notice the slight increase in your credit card bill? If you're really intent on making the purchase after careful consideration, call a couple of local stores or a mail-order catalog to find out how much a similar item would cost if you paid cash or chose in-store financing.

See No Products, Buy No Products

❖ To keep temptation at bay, write your credit card company or call the company's toll-free customer service number and request that you be sent no more promotional materials, just the bill.

BIG-TICKET ITEMS: CARS, HOMES, TAXES

Could You Bank On It?

❖ Furniture showrooms, car dealerships, electronics stores—all of them occasionally offer great financing deals. The problem is, deal or no, sometimes more debt is more than you should take on. To get a more conservative view of the purchase, call your bank or credit union. Find out whether it would lend you a similar amount of money, given your current debt load.

Take the Terror Out of Tax Time

❖ To qualify for some home loans, a bank or credit union may require regular payments to an escrow account, stocked with money for property taxes and home insurance, which the financial institution then pays for you. If you pay your own property taxes and home insurance annually, it can be tough to come up with the money in one fell swoop. Instead of borrowing that money, create your own escrow account, dividing the money you know you'll need at tax time into 12 payments and setting them aside in a separate savings account.

❖ So that you're able to handle the increase in savings psychologically, consider it a slight increase in your house payment. Pay it at the same time and, if you can, have it deposited directly into your escrow account.

Do Pay before the Payment Is Due

❖ If you've bought into one of those "no payments for a year" deals so popular among furniture and appliance stores, don't run the risk of falling short when the payments come due—and the interest starts accruing. Save a portion of next year's payments each month in a Christmas club account.

THREE WAYS TO WIN WITH PUSHY SALESPEOPLE

Salespeople are conditioned to close the sale—sometimes before you're sure what you want to do. Here are some assertive, honest remarks that can defuse the pressure.

1. "I'm not buying today, but if I decide to buy, I'll ask for you." When salespeople are on commission, they worry that they'll do all the work and someone else will make the sale—and the money. State this up front, and you'll get a more valuable interaction than you would if you said, "I'm just looking."

2. "I have a very strict 5-year financial plan, and I need to see if these payments will fit in with it." This remark portrays you as finan-

cially responsible (and a good credit risk), without giving the salesperson false hopes. Don't misrepresent yourself with a statement like "I probably can't afford this." If it's true, it's nobody's business. If not, it undermines your negotiating power.

3. "I just won't buy on impulse. It's too much hassle to return things. I'll come back if I decide I want this." This comment serves as a gentle reminder that you won't be pressured into buying until you're sure you want the item, and it reinforces the idea that you will return an item that doesn't suit you. It works much better than a lame remark such as "I'm not sure about pink."

SECRETS OF A DEBT-FREE LIFE

Use that money as a "down payment" when the first invoice makes its appearance, then keep paying the same amount that you had been saving each month toward the purchase. If you've managed to get enough of a head start with your savings program, you may not even have to increase the Christmas club amount to meet the store's required payments—or you might be able to pay off the bill early.

FAMILY STRATEGIES

Charges Begin at Home

❖ If several family members can use a certain credit card, keep all versions of the card at home in a cookie tin or cigar

WHAT'S THE BEST MONEY SAVER?

Which Debt Is in Your Best Interest?

Mr. Hall wants a new lawn mower, which costs $800. He could pay cash, using the money he's saved for utility bills in the summer. But then he'd have to take the utility money from the grocery budget and charge groceries on his Visa card for 4 months until his scheduled raise. Alternatively, the lawn dealership will finance the mower for 8 months and give him 60 days to start paying. The credit card and the lawn dealership charge the same interest.

What should Mr. Hall do?

A. Use the cash and charge groceries for 4 months

B. Finance the mower for 8 months

Even if he could pay the credit card bill in less than 8 months, Mr. Hall should (B) finance the mower for 8 months. Here's why: He'll consume the groceries immediately. Should he become unable to make his credit card payments, he'd have nothing to resell. If he can't pay the mower financing, he can always come up with the money by selling the mower (or the company can repossess it). In addition, the 8-month financing is closed-ended, so Mr. Hall can't choose to extend it. Last, Mr. Hall should keep his credit card balance freed up for real emergencies. A brand-new lawn mower doesn't fall into that category.

box. Keep a sign-out list by the box, with columns for name, date, intended purchase, and amount. Require another family member to initial the entry before a purchase is made and again when the card is returned (checking the receipt, which is placed in the box). The hassle alone may keep someone from making an unnecessary purchase, and impulse buys will be more difficult to disguise.

Let's See How We're Doing

❖ Keep a tally for all to see how well the family is doing on curtailing credit card purchases. Reserve a portion of the kitchen bulletin board the same width as two playing cards and a couple of inches longer. At the top, tap in a 2-inch nail at the center of each space. At the bottom, attach a piece of masking tape labeled in bold letters Days without a Credit Card Purchase. Then take a defunct deck of cards and use a hole puncher to make a small hole in the top center of the ace through number 10 cards, as well as a joker (for a zero). Hang the cards on the nails to designate the number of days the family has avoided the credit card menace, using both nails when you get into double digits.

Let everyone know how long it's been since you made a credit card purchase by posting it on a bulletin board.

This Isn't Very Convenient

❖ Convenience store purchases on the road or before or after work can really add up on a credit card bill, so curtail the habit. When anyone in the family uses a credit card at a convenience store, require that person to forfeit a dollar to a collection jar at home. Before long, you should amass enough money so that family members can borrow cash from the jar for the convenience store (signing an IOU, of course). That will cost them only an extra dime on repayment.

❖ To make sure the idea doesn't lose steam, put a child in charge of collecting the fees and pay her 10 percent of the collections.

A DEBT-FREE CHRISTMAS

This One's for Whom?

❖ Are you one of those bargain hunters who indiscriminately snaps up sales items, intending to give them out next Christmas? But when next year rolls around, you discover that they aren't appropriate for some of the people on your list, and you have to charge several last-minute gifts. Buy specific gifts for specific people, no matter how much money you think you're saving.

Yuck, It's Perfect

❖ When you're trying to pace your spending by buying Christmas gifts ahead of time, purchase only things that you don't particularly need or want yourself. That will keep you from investing in two of the same item or using the item yourself, then having to buy another gift, which can result in last-minute credit card charges.

Push the Limit

❖ If a group of friends or family members regularly sets a dollar limit for a gift exchange, great! But before you determine that the gift you'd like to give is within the range, add the interest charges you'll pay to the purchase price of the item. It may not seem so affordable.

CHAPTER 6

DO-IT-YOURSELF SAVINGS

*E*very week or month, your household income seems to fly in and out of your bank account, hardly touching down, let alone nesting. With regular bills to pay, not to mention unexpected expenses, how can you possibly save a dime? You can—but the key is saving one dime at a time. Saving small amounts regularly has two advantages. First, small amounts are pretty easy to handle; you are unlikely to miss a little loose change here and there. That means that you will be more likely to stick to the savings habit you start. Second, small amounts add up to large ones. You can use those larger amounts to purchase special items or transfer the balance to longer-term savings targeted for college, a house, or retirement.

The first way to start building a nest egg is to pay yourself; after all, you're worth it! If you work outside the home, shave off a percentage of every paycheck and deposit it in your savings account. There are lots of other ways to pay yourself, and we'll show you how. For instance, brew your morning coffee at home instead of stopping by the coffee shop every day, then deposit your savings in an empty coffee can in your kitchen cupboard. Or pay yourself for household chores and deposit the money in a savings account.

The second way to build your nest egg is to save change. For example, at the end of each day, empty your pockets or wallet of loose change and toss it all into a jar (or some other, more creative container). Or make grocery coupons really count by depositing the amount you save on each item in a jar. Save larger chunks of change, too, such as tax refund checks. Before you know it, your nest egg will be nice and plump.

KEEP THE SAVINGS

Buy Yourself a Cup of Coffee

❖ Can't do without that cup of joe on your way to work or at the office cafeteria? You can still have your morning jolt but increase your savings by making a small change in your daily habit. Instead of visiting the coffee shop, make your coffee at home and fill an insulated travel mug or thermos for your trip to work. Keep an empty coffee can in your kitchen cupboard and toss the amount you'd otherwise be paying for a cup of coffee in the can. You'll be surprised how quickly the cents will add up.

❖ If you're the type who thinks you can't go without your gourmet coffee fix, try these simple ways to make your own fancy coffee. Add a half teaspoon or so of ground cinnamon or cocoa powder (or a quarter teaspoon or so of each) to the ground beans for your pot. A drop of vanilla, almond, or cherry extract added to a cup of coffee will give it a little zing, too. Look for flavored extracts in the baking aisle of your grocery store. You'll find a wide range of flavorings to experiment with.

I Gave at the Office

❖ Every time you make a donation to a charity, donate the same amount to your own savings account. Your savings donation isn't tax deductible, but it will make you feel just as good.

Offer a Reward

❖ When you see something you've just got to have—a pair of shoes or a compact disc, for example—resist the impulse to buy, then reward yourself. Deposit the price of the item into your savings account. At the end of a year, you'll be amazed at the amount of money you've saved.

Check This Out

❖ Here's a great way for book lovers to save. Every time you check a current book out of the library—say, a novel on the bestseller list—look on the jacket for the book's list price. Then deposit the price of the book in your savings

WORLD-CLASS FRUGALITY
A Picture That's Worth 50 Cents

To my mother, there was no such thing as a nest egg. When I was a child, just before the Depression, people didn't have much money—not in Harvard, Nebraska, anyway. My mother set aside the money she needed for groceries, and if there was 50 cents left over, nobody knew it. She hid those coins, tucking them behind the pictures hanging in the living room. Extra money never got out in the open.

Other people hid money in the sugar bowl or a dish that sat in the cupboard and didn't get used much. It was just rainy day change for emergencies. If the money accumulated, you could buy something you needed, such as shoes or a coat, or something extra.

When I became a wife and a mother, I also hid extra money behind pictures around the house—at least for a few years. Like my mother, I had quarters and nickels stashed everywhere. When my mother got older, she was afraid she'd die before she could tell us where she'd hidden her money. Luckily, my sisters were with her before she died. She wanted us to have the money she'd saved, and she told my sisters which pictures and knickknacks had pennies in them.

They found $10 or $20 in change, and we split it, because that's what my mother wanted. It wasn't much, but all those years she felt safe because it was nearby.

—**Mildred Jensen**
Hastings, Nebraska

account. Instead of buying the book, you've read it for free—and saved the purchase price.

Eat In

❖ If you crave a gourmet meal, go for it—but don't pay restaurant prices. Instead, hire yourself as chef for the evening. Cook your (or your spouse's) favorite meal at home; it's okay to splurge on the best ingredients, even a bottle of wine. Don't forget to use the good dishes, place mats, and cloth napkins. Even light a candle or two for atmosphere. Then deposit the amount you would have spent at your favorite restaurant in your savings account. Your appetite—and your savings account—will be satisfied.

FRUGAL FORMULAS
AGE COUNTS

You want to put aside some money for your child or grandchild, but you don't have enough cash on hand right now to invest in a certificate of deposit (CD), mutual fund, or other option offered by financial institutions. Don't worry; here's a simple, painless formula for getting started. Weekly or monthly, set aside the amount of the child's age on his or her next birthday. If your grandson is going to be 5, for example, deposit $5 in a savings account each week or month for the entire year. Don't think it will add up to very much? Wrong! Take a look at this table, showing how much you'll save each year, not including interest.

Age	Monthly	Weekly
1	$12	$52
2	$24	$104
3	$36	$156
4	$48	$208
5	$60	$260
6	$72	$312
7	$84	$364
8	$96	$416
9	$108	$468
10	$120	$520
Total	$660	$2,860

Now let's say you stop contributing after age 10 and transfer the savings to an 8-year CD or other low-risk investment that yields about 8 percent annually. In 8 years, that $660 will just about double, and the $2,860 will amount to more than $5,200.

Turn Pro

❖ So you're not a professional painter or wallpaper hanger, but you're so good that you could be. You're pretty good at swinging a hammer, too. Here's how to turn that know-how into savings. Every time your house needs work—carpentry, painting, wallpapering, plumbing—for which you have the skills, do it yourself. But here's the important part: Pay yourself for the job. Determine how much it would cost to hire a professional, then pay yourself the going rate by depositing the amount in your savings account. When you really need to hire someone—say, to put on a new roof—the money will be waiting for you.

❖ If you can't afford the going rate for a particular service, pay yourself half.

Scale Down

❖ Pay yourself, instead of a weight loss center, for every pound you lose while on a weight loss program. Decide on a rate that's comfortable for you—$1, $2, or $5 per pound—and deposit the appropriate amount in savings each time you record a weight loss. By the time you reach your goal, your savings, rather than your body, will be plump.

Exercise This Option

❖ Fitness centers can be very expensive to join. They usually charge an initiation fee, then a monthly fee that can total as much as $1,000 per year. Instead of paying the gym to help you get fit, pay yourself. Choose a home fitness program—walking, riding your bike, following along with a television exercise program or video—then make weekly or monthly deposits in your savings account equal to the going rate at your local gym. At the end of the year, you'll be fit and rich.

Be a Cardsharp

❖ Greeting cards cost a mint these days, and most get tossed as soon as they're read. Here's a way to send your sentiments and add to your savings at the same time. Make your own cards from wrapping paper, wallpaper scraps, discarded gift bags, and the like. Buy packets of inexpensive envelopes at a discount store or office supply store. Then each time you send or give one of these cards, deposit $2 to $3 in your savings account. You'll be amazed at how much card money you'll accumulate throughout the year— enough, perhaps, to buy holiday gifts when the season rolls around.

Read It and Reap

❖ Magazine and newspaper subscriptions really add up, and most of us don't even read all of them on a regular basis. So cancel them. Instead, deposit the price of each subscription in your savings account and head to the library to read your favorite rags for free.

Clip and Save

❖ Make grocery coupons do double duty by treating the amount you save on each item as change. Toss it in a jar and see how your savings add up.

REIMBURSEMENTS, REBATES, AND REFUNDS

Travel Light

❖ If you travel for your job, you have yet another opportunity to save money. When you receive reimbursement for your expenses from your employer, deposit the check in a savings account. When you've saved enough, use the money to pay for a family vacation.

Taxi down the Refund Way

❖ When you get a tax refund, don't spend it—save it. Depending on the amount of the return, you may be able to buy a savings bond, deposit it in a certificate of deposit, or invest in a mutual fund.

❖ If the amount is small, toss it right into your regular savings account. If you do this year after year, those dollars Uncle Sam has returned to you will add up.

Save the Daily Bread

❖ The great thing about saving is that every penny counts; no sum is too small to save. Put a dollar a day into a jar, and at the end of a year you'll have $365 (or $366) you didn't have before. Next year, try saving $2 a day.

IT WORKED FOR ME
Small Change, Big Plans

My wife, Sue, used to think I was nuts. Whenever we went shopping, to a restaurant, or even out for a newspaper, I refused to pay with exact change. If an item cost $5.48, Sue would root through her pockets for the exact amount. Not me. I'd drop another paper bill on the counter, even if I had a dollar's worth of change in my pocket. On an average day, I'd come home with 75 cents to a $1.50 in nickels, dimes, quarters, and pennies.

For a long time, there was change everywhere—in ashtrays, coffee mugs, and candy dishes. Small piles and stacks of change cluttered up windowsills, dressers, and end tables. Sue was beside herself, especially when the vacuum cleaner went into seizures as the odd penny ricocheted inside it. When she became pregnant, I realized that we'd have to adjust our lifestyle— even I knew that small children and small change don't mix.

One day I brought home an empty 5-gallon plastic watercooler bottle. The delivery guy who serviced my office said it had a pinhole leak and was useless. It couldn't hold water, but it could hold my coin collection.

My wife and I gathered up all the change and deposited it in the bottle, making our home baby-proof. When we were finished, the bottle was a third full; within months it was half full. Since then, every year or so we cash in the change, netting several hundred dollars. We usually use this money to supplement our vacation fund. One year we spent a long weekend at a casino on just our spare change.

—Tom Donnelly
Flushing, New York

Have a Change of Plan

❖ You've probably already signed up for one of those telephone plans that promise you savings. (If not, review your existing plan to see whether another one would save you more on calls.) The great thing about this is that phone companies, as part of their marketing ploys, usually spell out how much you've saved on your bill each month. Make those savings real: When you pay your phone bill, deposit the savings into an interest-bearing bank account, even if it's only a few dollars. At the end of the year, you may have saved enough cash to visit Mom or Grandma instead of calling them.

Do-It-Yourself Banking Jr.

❖ Most kids love the idea of saving money. Don't defeat the purpose by buying an expensive piggy bank. Instead, let your little ones make their own. Find an empty shoe box with a lid, then cut a slot about 2 inches long in the top for them to slide their money through. Or add a clever touch by cutting several slots in the top—one each for bills, quarters, dimes, nickels, and pennies. Have kids decorate their banks any way they want, with crayons, markers, fabric, buttons, glitter, or whatever.

THE YANKEE MISER RECOMMENDS . . .
Turning Chores into Dollars

I hate doing household chores. I love saving money. So I combine the two. I set a fee schedule for routine chores—ironing, vacuuming, dusting, making beds, doing laundry, taking out the trash, and so forth. Then I pay myself in cash for doing the chores. I put the money in a jar, and at the end of each week, I head to the bank with my bundle of cash. This way, I'm motivated to do even the crummiest chores, like cleaning the bathrooms (I pay myself plenty for doing that). The house gets cleaned, and my savings account gets fatter.

OTHER SAVING IDEAS

Stake Your Claim

❖ You think you know where every penny you've earned has gone, but maybe you don't. If you have moved at any time, are you certain you closed all your bank accounts and transferred the balances to a new bank? Did you leave behind any certificates of deposit or treasury bills that hadn't yet matured? How about your individual retirement account? Double-check with every bank where you once had accounts. You may have accumulated savings that you didn't even know about.

Keep the Gift That Keeps on Giving

❖ When your child receives a gift of money—$5 from Grandpa in a Valentine's Day card, $10 from Aunt Peg on a birthday, or even larger cash gifts on graduation day—encourage him to put it in a savings account instead of buying something. Over time, these small gifts will add up to significant savings.

Join the Club

❖ Christmas clubs, which are special savings accounts set up by banks to facilitate saving for holiday expenses, can be a great way to accumulate funds on a regular basis. Contact your bank for specifics (or shop around for the best interest rates). Most clubs start in October and continue through the following September, so participants receive their money in plenty of time to shop for the holidays. When you sign up, you commit to depositing a certain amount in your account each week—$5, $10, or even more. The amount is usually up to you.

❖ Alternatively, establish your own savings club. Open a savings account and commit to depositing a certain amount each week throughout the year. Use the money for holiday shopping or just let it accumulate indefinitely.

CHAPTER 7

TRIMMING TAXES AND FINANCIAL FEES

a frugal person can really shine in the world of high finance. That's because those who set the fees, loan the money, and collect the taxes are constantly coming up with new deals, new ripples, and new rules. And that favors those of us who are willing to stay on top of things—to mind our business, if you will. Everyone has the same ability to tap the best offers and avoid the pitfalls, but you, as a Yankee watchdog, will persevere and benefit from the ever-changing realm of possibilities.

Here's just one example. Studies show that the interest banks pay on certificates of deposit and savings accounts vary by as much as 2 percent—maybe thousands of dollars a year, which can go into your pocket if you find the right savings account. This illustrates the direct path to making the most of your financial interactions: Do your homework, and not only on interest rates. Keep current on bank fees, credit card charges, and potential tax deductions.

Your first task is to find out about your credit rating and take any steps necessary to make it strong and clear. If you think you're in good shape, keep this in mind: About half of all consumers have errors in their credit files, and 1 in 10 errors is serious enough to cause them to be denied credit. Even if you're not looking for good loan rates, it's critical to have a solid credit rating, because those who do, earn the right to earn the highest interest, pay the lowest fees, and choose from the most options. In short, financial institutions have a stake in offering creditworthy customers the best they have to offer.

One other thing: Keep careful records of your financial interactions, particularly those that involve your tax returns. That way, you'll never lose money because you don't have the records to support the tax breaks you've taken. You'll know precisely where you stand with each financial improvement you're working to achieve, and you can show your progress to anyone who can help you on your way.

SAVING MONEY AT THE BANK

Let's Keep This between Us

❖ If you can, do all your business at one bank or credit union. When you have all your funds in one bank, it will usually charge you less for services. Just as important, you'll have more power (the implied threat of losing all your business) when it comes time to negotiate a loan, ask for an increased credit card limit, or request reduced fees for bank services such as traveler's checks.

This Just Looks Like a Credit Card

❖ So that you don't have to pay an automatic teller machine fee every time you need substantial cash, such as for groceries or a car repair, seek a bank that offers a debit card with a credit card logo, such as Visa or MasterCard. These charges are deducted from your checking account, sometimes immediately and sometimes at around the same speed as checks. You can't charge items worth more than is in your checking account, but the debit card is accepted wherever the credit card is, usually without a fee from the bank or the merchant.

Stamp Out Designer Checks

❖ If you have the fee for your supply of checks automatically deducted from your account, you may not realize how much more you're paying for the enjoyment of paying bills with checks that have say, sailboats on them. They could cost $4 or $5 per box more than plain checks. And who sees those checks, anyway, besides you and your creditors? Switch to the plainest checks (or at least the cheapest checks) you can buy, then perk them up yourself with a small rubber stamp, taking care to avoid any bar codes or account numbers across the bottom of the checks. You can find an elegant stamp at a craft supply store or upscale bookstore, or stop by a discount store to buy one of those newfangled "stamp markers" that companies such as Crayola manufacture.

Mail-Order Checklist

❖ Ordering checks from a mail-order company can save you some money, but make sure to answer these questions

FOUR WAYS TO FIND A CREDIT UNION

Credit unions can be a great deal if you can join one, but stiff laws regulate the field of membership. If your company doesn't sponsor its own credit union or offer someone else's, here are four other things to try.

I. Rate your state. Call your state's credit union league and find out which credit unions in your area might be open to you. The Credit Union National Association, listed in toll-free directory assistance (800-555-1212), can steer you to your state league or association. Or search the Internet using the keywords "credit union league" or "Credit Union National Association."

2. Shake the family tree. Most credit unions allow other family members to have separate accounts. That may mean immediate family members, or it may extend to siblings, grandparents, aunts and uncles, and even cousins.

3. Geography, not biology. Some credit unions serve people who live in a particular geographical region. Ask your neighbors and call the local chamber of commerce, usually listed in the White Pages, to see what you can turn up.

4. Check in with "Old Yeller." Check the Yellow Pages and see which credit unions are advertised. They rarely do more extensive promotions.

Mr. Tate is a pipe fitter and can join Pipetapper Credit Union. There he would have to keep $250 in savings as a "share" of the credit union, but his checking account would be free. At Your Town Bank, he would receive free checking and earn standard interest, as long as his average daily balance never fell below $500; otherwise, he'd pay $5 a month. Which option is the better deal for Mr. Tate?

A. Pipetapper Credit Union

B. Your Town Bank

If Mr. Tate's checking balance varies greatly, the answer is (A) Pipetapper Credit Union. There Mr. Tate's untouchable $250 does pay interest, and he will get it back if he quits the credit union. Also, he'll earn interest on anything above that $250. At Your Town Bank, he would have to keep $500 inactive ($250 more than the credit union requires) to earn interest. Should he fall below $500 for even 1 month, he would lose interest on all the funds between $0 and $499, and he would forfeit an additional $5—money he'll never see again. If Mr. Tate keeps a lot of money in the bank, Your Town Bank is the better alternative. But if he has the funds to maintain a balance higher than $500, he might want to look at a savings vehicle that yields higher interest than a checking account.

before you sign on: How much will I pay for shipping and handling? What's the price increase after my first order? Do I pay extra for deposit slips or checkbook covers? If the company requires a two-box minimum per order, am I planning to have this account long enough to use all those checks? How many checks will I get per box, compared with what I get now? If my order will take longer to fill than it would at my bank, will that cost me time (filling out counter checks), money (late fees), or credibility (many establishments won't allow you to write a counter check)?

No, Sir, No Surcharges

❖ For a listing of automatic teller machines in your area that don't require a surcharge, contact your state's credit union league. To find its number, contact the Credit Union National Association by calling toll-free directory assistance at (800) 555-1212. Or search online on the key-words "Credit Union League" or "Credit Union National Association."

No Substitute for a Good Credit Union

❖ Credit unions uniformly save you money on fees and loans. As nonprofits, they can afford to. But if you've exhausted your options and still can't seem to find a credit union that can legally accept you as a member, consider a little creative career hopping. Sign up as a substitute teacher in your school system. If you don't have another full-time job, work a couple of days a month. If you do work elsewhere regularly, use a few vacation days to substitute teach. That should qualify you for membership in some teachers credit unions, and the standard approach is "once a member, always a member." Just call the credit union to check on membership requirements before taking such a drastic step.

❖ Can't see yourself in front of a classroom? See if you can become a part-time employee by filling in on a bus route as a driver for a week or two one year, or sign up to substitute as a school system clerk, typist, or teacher's aide.

CONTROLLING CREDIT CARD FEES

Go for the Gold?

❖ Before you pay a higher annual fee for a Gold Card, list its advantages over your ordinary card and how much money you'll save overall. Then ask yourself, "Am I already getting this perk somewhere else? Or could I, less expensively?" For example, your standard auto insurance may already cover the collision damage waiver on rental cars, and another card in your possession might offer an extended warranty on purchases without an additional fee.

❖ Is it the higher credit limit that has you yearning for the higher-fee Gold Card? Ordinarily, if your credit record is so good that Gold Card issuers are approaching you, you will qualify for a higher credit limit with your existing card. So ask that company first.

900 Reasons Not to Respond to This Ad

❖ If you would like to find out about low-interest or no-annual-fee credit cards, go online and search on the key-words "low fee credit cards." Or call your local library and ask how you can find a current list offline. You also might ask your bank about its cards or request a referral. Avoid TV and print ads, as well as telemarketers, that promise a guaranteed MasterCard or Visa if you'll call a 900 number. Usually, you'll pay top dollar for the call and may get nothing more than an offer that requires you to pay up front for a secured card or, worse, a list of banks that issue secured cards.

WORLD-CLASS FRUGALITY
I Want My Credit Back!

Like so many people, Tom Malloy went deeply into debt when he got divorced, racking up $10,000 just in local, state, and federal taxes. He did manage to pay off his debts after 7 years, but his credit reports still reflected his problems, with long lists of late payments and even tax liens. Tired of getting turned down for credit cards, Tom, who lives in Lansdale, Pennsylvania, systematically attacked his credit report.

He estimates that he spent 1,000 hours writing letters to his former creditors, clearing up small errors and exaggerations, and asking them to take references about late payments off the record. He even sent flowers or notes to people who helped his cause. The results of 10 months' worth of effort? Tom had 39 derogatory references struck from his report, and now he has 15 credit cards. That's a few too many for our taste, but we figure he can handle it—who would want to go through that again?

Pretty Logos, Ugly Interest Rates

❖ You know those solicitations from your favorite charity or alumni organization asking you to apply for a credit card that will have the organization's logo printed on it and saying that a certain percentage of your charges will be donated to the organization? Tread carefully here. If the card has all the features you want and rates as low as any other card you have, go for it. But don't let guilt or wanting that prestigious logo cloud your judgment. Typically, the "donations" to your cause come from higher interest rates, and a negligible portion of your charges (sometimes as little as 50 cents of every $100) is donated to the organization. Last, consider making a comparable

ONLINE BANKS, OFFLINE SAVINGS

A re you constantly in Dutch because of late or nearly late payments? Do you occasionally run the risk of bouncing a check? Do you rarely have much money left over after you pay your bills? If you're online and paying for unlimited usage, you might want to consider online banking and bill paying. Typically, banks charge a few dollars a month for the service (credit unions may offer it for free). You can earn the fee back by minimizing these other costs.

I. Bounced checks. With online banking, you're able to check your balance daily and have a complete list of which checks have cleared at your fingertips, so you shouldn't be bouncing any more checks.

2. New checks. When you pay bills electronically, you don't have to buy as many checks.

3. Postage. Paying bills online will help you save on postage costs, which can add up.

4. Late fees. When you pay bills electronically, the funds arrive immediately at the vendor or service provider. You can wait until the last day without risking late-payment fees or worrying about whether a particular check has cleared (the amount comes out of your account immediately).

5. Transfers. If you need funds to cover a payment, you can usually shift money from one account to another without a trip to the bank. That saves on gas and shoe leather, too.

donation to the organization instead of taking on the card. Such a donation is tax deductible for most people who itemize.

What Does It Mean When You Say "Grace"?

❖ Your credit card's grace period—the time you have to pay without incurring interest or late fees—starts on the date printed on the bill, not the date you get the bill. So put that date on your calendar for the next 3 or 4 months (typically, it's the same day each month) without waiting for the bill to arrive. When the bill does come, double-check to make certain the date hasn't changed. This little exercise is well worth your time when you consider that a typical late-payment fee can be more than $20, in addition to interest charges.

Not-So-Amazing Grace Periods

❖ It's not enough to know how long the grace period is. You also need to find out how your credit card company, or any issuer you're considering, calculates the grace period on new purchases. Avoid companies that don't charge interest only in months when you have no previous balance. Find a bank that gives you the stated grace period on all new purchases, even if you have a balance from the previous month, and you can save an astonishing amount on interest.

And Now for the Small Print

❖ Unless you pay an annual fee and must renew your credit card, the issuer has no obligation to draw your attention to any changes in fees or interest rates. So make a list of all your credit cards in a notebook, leaving space to put the interest rates, grace periods, and annual fees. Then each month when your bill arrives, look at the table on the back of the bill and note any changes in your notebook. This not only will help you plan better, but it will readily show which cards are charging the most—and should be paid off and cut up first.

CLEAN UP YOUR CREDIT RATING

Make Sure They Get Good News

❖ To strengthen your credit report, ask the organizations you pay regularly and on time to report your activities to a credit bureau. Include a note with your next payment specifying which of the three American credit-reporting agencies you're most interested in satisfying. Ask the company to write back and confirm that it will start reporting your payments, if it doesn't already. Consider making the request of utility companies, cable companies, and mobile or cell phone providers, too.

Let the Agency Play FBI

❖ Should you find an error in your credit report, write to the reporting agency immediately. State which information in the report you are disputing and why. By law, if the company can't verify the information within 30 days, it must remove the item.

Let Me Explain

❖ Ever just let a bill slide indefinitely? You know, the vendor was hostile or overcharged; you never bought the charged item; or the product didn't perform well. If such an item shows up on your credit report, contact the credit-reporting agency immediately and exercise your legal right to have a 100-word statement explaining the situation attached to your credit report.

Purge It if It Isn't Perfect

❖ If a credit report reflects something you did do—pay late, have a card taken away—make sure to correct any other erroneous information within that item. For instance, always protest a report that says an account is open when it isn't or that incorrectly reports the original date of delinquency. Lending agencies will use this information to evaluate your applications for credit, so make sure all of it is correct.

❖ If you have the time and energy, protest if you find that an amount is slightly wrong, a lender's name is off by a bit, or there's another small discrepancy. This won't help your cause with lenders, but you might luck out, and the credit agency will strike the entire reference because it can't run down the information in question within the 30-day time limit.

That's All behind Me Now

❖ Look for items in your credit report that are beyond the statute of limitations. By law, an item that demonstrates poor credit can stay on your report for 7 years; a record of filing for bankruptcy can live on for 10 years.

TAX SAVINGS: CHARITABLE DONATIONS

Keep Up the Good Works

❖ To motivate yourself to get the best tax deductions for your charity dollar, plow your "earnings" back into the charity of your choice.

YOU CALL IT CHARITY?
THE IRS CALLS IT TAXABLE

These expenditures do not qualify for a charitable contribution tax break per IRS standards.

I. Money that was paid directly to a needy person

2. Blood donated to an individual or blood bank

3. Dues paid to alumni associations, fraternal organizations, country clubs, lodges, or social or sports clubs

4. Bingo tickets, raffle tickets, or lottery tickets

5. Donations or in-kind services given to chambers of commerce, political candidates, or lobbying organizations

6. Donations to foreign charities (unless an American charity funnels the funds to them)

7. Private or parochial school tuition

The IRS Says Okay Online

❖ Make sure you're giving to an IRS-approved charity before tax time by viewing the IRS's list of charities that have passed muster. You can find the list online by searching on the keywords "IRS" and "tax-exempt charities." (If you don't have a computer, head to your library, which almost certainly does.) Once you find the list, search for the organization you'd like to check by name or by city and state.

❖ No access to online services? After checking to make sure your local library's reference desk or business library doesn't have a hard copy of the list on hand, call the IRS's toll-free number (call toll-free directory assistance at 800-555-1212) and request Publication 78. This is a list of tax-exempt organizations, but it might not be as up-to-date as the online list.

❖ Before you say yes to those firefighters bearing tickets, ask them—or any other organization sponsoring a benefit—to spell out in writing what portion of the ticket cost is deductible.

Check Out This Donation

❖ When you deduct a Noncash Charitable Contribution, the IRS will want to know how you established the donation's fair market value. If you have books that are in good shape and would appeal to a fairly broad audience, consider donating them to a public or school library instead of Goodwill. That way, you can use the cost of replacing the book at the library as your method for establishing fair market value, instead of the thrift store price, which is almost always several dollars lower.

Let Your Veggies Eat Your Taxes

❖ Has it been a banner year for the fresh produce from your garden? Once you and your neighbors have tired of the excess, consider calling a homeless shelter or community kitchen to ask whether it can use your surplus. If so, you can consider the fair market value of your donation to be the grocery store price for comparable produce.

❖ If your local shelter is inundated with, say, zucchini in late summer, consider freezing, pickling, or canning the excess. Then make a donation later in the year, when the shelter needs more food.

Drive Miles, Then Take a Write-(Off)

❖ Don't forget to note the mileage, date, and reason when you drive for charity, whether you're dropping off Thanksgiving baskets or attending a leadership seminar as a representative of a nonprofit organization. Even a 20-mile trip can result in more than a $5 write-off, which will yield at least $1 off your taxes—almost enough for a gallon of gas.

THE YANKEE MISER RECOMMENDS . . .
Winning the Tax Race by an Heir(loom)

I'll wager I'm not the only one who's ever inherited a piece of jewelry or art that was quite valuable but just not my style. Recently, I decided that one particularly disagreeable set could help the charity of my choice, reduce my taxes considerably, and honor the aunt I inherited it from, all in one fell swoop. Here's what I did. I donated the ring and matching necklace to a charity in my aunt's memory. When I inherited the set, it was worth $1,000. I'd had it for some years, and it was then worth $3,000. If I'd sold it, I would have paid a capital gains tax on that increase in value. But because I donated the items, I avoided the capital gains tax and was able to take the charitable contributions deduction based on the jewelry set's fair market value—$3,000.

You can usually donate antique jewelry and art in this way if you've owned it for more than a year. The IRS also limits deductions for "ordinary income property." That's just a fancy way to say that you can't take the full market value of things that you'd ordinarily use to produce income, such as art you created yourself or inventory. In those cases, you can deduct only a percentage of your actual costs.

TAX SAVINGS: RETIREMENT FUNDS

My, How You'll Grow!

❖ It's easy to lose sight of the fact that your individual retirement account (IRA) or 401(k) contributions will grow enormously over time and are a fine investment in your future. To assign some cold, hard numbers to the vague feeling that you'll have more money later on, go online and summon a free 401(k) or IRA calculator by searching on the keywords "IRA" and "taxes." Enter your contribution, your employer's match, your investment rate, and your projected salary increase. The calculator will compute your projected IRA balance for each of the years during the period in which you are interested.

Go (Re)figure

❖ Each year when you get your individual retirement account (IRA) or 401(k) statement, revisit the online calculator to see how your projections compare to the actual performance.

WHAT'S THE BEST MONEY SAVER?
Reconsider the Rebate

Tom and Bill have shopped for credit cards, and since both have high long-distance telephone bills, both have settled on cards offered by long-distance carriers. Who is the smarter shopper?

A. Tom, who receives a 5 percent discount on all calls from Phone Home Enterprises

B. Bill, who receives a 5 percent rebate on all calls from Dial M, Inc.

The answer is (A) Tom, because a discount up front is worth more than a rebate at a later date, all other factors being equal. Keep in mind, too, that many rebates aren't figured until the end of the year, which makes you lose interest on the money you paid up front. Last, check out the fine print on discounts or rebates. Often the best rate applies only to purchases over a certain annual amount.

❖ Use play money to update your 5-year projection each year. For added spice after the first year, write a reward— a candy bar, movie, or weekend away—on the back of 5 or 10 of the spare bills at random, then shuffle them. Each year when you dole out more bills, treat yourself to the specified reward if you earn a bill with one written on the back.

I Retire a Little Every Year

❖ To continually reinforce the benefits of making contributions, each year when you receive your annual individual retirement account (IRA) or 401(k) earnings statement, have a special dinner with your spouse or family. At the end, say a few words about how well the fund is doing (no need to divulge figures unless you'd like to) and how it will help you meet your retirement goals. If you like, give the dinner a retirement-based theme—a fish dinner, for example, or Florida cuisine.

❖ If your fund has done well, you might want to match 1 to 3 percent of the earnings and spring for an early retirement present or activity. If your retirement dream is to sail around the Caribbean, for example, rent a sailboat for a weekend.

TAX SAVINGS: MISCELLANEOUS

That Mortgage Interest Isn't All That Interesting

❖ To deduct mortgage interest for "Business Use of a Home," make sure that it's interest on a loan that benefits the home, such as a new central heating system or storm windows. When you use your line of equity for consumer goods such as cars, Christmas presents, restaurant meals, and the like, you can't deduct the interest you pay on that portion of the debt as mortgage interest for "Business Use of a Home."

TRIMMING TAXES AND FINANCIAL FEES

A Record Year for This Home Business

❖ If you're considering claiming that you used a portion of your home as a consistent and primary location for a business or as an unreimbursed employee expense (home office), keep a regular record of your business activities and expenditures: utility bills, with separate accounts for water, electricity, heat, and gas; mortgage interest, if the loan benefited your home; real estate taxes; home owner's insurance; your rent (if you rent rather than own your home); repairs and maintenance, and whether they benefited the business part of your home only or were part of keeping up and running your entire home; and any improvements or additions, and whether they benefited the business part of your home only or were part of keeping up and running your entire home. In addition, record the square footage of your home, including garages and sheds, if applicable; the percentage of your home that you used for business only; and the date you started using your home for business.

RECORD KEEPING 101

Don't Wine about Keeping Records

❖ No one says you have to have a fancy file cabinet to save the receipts and invoices you need to do your taxes at the end of the quarter or year. Instead, consider adapting a wine box, which you can obtain from a restaurant or liquor store. Write the names of the months on index cards, then staple one card inside the opening of each square compartment. Drop in that month's utility bills, phone bills, credit card bills, receipts, and mileage. If you can spare it, also include the appropriate page from your business calendar.

Transform a wine box into a receipt storage device.

CHAPTER 8

FINDING MONEY FOR EDUCATION, RETIREMENT, AND OTHER LARGE EXPENSES

Saving the odd dollar here and there can be fun. But when you set out to save for a bigger purchase or a long-term commitment such as retirement, the stakes go up. Along with your already fine-tuned ability to be frugal, you'll need strategies to stay motivated over the long haul.

To get a grip on the psychology required for long-term, big-money saving, consider this: Ever notice how much easier it is to be on time for an event you have selected yourself than for a work event where attendance is mandatory? Or that you don't mind emptying your wallet nearly as much for a cause you believe in as for yet another grapefruit sale to support the local high school band? Or that you can work more cheerfully on your garden, or even a cluttered living room, when you envision the beautiful blooms next spring or relaxing in that clean room?

The same thinking applies to saving money for big purchases or long-term goals. It's much easier to save when you choose what you're willing to sacrifice for, instead of saving because it's something you should do. It also helps to be convinced of the worthiness of your cause and to be able to link today's deprivation to tomorrow's payoff.

That's why it's so important to start any big savings project by determining just what you'd like to achieve. For example: "I would like to retire and be able to have the same standard of living I enjoy now." Or, "In two years, I'd

like to purchase a brand-new car." Then set a few short-term goals to help you achieve your vision. For instance: "I need to start contributing 50 percent more to my 401(k)." Or, "I'll start setting aside 10 percent of the down payment each month." Next plan the specific actions you must take to reach those goals.

Then, and only then, are you ready for some of the tactics that will help you save—sometimes without being aware that you are doing so. Some of these approaches are simple and straightforward, such as completing the paperwork so that your employer will automatically deposit a portion of your check into savings each pay period. Other ideas are a little more creative, like selling your change to the local convenience store or encouraging your kid to grow loofah sponges for a college fund. The trick is to try the tips that fit your savings style, as you continue to pursue the dreams that are dependent on cold, hard cash to come true.

THE PSYCHOLOGY OF SAVING BIG

This Little Dollar Goes to Vacation

❖ Instead of putting all your savings in one big pot, decide precisely what you're saving for and how much you'll need for each savings goal. That makes it a lot easier to concentrate on what you'll get if you save, instead of just getting a general sense that you're saving because it's something you should do—like flossing.

Savings, Sealed and Delivered

❖ Almost any long-term savings project worth its salt will require at lease one envelope, labeled with the savings goal, for cash, IOUs, records of payments, and price comparisons. No need to buy new envelopes for this purpose, especially if your town has just held an election. Political campaigns frequently print up a passel of time-sensitive envelopes. Head for headquarters and ask if you can have any extras after election day.

How Much Is That Model in the Showroom?

❖ Before you start putting money away for a big-ticket item, find out just how much the make and model you want costs. If there are several options, write each one and its price on the outside of your savings envelope or passbook. That way, you'll have a constant reminder of how close you are or how far you still have to go.

Out of Sight, Out of Mind

❖ One of the simplest ways to save money for big purchases is to put it away before you see it. If your employer offers a direct-deposit program, complete the paperwork so that a portion of your check will automatically be deposited into your savings account each pay period.

When Wendy's Braces Come Off, We're Ready

❖ Is the end in sight for a long-term expense that has required regular payments—for example, orthodontia, ballet lessons, a car, or night school tuition? If another expense won't immediately fill the void, the end of these payments could signal the start of a great savings possibility. Decide at least a month ahead of time how much of this money can go into savings, which savings goal you'll apply it to, and how (by check, direct deposit, or with cash in an envelope, for example). If you don't plan ahead, you'll be amazed at how quickly the money is absorbed into your everyday household budget, with no added benefit.

❖ If you're planning to redirect that money into savings, give yourself an immediate reward. After all, you've probably worked hard to pay that expense all these months or years. Either blow the equivalent of one payment before switching to the savings plan or put 10 percent into a short-term "family fun" budget.

Succeed in Stages

❖ To stay motivated to save over the long haul, match a long-term savings project with a related short-term goal

that you'll reach within a few weeks or every few weeks. For example, if you're saving $25 a week toward $1,000 worth of exercise equipment, put $5 a week toward a session with a massage therapist.

Our Stock Splits

❖ As you save money for a particularly big endeavor, such as a new car or college tuition, pay yourself a portion of the interest you earn as a "dividend." Establish ahead of time what percentage of the interest will come back to you—say, 2 percent if you're earning thousands annually, 5 percent if you're earning hundreds. It's important to have some funds with no strings attached so that you can either spend the dividend frivolously or apply it to one of your lesser, short-term savings goals.

BETTER BANK TACTICS

Save Me Several Accounts

❖ For each big-ticket purchase or goal, open a separate savings account—if you can open multiple accounts for free. If your bank doesn't endorse the idea, call around and try to find a bank that does.

Make It a Mommy-and-Me Account

❖ If you have young children, you can gain some extra savings accounts by opening accounts in their names with you as cosigner. Remember, though, if it's your money, you'll be expected to pay taxes on the interest earned.

Let the Bank (Lines) Hold You Up

❖ Open at least one savings account (but not a checking account) at a financial institution without completing the paperwork for an automatic teller machine card. That way, you'll have to go to the bank to make withdrawals, which can slow down impulse purchases using funds from your savings account.

The Nonbinding Bond

❖ Many mutual funds and certificates of deposit require large deposits to reap higher interest rates. Go ahead and combine various savings vehicles, even from different family members, to open these accounts. But make sure you keep a written record of how much money you contribute from each account and how much interest should result. A good way to keep it straight: Create your own certificates for each account or person who contributes, spelling out the

FOUR EARLY-EARNING PROJECTS

Even a child as young as 7 or 8 can earn a little extra pocket change. Encourage your child to put part of that money—say, half—toward his college fund. Here are some moneymaking projects suitable for the younger set.

1. Snip 'n' save. If you use grocery store coupons, let your child be responsible for clipping them, organizing them, and making sure the right ones make it to the store. Let the child pocket the savings at the checkout counter.

2. Can it. If you have an outlet that buys aluminum by the pound, let your child collect aluminum cans, foil, and pie and frozen food containers.

3. Are you out of your gourd? If children get started early enough in areas with a short growing season, they can grow birdhouse gourds for fun and profit. If you don't have a lot of space on the ground, trellis the gourds or grow them in garbage cans or whiskey barrels. Usually, your local extension office can tell you where to get the seeds. When your child is ready to sell the gourds (most fetch a couple of dollars each), contact your local ornithological society, run a classified ad in the paper, or see if the extension office will announce that she has gourds for sale.

4. You clean my back. Loofah sponges are actually a variety of dried gourd that grows readily in most climates. Your child can easily grow them and then sell them at the local health food store, farmers' market, or roadside stand. Ask your local extension office where you can buy seeds, or purchase them at a local nursery or from an upscale seed catalog, such as Shepherd's Garden Seeds.

amount, the "mature" amount, and the dates of deposit and maturity. A few sentences typed in a fancy typeface and signed by your family treasurer will suffice, or use the stationery templates available in most current word processing programs.

GETTING THE FAMILY INVOLVED

Change Your Ways

❖ You may be surprised to learn that those machines in grocery stores that convert change to cash charge as much as seven cents on the dollar. At the same time, a lot of banks accept change from their customers only, and some credit unions don't keep cash on the premises, so they can't accept change at all. So what's a coin-bearing Yankee to do? Sell your coins to the local convenience store. The store will be happy to have the money, since the bank charges it extra for rolls of change. The store will likely provide you with free change rollers (whereas your local discount store will

WORLD-CLASS FRUGALITY
Running for the . . . Small Change

When Craig Davidson runs, he has two goals in mind: getting fit for marathons and earning money for vacation. Every day, Craig runs along busy Bell Road in Phoenix, Arizona, and picks up every coin he spots. Between 1981 and 1999, he scooped up $5,700, including two $100 bills. More often, his take is about 70 cents a day, which he saves for family vacations. In 1991, the street change paid for a trip to Hawaii for Craig and his wife, Irene.

Another of Craig's collectibles is empty cigarette packages, which he redeems for prizes. The largest and most expensive was a satellite dish, but he's been known to cash in others for high-end Christmas presents and gifts for himself, such as a camera, a telescope, and a lantern—which he will not use for nighttime change-gathering expeditions.

charge around three cents each for rollers). And since you'll need to give the store your phone number, you won't have to go to the trouble of writing your name and account number on each roll as you would at most banks.

Raising Scrooge

❖ Some kids take the whole savings concept a little too far, squirreling away every penny. This may seem like a great habit, but it's important for a child to learn the enjoyment—and the responsibility—of spending money on something he really needs or wants. And just like adults, children need to recognize the benefits of setting a meaningful goal and attaining it, instead of saving just so you can say you do. So encourage your child to save with a purpose in mind. Also, make it a requirement that he spend at least a tenth of any gift money or allowance within 3 weeks of receiving it. Make a special savings jar for that money, labeled with the date by which it must be spent.

IRS RULES AND REGULATIONS

Do 3 to 6 Months in My IRA

❖ The recommended 3 to 6 months' living expenses is one of the most difficult things to save for—and one of the easiest accounts to siphon from, since it's accessible. If you have a traditional individual retirement account (IRA) and aren't already contributing the maximum amount, consider saving your living expenses within your IRA. That way, it can earn the usually higher interest associated with an IRA tax-free until you withdraw it. You do pay a 10 percent penalty if you must take it out before you retire, but that slows down frivolous borrowing. And with any luck, the penalty will be offset by years of interest earned before you must tap those funds in a true emergency. Before you try this approach, make sure your IRA allows you access to early payouts, and find out how often you can withdraw funds from the account.

Need a Home Loan? Ask Your IRA

❖ Not maxed out on your individual retirement account (IRA) contribution? If a new house or college is in your future, consider putting a portion of your home or school savings into your IRA until you reach the maximum. New laws allow you to tap your IRA penalty-free to buy a qualified first home or pay college expenses. Just run through the details with your tax advisor and IRA provider before you move any funds.

SALARY STRATEGIES

Don't Go into Overtime (Pay)

❖ Instead of considering overtime pay part of your salary package, budget to live on your base pay. Then create a savings budget each pay period to direct your extra income into the appropriate savings fund.

Assign Your Bonus

❖ Expecting a bonus? A few weeks before the payment, plan how each penny will figure in your savings plan, leaving a good 10 to 20 percent out of the plan so that you can splurge on some instant gratification. Even if you've worked very hard at a thankless job to earn the bonus, resist the temptation to think of it as a reward you should blow. And try not to anticipate the bonus months in advance, or you'll find that you've "spent" it before it arrives or gradually come to count on it as part of the everyday household budget. Instead, consider a bonus as a windfall that can help you reach your savings goals.

Look Forward to Five-Monday Months

❖ If you're paid every two weeks, budget so that you pay all your bills with two paychecks each month. That way, twice a year (mark your calendar), you'll have two "extra" paychecks. Plan how much of each check you'll contribute to each savings fund you have.

❖ If you're paid once a week, use just four paychecks a month, and you'll have four "extras" each year.

SAVING FOR A VACATION

Saving: Don't Leave Home without It

❖ To fan interest in the power of saving, create a menu of vacation options, with the savings required for each, and post it where all family members can see it. For example: "If we save $1 a week, in 6 months we can all go to the local zoo. If we save $10 a week, one of us can go on a cruise," and so forth. If you like, cut out appropriate magazine photos and paste them on the list to reinforce the message.

One Fewer Meal Out, One More Vacation Day

❖ Create a vacation budget, then save for different activities in different envelopes. Small sacrifices are easier to bear when you can see why you're making them. For instance, it'll be easier to give up that six-pack of beer each week when you know that doing so will pay for your moped rental during vacation.

❖ If you can, pair a savings sacrifice with a related vacation activity. For example, if you're giving up your afternoon soda every day for the vacation fund, put that money in the "meals out" envelope.

Let Disney Pay for the Beach

❖ When you're saving for a vacation, make a budget with ample padding. That way, you can splurge a little. You can even take it one step further: Anytime you go under budget while on vacation—you use a hotel coupon or skip a meal; it rains and you can't do an activity you budgeted for—set the money aside and take it home. Use it to start next year's vacation fund.

SAVING FOR COLLEGE

Back to School Can Pay You Back

❖ If you're planning to return to school, remember that you might save money on medical care by joining the student health plan. You also may be able to cut down on entertainment costs, since so many free or low-cost activities are offered at colleges, and on health club dues, since most schools have their own facilities. Although all of these things might require payment of fees, these costs are usually lower than their real-world equivalents. Rejoice over the savings, but also plan to funnel them back into the savings vehicle for your ongoing education.

Alms for the Alma Mater

❖ Hoping your children or grandchildren will eventually attend your alma mater? Sock away $10 every time your school wins a football game (or a match in any other sport you follow).

Expect Checks from Your Ex?

❖ If your divorce agreement spells out that your ex-spouse will pay for your children's college education (or will try to), check the law in your state to see whether it is possible to enforce the agreement before you rely on that money. Consult the reference librarian at your local library to find applicable portions of your state code or ask your attorney.

Who Gets Custody of the College Account?

❖ If you're still negotiating a divorce agreement, ask your attorney or mediator if both spouses can be required to contribute a certain portion of their income (or a flat fee) annually to an established savings vehicle for the children's college expenses. Such an agreement is much easier to abide by and enforce than simply requiring one or both spouses to pay for the children's college education 10 or 15 years in the future.

❖ If you can make such an arrangement, specify that the money will revert to the parents—with interest, in the same proportions contributed—should a child not attend college or not use all the money.

10 to Go (to College) On

❖ Starting as early as you start paying your child an allowance, increase the amount you would ordinarily pay by 10 percent, which your child will then deposit into a designated savings account for college. This reinforces both the

WORLD-CLASS FRUGALITY
This Wedding Is Brought to You By . . .

Frugal? Yes. Romantic? Not exactly. Sabrina Root and Tom Anderson of Philadelphia substantially reduced the amount of money they needed to save for their $25,000 wedding by having, um, sponsors pay for about half of it. The couple came up with the idea because Tom, who is a bartender, persuaded friends in the restaurant business to supply the food in exchange for promotional consideration. From there, the concept expanded to invitations, formal wear, and even the honeymoon (for which a friend donated his condo share in Cancún). In return, a list of the sponsors appeared in the calligraphic invitations and on T-shirts wedding guests took home.

At the reception, each company's name and logo appeared prominently in front of their donation to the big day. The way the couple sees it, having sponsors for a portion of their wedding allowed them to concentrate on saving for all the extras they needed to make the day really special: the service staff, limos, and photographer. Sabrina, who is a hairstylist, also insisted on paying for her own $1,800 wedding dress.

Selling sponsorships to pay for a wedding? It worked for this clever couple.

idea that your child will attend college and that she will shoulder some of the responsibility for paying for her schooling.

Nine for You, One for the U

❖ Make it a rule that your child will deposit at least 10 percent of every monetary gift into his college fund, starting as soon as he is old enough to understand the concept of money (for some, this is as early as age 5 or 6). Make filling out a deposit slip and taking it down to the bank a ritual, even if your child is depositing only 50 cents.

The Ivy Is Extra

❖ When your child is evaluating colleges to attend, sit down with her and review precisely how much savings you have amassed for her continued schooling. Then compare the cost of each college to that amount, in a table format. Don't forget to include housing, food, and travel expenses. Tabulate the shortfall between what you've already socked away and what's needed for each school. If your child is still interested in a school that is beyond your means, rough out precisely how much she would have to earn to make up the difference and how much time she has to do it.

To the Bank, James

❖ If your child starts a part-time job before he can drive, charge him a portion of his earnings for chauffeur service and add the money to his college fund. To decide what rate to charge, consider half of the going rate for a taxi, the equivalent of bus or subway fare, or the rate the IRS allows for mileage deductions (which, alas, you won't be able to take for this activity).

CHAPTER 9

EASY WAYS TO INCREASE YOUR INCOME

*E*veryone could use a little extra money, and some of us could use a whole lot. Whether you need to catch up on the utility bills or save for a vacation, it's great to have an easy way to earn extra money—without giving up all your free time. Don't you wish there were a little switch you could flip that would automatically increase your income? Well, most of the following advice doesn't work as simply as that, but with just a little effort, you can have more money in your pocket at the end of each week.

You may have one job, but you probably have many interests. If you keep a few basic points in mind, your choices for extra income can be as varied as your talents. First, do what you love. It's a cliché, but it's true, especially when you're talking about making extra money in addition to your primary income. Earning money by taking advantage of something you already enjoy doing (like a hobby) might not move you into the next tax bracket, but it may bring in a few extra bucks. For instance, if you're the one who's always asked to take the snapshots at family gatherings, why not try your hand as a professional wedding photographer?

Almost as important as knowing what you like to do is knowing what you don't like to do. Don't try to make extra money by doing something you know you'll hate just because there's a market for it. You'll probably just give it up. For example, don't become a dog walker if you don't like

dogs—even if everyone on your block owns one. No matter what you decide to do, don't be surprised if some of our tips work so well that you begin to think about quitting your day job and doing this work instead.

MONEYMAKING BASICS

Baby, You Can Drive Your Car

Turn your car into free ad space.

❖ If you use your car to make deliveries (and even if you don't), advertise like the pros with a sign on your car door. For a sign you can remove easily, make it out of poster board and attach it with painter's nonmarring masking tape (which you can get at any hardware store). Cover the sign with clear contact paper to make it waterproof. As you drive around town, your neighbors will know whom to call when they need your specialty service.

Research Your Market

❖ How can you know whether you'll be able to make extra money walking dogs or babysitting? By doing a little market research. That's a fancy way of saying that you should take a look around and find out what services or products your community is lacking. Large companies do it all the time, so why shouldn't you? For example, before you plan to make your first million selling custom-made dog leashes, you may want to head to city hall and find out how many dogs there are in your community. If the number is very low, make other plans for earning your fortune.

It Pays to Advertise

❖ Don't hide your light under a bushel basket when you're trying to make an extra buck; let it shine. How will your potential customers know what wonderful custom-built doghouses you make if you don't tell them? Word-of-mouth advertising is the least expensive—and sometimes the most effective—kind. If you've made a doghouse for a friend and he's happy with it, ask him to pass the word along to other dog owners. Whenever you can, mention the fact that you make doghouses—at parties, at PTA meetings, or when talking to your mailman.

Hear Ye, Hear Ye

❖ Do you remember the folks who used to walk around with sandwich boards, ringing a bell and handing out leaflets advertising this and that? You can make your own set of boards. You need a couple of pieces of heavy cardboard (such as the sides of an appliance carton), some

IT WORKED FOR ME
Up, Up, and Away

It was time to clean out the garage, and I thought that, while I was at it, I'd make a few bucks with a garage sale. I was afraid that even with the directions on the circulars I put up in town, however, my customers would have a hard time finding me. Our home is surrounded by fields, and visitors would have to take a few winding country roads to get here. My husband told me to "Go fly a kite." Luckily, that sarcastic comment gave me an idea.

To guide people to my sale, I'd need something visible from a distance, like those helium-filled miniblimps you see in front of used car dealerships. My florist sells helium balloons, so I bought a dozen. I put them in an oversize, clear garbage bag and tied them together to the end of a spool of kite string. For an extra flourish, I added some leftover ribbons as long, flowing streamers. I let them sail way up over the house. Not only did this signal where the place was to people looking for it, but more than one person told me that they were just out for a drive, saw the balloons, and got curious.

Balloons away!

—Sheila Serbay
West Burlington, New York

A homemade sandwich board is a real attention grabber.

poster paint, and two pieces of clothesline, each about a foot long. Punch two holes, shoulder width apart, at the top of each piece of cardboard. To make each shoulder strap, thread a length of clothesline through each set of two holes from front to back and knot it. Add to the attraction by dressing up in a costume, putting on clown makeup, ringing a bell, or blowing a bicycle horn. If you're the shy type, hire a student to wear the sign for you.

GARAGE, YARD, AND APARTMENT SALES

Just Like Burma-Shave

❖ Want the whole town to know about your garage, yard, or apartment sale? Here's a cheap way to attract attention to your event using materials you may already have on hand. Think up a clever verse or adapt one that everyone knows. ("Out for a drive? Then beat a trail. It's up ahead. Our garage sale.") Write a few lines each on large pieces of cardboard, then attach the signs to power poles or plant stakes purchased at the garden center. It worked for Burma-Shave, didn't it?

Footprints on the Pavement

❖ Here's a cute way to tell folks where your sale is. With a 2-inch paintbrush and water-based tempera paint, draw a trail of footprints on the sidewalk leading right to your sale. To make the prints uniform, make a stencil out of a scrap of vinyl wallpaper. Remember that the prints, though not permanent, may last for a while. Don't be surprised if a curious visitor or two show up a week after the fact.

Sandwich It In

❖ The shopkeepers in town use freestanding sandwich boards to draw you into their stores, so why shouldn't you? Here's how to make your own. Hinge two 3- by 4-foot pieces of ½-inch scrap plywood along one side with an old door hinge. Put an eye-catching poster advertising your sale on both sides. Make sure you include your address. Stand the sign near the curb or in front of your building, being careful not to block traffic. To be on the safe side, check your local laws to make sure such signs are permitted.

Give It a Little Juice

❖ Your yard sale customers will be more likely to buy an electrical appliance if they know it works. On the day of the sale (as long as it isn't raining), set out a long extension cord so customers can test that old phonograph or can opener.

Capture the Moment

❖ You're just about to sell that old sofa, when your potential customer decides she can't buy it until she consults her husband. But he's on the other side of town. The solution? Keep that Polaroid camera loaded with film. You can give your customers photos of potential purchases so that they can take them home and mull them over later.

SELLING YOUR SKILLS

Hair Today, Gone Tomorrow

❖ Does everyone in the neighborhood come to you for a cheap or free haircut? Do you spend your Saturdays setting the hair of friends? If you can style hair and don't need to carry on a conversation while you work, there may be a job

IT WORKED FOR ME

A Plan
for Extra Earning

I'm the maintenance man for a business owned by a large corporation. The Occupational Safety and Health Administration (OSHA) requires that our company's site-specific plan for emergencies include a floor plan indicating where emergency exits and fire extinguishers are located. I'm no architect, but I took architectural drawing classes in high school and did some drafting in the navy. When I heard that the company needed someone to do the drawings, I jumped at the chance. I took on the job as an after-hours assignment—for a fee, of course. Because the company liked my work (and the fact that I was a lot cheaper than an architect) so much, they've since asked me to draw up the floor plans for their other sites as well. Now whenever the company acquires a new property, I get a chance to make a few extra bucks.

—**Tom Donnelly**
Flushing, New York

for you. Some funeral homes hire part-time hairstylists to work on their, um, clients. Even though funeral directors are trained in the restorative arts, they often need help when it comes to styling hair. If you're interested, call the funeral homes near you. The manager will probably ask you in for an interview and give you a tour. If you're lucky, you could be making some extra cash soon.

You Ought to Be in Pictures

❖ Are you a ham? Does your little girl always get the lead in the school play? If so, both of you might get work acting in commercials. Not everyone on TV is a supermodel. In fact, most television and radio commercials, especially advertisements for local businesses, feature regular folks. Look in the Yellow Pages under Theatrical Agents; they're the folks who can get you work. You'll need some good pictures—close-ups and full-body shots. Keep them natural (no silly candid photographs) and don't hire a professional photographer. Take the pictures yourself or have a friend do it. (You don't want to sink a lot of money into something that isn't a sure thing.) Choose 10 of the best pictures and attach a brief note about you or your child (or both). Include your height, weight, hair and eye color, and age, along with a brief description of your interests and experience.

❖ If an agent asks for money up front, find someone else. Agents work for a percentage of the work they get for you, not for a fee. If you live near a big city, call the local chapter of the Screen Actors Guild or the American Federation of Television and Radio Artists for more information. They'll tell you specifically what you need to do to find work in television and radio commercials.

Unofficial Overtime

❖ Here's a novel idea. If you like what you do for work, do more of it on your own time. Call it unofficial overtime. For instance, if you work as a short-order cook during the week, there's no reason you can't be a caterer on the weekends. If you're a secretary, start a résumé-designing service. If you're an ace bookkeeper, you can keep the records part-time for a small business. This works for homemakers as well. In the old days, a common way for Grandma to make a few extra dollars was to take in the neighbors' laundry. After all, what's a few more loads?

Ring Those Wedding Bells

❖ Any bride will tell you that the hardest part of getting married is the planning. Plenty of folks are willing to pay someone to help them with the planning or even take over the entire operation. If you're organized and a good listener, this could be the job for you. Wedding consultants have to deal with invitations, thank-you notes, and everything in between. One way to get started is to leave some business cards with the jeweler in your area. This way, you'll attract couples shopping for engagement rings.

Favor Them with Your Talents

❖ If you are artistic and like to work in multiples, here's a fun way to make some extra dough. Many couples like to give wedding guests a small token to commemorate the day. These gifts can be simple, such as a cluster of candied al-

---

THE YANKEE MISER RECOMMENDS . . .
Making Speedy Deliveries

Don't turn up your nose at making deliveries as a source of extra income. Many businesses need or would like to make deliveries but can't afford to hire a full-time delivery person. If you (or your mature teen) have a flexible schedule and a vehicle, think about arranging to be on call for any or all of the following businesses.

1. Local bakeries that supply bread to delis and restaurants
2. Florists
3. Printers
4. Frame shops
5. Antique dealers
6. Delis and other small restaurants

monds wrapped in tulle, or more elaborate and personalized. If you're creative and come up with a few stock designs, you can leave samples at the local bridal shop. Strike a commission deal with the shop for any business it refers to you.

Party!

❖ Some people just know how to throw a party. If you're one of the lucky ones, you can hone your gift into a part-

---

WORLD-CLASS FRUGALITY
It All Started When . . .

Convinced that your at-home, part-time business won't go anywhere? These four companies started in a garage (or a kitchen or bedroom) and ended up as household names.

1. Hi, Mac. In 1976, buddies Steve Jobs and Steve Wozniak were on the verge of starting the personal computer revolution. For their first order of 50 Apple computers, they bought parts on credit and spent marathon sessions soldering in Jobs's garage.

2. Dingdong. The Avon lady, mother of all door-to-door sales representatives, was originally a man. (No, it's not what you're thinking.) In 1886, David McConnell, a door-to-door book salesman from Suffern, New York, gave away as a sales premium vials of perfume that he and a chemist friend mixed themselves. The rest, as they say, is history.

3. What a card. In January 1910, Joyce Hall arrived in Kansas City, Missouri, with two shoe boxes full of picture postcards. From his base at the local YMCA (where he stored his inventory under his bed), he set up a mail-order business that evolved into Hallmark, the world-famous greeting card company.

4. To err is human. In the mid-1950s, Bette Nesmith Graham was a secretary with a problem. She was a poor typist who couldn't erase mistakes when she typed with the new electric typewriters. She decided that what she couldn't erase, she'd cover up—with a white, water-based paint. Graham's invention was so popular with other secretaries that she mixed up batches of Mistake Out in her kitchen and garage for them. In 1979, she sold the Liquid Paper Company for $47.5 million.

time profession. Lots of organizations (and plenty of individuals) hire professional event coordinators to organize affairs, large and small, such as awards ceremonies, fundraisers, retirement parties, and holiday events. A party planner is a take-charge type who dotes on details, can tell a mai tai from a Bloody Mary, and knows where to seat the chief executive officer. A planner also has more mundane responsibilities, such as renting a hall, sending out invitations, and hiring a caterer.

Those Who Can, Teach

❖ If you like to work with kids, set up a tutoring service. There are plenty of kids who need after-school help with homework and schoolwork that their parents, for a variety of reasons, can't provide. That's where you come in. You can hold sessions in your own home or travel to your students' homes. You don't need to be a college professor or even a college graduate. (A high school student can help a grammar school student, or a college student can help a high schooler.) You don't have to tutor in all subjects. If you're not a math whiz, don't tutor in math. To get started, call the local school with which you'd like to work and ask if it's okay to put up a sign there. Or distribute a circular at the next PTA meeting. Call the school to find out when that might be. The principal might even be able to recommend some students for you to work with and give you an idea of what the going pay rate is.

Pencil Yourself In

❖ A lot of people would love to learn how to paint a watercolor, fix a car, or speak French as well as you do, but they're too busy to fit a class into their schedules. You can help them out and make a few extra dollars at the same time. If you have a special skill, bill yourself as a freelance instructor and give a customized class (for a fee, of course). Let the students choose the time and place. They'll appreciate the fact that you're willing to accommodate them.

Tell Us a Story

❖ If you enjoy being around children, you've probably already considered babysitting as a way to make some extra cash. But the competition for babysitters might be a little stiff, especially if you live in a neighborhood with lots of teens. How can you make yourself stand out from the crowd? Bill yourself as a storyteller or story reader. Get started by hanging a sign at the local grammar school (get permission first) or distributing flyers at the next PTA meeting. Then head down to the library to pick up some children's books. Ask the librarian for a few recommendations. Choose a selection that includes the latest releases as well as some of the classics. Also include some of your own favorites to share with the next generation.

❖ If you have a theatrical bent, turn some of those old socks into puppets and incorporate them into your storytelling sessions.

Is That a Fact?

❖ If you're good at paying attention to details and like to spend time in the library, maybe you're cut out to be a researcher or a fact checker. Freelance writers often need help doing research and verifying information. Researchers work with the writer, digging up information, and fact checkers go to work after the writing is finished, verifying what the author has written. Both jobs usually involve making lots of phone calls to verify quotes, dates, phone numbers, and other information. To get started, contact some local publishers, listed in the Yellow Pages under Publishing or Publishers—Book. If you don't live near any large publishers, don't fret. With a computer and e-mail, you can work from just about anywhere.

He Ain't Heavy, He's My Paycheck

❖ Are you looking for a part-time job that requires only a couple of hours every so often? This one requires some lifting, but you share the load with five other guys. In the trade, they're known as porters, but most people call them pallbearers. Some funeral homes hire extra employees to assist at funerals. This involves moving the deceased (already in a casket) in and out of the hearse after the service at the funeral home, at a religious service, or at the cemetery. Although some funeral homes employ a full-time staff for this service, many hire contract workers. If you're interested, call around to the local funeral homes.

Pick a Card

❖ Do you find yourself buying a line of greeting cards because they really speak your language? One way to make some extra money is to speak *their* language. Greeting card companies often hire freelance writers to compose verses for their cards. You can get started by contacting your fa-

GLOBAL WORMING

This one's not for the squeamish, but it's not as outlandish as you might think. If you live in an area where fishing is popular, you might want to try your hand at worm farming. And if you have a backyard, you can get started tonight.

To keep a good supply of night crawlers—the ones that fishermen like to use as bait—you'll need a worm box. A 2- by 3- by 2-foot plastic storage bin will do. Fill it loosely with soil and place it in a shady spot in your yard. Come dusk, head out to your backyard and capture a bunch of night crawlers, then put them in the box, which will hold up to 700 of the little guys. Worms like their environment to be damp and cool, so keep a damp burlap sack or damp mulch on top of the box to keep the little squirmers happy.

Since this isn't your primary source of income, you can make money simply by undercutting the other bait stores in your area. You may even be able to sell worms to those bait shops. Just put up a sign, and you're in business.

Here's where the worm turns.

vorite companies (you'll often find the name and address on the back of a card). Ask whether they hire freelance writers. If so, request their writer's guidelines. Don't worry if you're not a great artist or designer. Most companies also hire illustrators and designers to produce the artwork.

SELLING YOUR HOBBIES

Money in Bloom

❖ If you have a green thumb, color your other fingers green by counting the cash that your hobby can bring you. Before you plant for the season, talk to the managers of local stores and restaurants about supplying them with fresh flowers. Be realistic about what you can grow, and don't expect to be paid until you deliver. You probably won't be able to compete with commercial nurseries and florists, but you might be able to cover the cost of your hobby.

SCHEMES AND SCAMS

One to Avoid

❖ Someone looking to make extra money may have considered a multilevel marketing business, sometimes known as a network marketing or pyramid scam. These businesses are designed not only to sell a product but also to involve other participants in selling the same product, usually with some commission scheme. When the emphasis is on signing up more representatives rather than on selling a product, you've stumbled onto a pyramid scam, which in most places is illegal. Here are some things to watch for: extravagant get-rich-quick claims; a requirement to pay a fee or make a large up-front purchase of a product before you can earn a commission; a requirement to sell unreasonable amounts of a product to other participants; or a plan that refuses to allow for the return of merchandise at the fair market value. If you spot one of these scams, steer clear of it.

PART III

Frugal Living Day-to-Day

SMART WAYS TO LEAD A THRIFTY LIFESTYLE

So YOU HAVE A BUNDLE of money in the bank. Your neighbor thinks you got a raise or a second job because you have a new wardrobe. But you don't seem to be working any harder. In fact, you seem to have more free time. Sound like a dream? It's not. You needn't win the lottery or get hooked into a get-rich-quick scheme to live that kind of life. All it takes is a heaping dose of good old Yankee ingenuity—and the strategies contained in this section. On the following pages, you'll find hundreds of clever—and painless—ideas to help you reduce your expenses and save money, up to thousands of dollars a year. Not only that, but you'll enjoy the fun and satisfaction of saving with such industriousness and ingenuity.

For instance, let's say that you and your family eat take-out food four times a week and that each of those meals costs $15. For $15 you can prepare two meals at home and eliminate two take-out meals. That's a savings of $30 a week or nearly $1,600 a year.

Now add to that another $300 in annual savings simply by turning your water heater down and wrapping it with a heater blanket. Want to hear more? The following pages are chock-full of practical ways to trim your everyday expenses, without feeling as though you're giving up the pleasures of life.

Of course, this wouldn't be much of a Yankee frugality book without a few surprises. Flip through this section to find a singularly Yankee way to adorn your home with fresh flowers almost every day for free. Check out our imaginative technique to burglar-proof and beautify your home. And don't pass up the clever method to turn newspapers into mulch. Or the recipe that shows you how to make your own brown sugar. Then there's . . . see—we told you this would be fun.

CHAPTER 10

SAVING ON EVERYDAY HOUSEHOLD EXPENSES

ome expenses seem unavoidable. Every month you spend money on electricity, water, and water heating. Every winter you pay to heat your home, and every month when the bills arrive, you have that nagging suspicion that they could be lower. Well, you're right. A little nosing around to find the seams and cracks that let cold air in will shave dollars off your heating bill. Heck, adding insulation will likely save money on your hot-water bill, too—if you know where to put it.

The thrifty home owner lives by the rule that knowledge isn't just power; it's money, too. Knowing where the fuse box or circuit breakers are, where to find the shutoff valves for your water, and where you stashed the flashlights can get you through an emergency.

If you know how the washing machine works, you'll also know whether the problem you're having requires a re-pairman and the $60 service charge that comes with him. Maybe you can solve it yourself with a 50-cent part from the hardware store and 10 minutes of effort. Now *that's* power.

SAVING ON WATER COSTS

Work the Night Shift

❖ One good way to save money is to run your dishwasher or washing machine at night. In many communities, the water rates are based on peak usage, which means that they are highest when people are using the most water. If you run your dishwasher just before you go to bed, you'll be billed at a lower rate. To find out if you live in one of those communities, locate the customer service number on your water bill and give the company a call.

Don't Be So Picky

❖ If you are in the habit of rinsing your dishes before you put them in the dishwasher, use a shorter wash cycle. The dishes will get just as clean, but you'll save money on both water and water-heating costs.

Saving in the Rain

❖ The only water that's free is the kind that falls from the sky. Your gutters collect it naturally, so don't waste it. Place a rain barrel under your gutters to collect the runoff and use it to wash your car, rinse dirt off your sidewalk or front porch, and water your garden during dry spells.

❖ Be sure to keep the barrel covered after the rain stops. This will slow evaporation, keep kids from falling in, and prevent mosquitoes from breeding on the surface of the water.

WHAT'S THE BEST MONEY SAVER?
The Bright Stuff

You're ready to buy a new light bulb for your favorite reading lamp. The hardware store has three possibilities.

A. An incandescent bulb
B. A halogen lamp
C. A compact fluorescent bulb

Believe it or not, the best choice is (C) a compact fluorescent bulb, which will burn 10 times as long as the normal incandescent bulb. It will use only one-fifth the energy, too. This will save you money on both replacement bulbs and your electric bill. Halogen lamps seem bright and snazzy, but they cost a lot more. Light already accounts for about 10 percent of your electric bill, so why add to the bill when you can reduce it?

Warm Up the Pipes

❖ The reason the water isn't hot when you first turn it on is that the heated water in your tank has to travel through unheated pipes. You can reduce the amount of water wasted on this journey by insulating your hot-water pipes. The water that sits in the pipes will stay warmer longer, and the pipes won't get as cold in the wintertime. Pipe insulation is available at most hardware stores.

❖ Instead of buying pipe insulation, if you have some insulation lying around, cut it into strips and use duct tape to fasten it to the pipes.

Throw Cold Water on It

❖ Most of the energy your washing machine uses is in heating the water. Wash your clothes at a lower temperature—warm or even cold settings are best—and you'll save on hot-water costs.

Security Blankets

❖ Check to see whether your water heater has an insulating blanket. (Most newer water heaters have built-in insulation.) If the water heater is warm to the touch, it needs more insulation. Precut heater blankets or jackets for electric water heaters are available at hardware stores starting at less than $30, which is a lot less than you'll save in the long run. Keep in mind that it can be dangerous to cover a gas water heater, so don't make a move without calling an expert for advice.

❖ If you don't want to pay retail for an insulating blanket, check with your utility company to see whether it sells these blankets at a lower price. The company also may install the blankets for free as part of an energy-saving program.

❖ Don't cheap out and try to attach a regular blanket to your water heater. It's not a good idea for a couple of reasons. First, there's a potential fire hazard. Second, although you can cover an electric water heater completely, you must leave the top of a gas or oil heater uncovered. It's better to get the right blanket for your specific heater.

Turn It Down

❖ Most manufacturers use 140°F as a standard setting for water heaters. Some set them as high as 180°F. You'll never use water that hot—unless you're running a dishwasher that doesn't have a booster heater. If you don't have a dishwasher, the easiest way to save money on your heating bill is to turn down the temperature to a more manageable 120°F. That's still plenty hot for a shower or for washing dishes. You can save 3 to 6 percent on your bill for every 10°F you reduce the temperature.

❖ If you do have a dishwasher and it doesn't have a booster heater, you might want to check into buying one. The booster will heat only the water that your dishwasher uses, so it will cost much less than having your entire water tank heated to 140°F.

Give It a Rest

❖ Does your furnace also heat your hot water? If so, when you go on vacation in the summer, there's no need to keep your furnace running. Even when it isn't heating your home, it's still coming on several times day and night to

WORLD-CLASS FRUGALITY
He Knows How to Pamper His Furnace

Charlie MacArthur of Sangerville, Maine, thought he'd figured out the best way to reuse solid waste when he built a car engine that would run on chicken fat. Then when his children came along, he had a better idea. He modified his furnace to burn dirty diapers. Not only did the invention reduce his heating bill, but it also cut down on trips to the dump.

keep your water hot. Turn it off before you leave town, and you'll save money.

❖ But be sure to leave yourself a note to turn the furnace back on as soon as you get home. Otherwise, that first shower will be mighty cold.

❖ Remember that this is not a good idea for your winter vacation, because there's an increased risk that your pipes will freeze.

USE IT UP

Keep your money from going down the drain by catching the water that runs just before you wash your hands or the dishes. Put it in the:

1. Humidifier
2. Watering can
3. Mop bucket
4. Fish tank
5. Dog dish

SAVING ON HEATING COSTS

Prevent Oily Buildup

❖ The best way to keep an oil-burning furnace working properly is to have it cleaned once a year. As a furnace runs, the by-products of combustion build up in the heat exchanger and act as an insulator. Eventually, that heat exchanger will be as full of gunk as it is of fuel; that can decrease your furnace's efficiency by up to 30 percent. The least expensive option for keeping your furnace clean may be a service contract. If your oil provider offers one that includes cleaning, consider taking it. If the service contract costs less than 10 percent of your annual oil bill—and it will—you will still be saving money.

When Neatness Counts

❖ Your mother told you to make your bed, but even she didn't know that it would save you money. If you have a water bed, that is. The covers act as insulation and will reduce the amount of energy the bed needs to heat itself.

Be a Draft Dodger

❖ You insulate your attic, right? Well, you should also seal up the heat leaks in the rest of your house. The biggest culprit is usually your plumbing. When your house was being constructed, the plumbers probably cut fairly roomy holes in the walls and floors before installing the pipes. Taken together, those holes can add up to as much heat loss as an open window. Padding them with insulation will take dollars off your heating bill. Go into your basement or crawl space and tuck small strips of fiberglass insulation into the holes through which the pipes travel up into your bathroom and kitchen. Or get a spray can of insulation at the hardware store. The insulation looks like shaving cream as it comes out of the can, but it will dry hard and completely seal the hole.

❖ Other potential leaky spots in your home include the gaps around chimneys and recessed lights in insulated ceilings and the unfinished spaces behind cupboards and closets, although these are tougher to get to unless you're already doing some work there.

Get Audited

❖ One way to discover the heating and cooling leaks in your house is to hire an energy auditor to point out where the worst leaks are. The auditor will close the windows and doors, then evacuate the air and measure the drop in pressure. If the drop is substantial, your house is pretty tight. If not, you're losing valuable heat or cooling air somewhere. Check with your utility company; some companies provide free audits.

SAVING ON ELECTRICITY COSTS

Don't Keep Your Light under a Bushel

❖ Are all the lamps in your home turned on because you think that it's just too dark? Check the light bulbs; they may be dusty or dirty. If they are, they're emitting up to 20 percent less light than clean bulbs. That's quite a bit, actually, and that means money down the drain. Once in a while, when the bulbs are cool and the lamps are un-plugged, run a damp cloth over the bulbs to clean them. While you're at it, dust or vacuum the lamp shades, too. If each lamp emits more light, you'll need to turn on fewer lamps, and you could save about $5 per lamp each year.

Savings, Cubed

❖ Large appliances are often the culprits when it comes to wasted energy, but you can take some steps to save some money here. Take the freezer, for instance. A freezer that's

FRUGAL MEMORIES

Low-Rent Maintenance

The first house that my husband and I shared was a fixer-upper. The tiny kitchen had no cabinets. There was only one closet, and it wasn't in the bedroom. The roof leaked. There was no insulation. And we hated the carpeting, the wallpaper, and every single light fixture. But, hey, the rent was low. The good news was that my husband and I had met while working at a lumberyard, and we both knew our way around the hardware store. We went to our landlady and asked if we might make a few, uh, changes to the property. She said okay and invited us in for cookies.

Thereafter, we dropped off the rent every month and proposed more changes. The landlady always said, "Oh, you kids do whatever you want." We bulldozed the kitchen to make it bigger and added built—in cabinets. We moved walls and added closets to every room. We paved the driveway and built a garage. We shingled the roof, waterproofed the basement, and insulated the heck out of everything. People don't believe us when we say that we replaced every piece of plumbing in the house and every light fixture, but we did. And we did it without hiring a single repairman. Our rental became a kind of dream house.

Then one day we dropped off the rent check and the landlady told us she wanted to open a boutique, so she needed to sell our house. Did we know anyone who wanted to buy it? We sure did. We got it for a good price, too.

—**Carole Wilson**
Monticello, Illinois

at least half-full is more efficient than an empty one; that's because there's less air to escape when you open the freezer door. But what if you don't have enough food on hand to make a half-full freezer? Make a few extra trays of ice cubes, transfer them to plastic freezer bags, and place them in the freezer. The ice cubes also will keep food cold longer in the event of a power outage.

Refrigerators: Give 'Em a Rest

❖ The trouble with refrigerators is that they run all day, every day. Not only does this consume a lot of electricity, but condensation builds up behind the freezer box and can interfere with the fan—even on frost-free models. The best way to maintain your refrigerator—and keep it running quietly—is to give it a rest. Once a year, before you go on vacation, turn the fridge off and let it warm up. Then give it a good cleaning. Pull it away from the wall, remove the cardboard backing, and vacuum out the dust and gunk that's settled on the coils. When you return, your fridge will run much more efficiently.

CARING FOR APPLIANCES

A Solid Footing

❖ The parts that wear out most quickly on your dishwasher are the same parts that cause leaks in your sink— the rubber stoppers and footings that control the flow of water into the appliance. Checking those and replacing them every 2 years will reduce the leaks (read "save you money") and the chances that you'll have a flood in your kitchen.

❖ If you have a rustlike residue in your dishwasher, it's a sure sign that the gaskets and stoppers are falling apart and need to be replaced. The cost to you? A couple of cents. The long-term savings, however, could be great. A failed gasket could mean a flooded kitchen.

Debris Can Be a Drain

❖ The other area of your dishwasher that you should keep an eye on is the drain, located down in the basin, under the racks. Bits of food can easily get caught in the drain, and over time a buildup of debris can cause your dishwasher to flood or even burn itself out—not to mention the funky smell that will emanate from even a small amount of rotting food. Keeping the drain clear will help keep your dishwasher running efficiently.

DO-IT-YOURSELF PLUMBING

Don't Delay—Save Today

❖ When you notice a water leak, it's tempting to put off the repair until the weekend, when you'll have more time. But a running toilet, for example, can waste 1,000 gallons of water per day. In an area where water rates are high—say, $8 to $12 per 1,000 gallons—a 5-day delay in repairing it can be shockingly expensive. In this case, time really is money.

❖ If you're running out of the house to go to work when you notice the leak and can't stop to fix it right away, just reach below the tank and turn off the shutoff valve so that you're not wasting water all day.

Leaky Pipes Sound Off

❖ Some of the costliest leaks occur in supply lines or in the walls of your home, where they can do tremendous damage before they're discovered. If you suspect a leak that you can't

---

IT WORKED FOR ME

Tie Dye Your Toilet

If you think your toilet might be leaking, there's an easy way to be sure. Do this when the toilet has not been flushed recently so that it's not still quietly filling. Take the lid off the tank and put several drops of the food coloring you hate most into the tank. I think red is pretty awful, so I use red. Put the lid back on the tank. If the toilet is leaking, the colored water will leak into the bowl. Water enters almost all toilet bowls from under the rim, so you'll see a telltale streak of colored water coming down the side of the bowl. You can fix the leak by replacing the $2 stopper at the bottom of the tank.

—TJ Wilson
Monticello, Illinois

---

see, turn off all the faucets in the house and put your ear to the faucet in your bathtub or sink. Pipes are great transmitters of sound. If you can hear water running, then you have a leak.

❖ Alternatively, use an old plumber's trick. Put the blade of a screwdriver against a pipe and your ear to the end of the handle. It will transmit the sound right into your ear.

❖ If you suspect that the leak is inside the wall, it's time to call a plumber.

FRUGAL MEMORIES

Doing Without the Bare Necessities

During World War II, my mother worked in a rubber factory making raincoats for servicemen. In those days, we lived from ration book to ration book. Even after the war, there were lots of things we had to do without—like a bathroom, for instance.

The neighbors all had indoor plumbing, but we didn't. As a kid, I never thought to ask why. Instead, we had a hopper out on our unfinished, unheated back porch. The porch had walls of exposed beams and bare floors. It was pretty cold come January.

Of course, we had no bathtub with running water. My sister and I raced each other to the kitchen sink to wash up before school. On the weekend, we bathed in a huge tin tub that my mother carried in from the porch. She heated water in stockpots on the huge kitchen stove and poured it into our tub. We all washed quickly before the water got cold. Afterward, we carried the tub outside to empty it, then put it back on the porch.

When my friends came over, they looked at our makeshift bathroom out back and shook their heads. When they asked about it, I always told them that our bathroom was still under construction. Of course, we lived in that house and bathed in that tub until I was 18 years old. It was the slowest construction project in history.

—Ellen Bean
Somerville, Massachusetts

Burst Its Bubble

❖ If you have water dripping under the sink, you have to find the source before you can fix it. Chances are that the leak is so small that it's hard to tell exactly where the water is coming from. An easy way to find out is to dry the pipe, then smear a thin film of dishwashing liquid over the area where you think the leak might be. Turn the water on and look for bubbles, which will appear as the leaking water hits the soap.

Give Leaky Toilets a Valve Job

❖ The cure for continuously running toilets couldn't be simpler. The drain in the bottom of the tank has a rubber stopper that sits on it. Over time, rusty water or debris may settle on the rim under the stopper so that it doesn't sit snugly. To fix it, turn off the shutoff valve under the toilet and then flush. The toilet will empty, but it won't refill. You can then clean the tank, especially the drain, with any cleanser you like.

❖ To make your own cleanser, mix ¼ cup baking soda with 1 quart warm water. This light abrasive will clean any stains out of your toilet tank. For a little extra punch, pour a bit of baking soda directly on a sponge and scrub away.

❖ If the stopper itself is the problem, drop by the hardware store and buy a new one for about $2.

Make Do, So to Speak

❖ If you have a clogged toilet that hasn't responded to plunger therapy, it's probably time to use a snake. No snake? No problem. Just use a heavy-duty metal coat hanger (or any length of rigid wire). Bend the hanger until it is relatively straight, leaving the hook end intact. Holding the hook in one hand, send the other end down to do the dirty work. Twist the hook end around to mimic the drilling action you'd use with a snake, then work the hanger back and forth. Sometimes this is all it takes to get your toilet back in running order.

REPAIRING DOORS

Wobbly Knobs

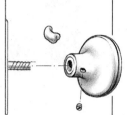

❖ If your doorknob rattles in the frame, it may not fit properly. Do not, under any circumstance, pay someone to fix this problem. Rather, do it yourself with modeling clay. Unscrew the knob, take it apart, and put a small piece of clay inside the knob before you put it back together. The clay will fill in the space around the thread and hold the knob in place.

A small piece of clay can stop your doorknobs from wobbling.

Screen In Holes

❖ If you have an old, damaged screen door, don't throw it away. Store it until the screen in your new door gets torn. When it does, you can use the old door to make a patch. First, trim the tear so that it has even edges. Then cut a piece out of the old screen that is one inch longer on each side than the hole. Remove two or three strands of wire from each side of the patch and bend the wire down. Simply stick the patch over the hole and fold the wire toward the center.

DO-IT-YOURSELF HOME SECURITY

Nip Burglaries in the Bud

❖ There's no need to invest in new locks and alarms to make your house safer. Just trim the bushes. Tall hedges that cover back doors and ground-floor windows may look decorative, but they provide cover for anyone trying to break in. Discourage burglars by giving your neighbors a clear view of your house.

A Thorny Solution

❖ Home safety is of paramount importance to all of us, but between installation and service, commercial security systems can cost a bundle. Here's one step you can take to discourage burglars and others from dropping in when you are asleep or not around. Visit your lawn and garden center and purchase plants or bushes with long thorns to plant around your windows and doors. Roses are a natural choice, but ask the garden center staff for advice about which plants will thrive in your area of the country. These plants will serve as a natural (and beautiful) barrier that discourages human—and animal—pests.

Have an Imaginary Friend

❖ Most times opening the door to a stranger isn't dangerous. But it's better to be safe than sorry. Don't be afraid to pretend that there's someone else at home when a

PUT THE GLIDE BACK IN STICKY DRAWERS

Fighting with your dresser drawers can be the most frustrating of domestic disputes. Left unaddressed, these little annoyances can evolve into broken handles, and the drawers themselves may even come apart. But there are three things you can do right now so that your drawers will always behave.

1. Take the drawers out and look at the edges. Are there shiny spots? Those are the areas that stick. Sand them down with some coarse sandpaper, and they should be fine.

2. If your drawer usually holds books

A few thumbtacks can restore the glide to a drawer.

or other heavy items, rub the frame of the drawer (the spots where the drawer glides into the frame) with candle wax, paraffin, or even an old bar of soap to give it a little extra glide.

3. If you take the drawer out, you may notice that the glide (the narrow piece of wood on which the drawer glides shut) is missing or worn down. If it's missing, the drawer will drag. You can give the drawer a lift by pushing three or four thumbtacks along the glide. The door should open and close with ease.

stranger comes calling. After all, he doesn't know for sure who lives with you. Be creative. When you open the door, excuse yourself and yell back over your shoulder, "Steve, shut off the eggs, will you?" You've established that there is a male inside your home who is old enough to cook—and who is holding a hot skillet.

Honk if You're Home

❖ Burglars depend on stealth, so loud noises usually chase them away. If you should wake up to the terrifying sound of someone trying to gain access to your home, nothing says "I know you're there" better than a blast from a U.S. Coast Guard–approved maritime air signal device. These portable compressed-air horns make a deafening racket—louder than most home alarm systems—and they're much less expensive. You can pick one up from any boat shop or sporting goods store.

Computer-Generated Security

❖ Just because you don't have an electronic alarm system doesn't mean everyone has to know that. Use your home computer and a color printer to design your own home security decals. Invent a name and a logo. Keep it simple, though. Remember, you want them to be believable. "Magnum .44 Laser-Guided ICBM Attack Squad Security Systems" might be a little over-the-top.

Nice Doggy

❖ Nothing may deter a thief more than the presence of a large dog. If you don't cohabitate with a canine, however, simply create the illusion that you own one of man's best friends. Leave a food dish outside your front door; hang a heavy-duty leash over the porch rail; scatter a few large dog toys around the yard. How about a bumper sticker that says, I Love My DEA-Trained Rottweiler!

CHAPTER 11

SPENDING LESS ON FURNITURE

Stretching your furniture dollar is definitely a case of "you get what you pay for." Buy well-made furniture and treat it right, and there is no reason it won't last you a lifetime.

Some pieces will last even longer. You may own your grandfather's rolltop desk or an heirloom side table. The craftsmanship responsible for that type of longevity hasn't disappeared; it's just less common than it once was.

Making the most of your furniture is a two-step process. First, you need to shop carefully and wisely. An inexpensive sofa that will last you 3 years is actually less of a bargain than a model at twice the price that will last 15 years. In short, you need to look at your furniture purchase as an investment as well as an expense. Second, regular care and maintenance will keep your furnishings looking good and serving their purpose for a long time to come.

FURNITURE-BUYING BASICS

Proper Planning

❖ No matter what type of furniture you plan to buy, a little preparation before you shop can save you a great deal of money. Measure the space you need to fill and decide on the type of wood, finish, and fabric. Then determine the budget you have for the piece. That way, you won't arrive home with a piece that is more than you need or that doesn't fit your decor.

❖ Don't forget to measure the spaces that your furniture will have to get through to arrive at its final destination. You'd be surprised how many folks aren't able to take delivery of their $2,000 sofa because it won't fit through the front door or around a tight corner. If you're not sure how to figure out those measurements, ask the salesperson to help you.

WORLD-CLASS FRUGALITY
Have a Seat, My Dear

When I was first dating my wife, Michelle, she didn't have very much furniture. Her living room was kind of empty, in fact, except for a futon that was supposed to be a couch and a broken-down chair in the corner. The chair sat on some spread-out newspaper. It had no cushions and seemed to be shedding its varnish. When I asked her about it, she said that she was refinishing it.

Six months later, I helped her move into a new apartment. She hadn't touched that old chair, and when I picked it up to move it, the arms came out and the dowels scattered across the floor. I gathered the wood into a pile and moved it to the new place. Michelle told me to put the chair on the back porch. I love woodworking and told her I'd fix it for her. She said

no, she'd get to it when the weather turned warm.

The chair sat out there for 3 years. Then last Christmas, Michelle went home to see her family in Nebraska. She gave me a key and asked me to pick up the mail for her while she was gone. Before I went over there the first day, I stopped off at a hardware store and picked up some sandpaper, stain, varnish, and wood glue. I worked every night for 2 weeks. The day before she came home, I bought cushions for the chair, put a big bow on it, and set it her living room.

She loved it but didn't recognize it. "Where did you find this?" she asked.

I shrugged and said, "Out on the back porch."

—**Larry Bean**
Medford, Massachusetts

Keep the Interest

❖ Regardless of the piece you are purchasing, save money by putting down as small a deposit as the store will allow. If the furniture takes 8 weeks to arrive, that's 8 weeks of interest you could be accruing in your savings account. If the store demands full payment in advance, use a credit card and ask that you not be charged until the piece is delivered. This also gives you leverage if delivery is unreasonably late.

Delayed Gratification

❖ Consider layaway as a less expensive way to buy compared to credit. Furniture stores are some of the last remaining retail outlets that offer this purchase plan. Layaway means you make a small down payment and monthly payments until the piece is paid for, at which time you take delivery. Although the pleasure of having your new furniture is put off, you avoid high interest rates.

A Sure Loser

❖ Avoid rent-to-own furniture. Not only do you end up paying much more for the furniture (sometimes double the price of an outright purchase from a furniture store), but disclosure laws and regulations are still somewhat lax for these types of agreements. Many people get burned by rent-to-own agreements that they can't get out of. If money is tight, consider a layaway plan instead.

Off the Floor

❖ If you find exactly the piece you want in the fabric you want on display in a retail furniture store, ask to buy it at a discount—10 to 20 percent off is reasonable. These pieces usually get little wear. And because retailers regularly change their displays, they are usually willing to sell a piece for less. Even if the salesperson is reluctant, ask her to call you when the store is ready to sell the floor samples. Furniture salespeople work on commission, and most will be happy to keep you in mind if they know you're likely to buy—even if it's down the road.

Why Not the Best?

❖ For a return on your investment, there is no substitute for wood. Cherry, maple, and oak are the most durable, although many people like the look of pine, a softer wood that is susceptible to nicks, dents, and scratches. Stay away from pressboard furniture. It's more unstable than wood, and the piece will have a much shorter life, which negates its lower price.

Avoid the Hard Sell

❖ Be leery of extended warranties offered by the store. First, determine how good the original warranty is. For instance, many sofas carry a 10- or 15-year manufacturer's warranty, or a limited lifetime warranty, which should cover the sofa through its reasonable life span. Then contact the manufacturer of the piece. It may offer an extended warranty with more coverage and a lower price than the store's. It's a dead giveaway when the salesperson works harder trying to sell you the warranty than trying to sell you the furniture.

FRUGAL FORMULAS
SIX COMMON WOOD BLEMISHES AND HOW TO REMOVE THEM

1. Water marks or rings. Cover the stain with a clean, thick blotter, press down with a warm iron, and repeat. You can also try rubbing with salad oil, mayonnaise, or white toothpaste.

2. White marks. Rub lightly with ashes mixed with lemon juice. Remove any excess and polish.

3. Milk stains. Rub with a cloth dampened with household ammonia.

4. Heat marks. Dampen a cloth with mineral spirits or turpentine and polish lightly with the grain. Dry the surface and buff.

5. Stuck paper. Soak the area with vegetable oil or olive oil, let sit a few minutes, and rub along the grain with a coarse towel or cheesecloth. Dry and finish with polish.

6. Gum. Hold an ice cube on the gum until it hardens. Use an old credit card to crack it off the surface, then polish.

JOINED FOR GOOD

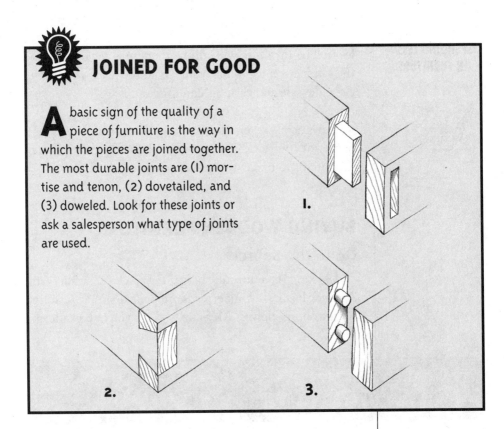

A basic sign of the quality of a piece of furniture is the way in which the pieces are joined together. The most durable joints are (1) mortise and tenon, (2) dovetailed, and (3) doweled. Look for these joints or ask a salesperson what type of joints are used.

1.

2.

3.

Slow Means Save

❖ You may be entitled to a delivery charge refund if the store does not deliver by the stated deadline. Check your receipt. Even if the salesperson did not record a date, the receipt often includes a phrase such as "delivery in 6 to 8 weeks." If the store doesn't meet that date, call and ask that the delivery charge be returned.

Save on Shipping

❖ Save on shipping costs by negotiating them down as part of the purchase. Do this before you buy the furniture. You should be able to get a reduction if, for example, you are buying more than one piece or are spending more than $1,000, or if you have another good argument that the delivery should be thrown in for free. Act reluctant to buy if the store won't budge on the shipping costs. You can even leave. The furniture will still be there in a day or two, and the salesperson will quickly understand what it will take to close the sale and earn his commission.

❖ Beware, however, of stores that offer free delivery as a matter of course. Those stores simply increase the costs of their items to make up the difference.

BUYING WOODEN FURNITURE

Go to the Source

❖ Looking for a furniture bargain? Try a local lumberyard. As a side business, lumberyards often make simple furniture such as bookshelves. Measure a piece you're considering

---

IT WORKED FOR ME

Making a Silk Purse Out of a Sow's Ear

I needed some shelves in my living room, but all the prefab shelving I found at home improvement centers looked plain, if not ugly. And those shelves were expensive to boot. Instead, I found the beauty in plywood.

I bought three plywood pieces out of the "extras" bin at my local lumberyard. These were odd pieces left over from large plywood sheets that were cut down for other projects. I had the three pieces cut to the same measurements. The shelves and cutting cost less than $10.

Then I bought a quart of clear, high-gloss polyurethane and a small jar of dry painter's pigment. You can buy painter's pigment in an incredible variety of colors at most art stores. I sanded the shelves, mixed a teaspoon of pigment into the polyurethane, and coated the plywood. I kept sanding and applying the tinted polyurethane until the wood was saturated and I could hardly see the grain.

I hung the shelves on standard white metal brackets. These stunning shelves match my decor and are unique as well.

—Carol Peterson
Sunnyvale, California

---

buying from a furniture store, then bring the measurements to the lumberyard. In most cases, it will beat the store's prices, and the furniture will be crafted by skilled woodworkers.

BUYING UPHOLSTERED FURNITURE

A Perfect Match

❖ You're less likely to replace furniture that fits in with your home decor, right? So when shopping for upholstered pieces such as a sofa and chairs, you should ask for fabric swatches to bring home and match them against your other furniture and painted surfaces. Be sure to request the grade of fabric you will ultimately buy because different grades will have subtle color differences.

The Lift Test

❖ Heavier furniture is usually a better buy than lightweight furniture because it will stand up to more abuse. Lift the edge of an upholstered couch or chair. If the piece is heavy and the frame doesn't bend or wobble, it is likely made of solid wood and will withstand many years of wear and tear.

The Light Test

❖ To save on upholstery repair, check the weave of any fabric you are considering for a couch or chair. Hold a swatch of the fabric up to a strong light: The more light you can see through the swatch, the thinner the fabric and the less durable it will be over the long run.

BUYING SECONDHAND AND ANTIQUE FURNITURE

Moving On

❖ Moving sales are some of the richest territory for thrifty furniture shoppers. Any sale held on a rainy day is likely to be a bonanza because fewer people venture out in bad weather to go to these sales. If you're not interested in a particular piece, arrive late, because anything that is left is sure to be radically discounted.

Do Your Homework

❖ Buying a piece of antique furniture is not just a purchase; it's an investment that could one day return a profit. Before you shop, decide on the periods and styles that most interest you and learn what distinguishes those pieces from earlier or later ones.

❖ Buy from a good source to ensure the best value. A knowledgeable antique dealer should be able to tell you something about the piece, including where it came from. In addition, the dealer should provide a guarantee if the piece is found to be a fake.

Spot a Fake

❖ Don't lose money on something that is not what it appears to be. Carefully inspect any antique you're considering buying. Be on the lookout for hardware that does not seem to go with the style of the piece, filled-in holes where hard-

THE YANKEE MISER RECOMMENDS . . .
Knowing the Value of Dirt

My motto when it comes to buying secondhand furniture is "You can't judge a book by its cover." Or maybe that should be, "You can't judge a sofa by its upholstery."

You may get a real buy if you find a secondhand piece that's filthy. Use the furniture's condition as a bargaining chip to get a lower price. Then call up a professional cleaning service (check in the Yellow Pages under Upholstery Cleaners or Furniture Cleaning) and have the piece cleaned. Typically, a cleaning service will charge about $25 to clean a love seat, depending on where you live. These services can work wonders, bringing even the dingiest and smelliest upholstery back to life.

ware was removed or changed, or lack of wear and tear, which is a normal sign of aging. When in doubt, don't buy, even if the price is great.

Written Protection

❖ When buying an antique, insure your investment with a detailed written receipt. This should provide the age and style of the piece and the price paid. You'll need the receipt for your home owner's or renter's insurance and as protection in the event the piece turns out to be a fraud.

Avoid Insects

❖ Woodworm holes can be a sign that a piece is not worth any price. If there are a dozen or more of these round holes in the surface of a piece, push a pin in. If the pin goes in easily, the interior of the wood may be largely eaten away, and you should shop for another piece.

WOODEN FURNITURE CARE AND MAINTENANCE

Finish It from Scratch

❖ Scratch in that table? There are plenty of expensive remedies on the market, but here's a solution that will cost only pennies: a box of wax crayons. You don't even need the name brand. Find the crayon that most closely matches the color of the finish. Rub it into the scratch, then buff it with a soft cloth, such as an old T-shirt. Start with a color that's lighter, rather than darker, than the furniture, because it's easy to darken a color, but almost impossible to make it lighter.

Healthy Humidity

❖ Hardwood furniture, even stained or painted pieces, absorbs moisture from the air. When the humidity is low, the wood dries out. If the humidity varies a great deal in your house, hardwood furniture will warp or experience other problems over time. So if you own a particularly valuable piece of furniture and the humidity is not relatively even year-round, use a humidifier in the winter and an air conditioner in the summer.

Smoothing the Way

❖ You can extend the life of wooden furniture that has drawers or sliding doors (such as a hutch) by protecting the areas where wood-on-wood contact is made. Every 6 months or so, coat drawer guides and rails, and the channels and sashes of sliding doors, with linseed oil. This will decrease friction between the moving surfaces and prevent moisture from entering the wood at those junctures.

Bleachy Keen

❖ Just as the sun can whiten the bedsheets that you hang out to dry, it can bleach your hardwood furniture, lightening the color over time. To prevent this from happening, keep your furniture out of continuous sunlight. If the furniture is near a window, draw the curtains occasionally. If the furniture is expensive, you should consider moving it.

THREE QUICK FIXES FOR SCRATCHES AND NICKS

You don't need to pay a furniture shop or restoration professional big bucks to repair fine furniture. You'll find many simple fixes right in your the house. Use these suggestions carefully, however; it's always better to use a light touch for the first application. If the shade doesn't match the finish, repeat the process until the blemish disappears.

I. Dark wood. Depending on the finish, rub the meat from a walnut or Brazil nut in the direction of the scratch. Wipe off any excess.

2. Cherry wood. Use iodine, applied with a cotton swab or thin artist's brush. Control the shade by applying more than one coat.

3. Light wood. Use a light-colored paste shoe polish, such as tan or natural, to fill the scratch.

Stay Together

❖ Store table leaves as near to the table as possible. Do not keep them in an attic or basement, or they will likely absorb more or less moisture than the table itself, making for a poor fit when the time comes to use the leaves.

❖ This goes for the amount of light they receive, too. A table kept in a bright room will lighten over time, but leaves kept under a bed won't. If you keep the pieces together, they'll be the same color when you put them together.

Location, Location, Location

❖ The quickest way to lose your investment in a piece of wooden furniture is to subject it to extremes of temperature. There's no better way to make table legs, seat backs, and cabinet panels warp and split. Keep your wooden furnishings away from radiators or baseboard heating and at least 10 feet from the fireplace.

Smooth Move

❖ Wooden furniture can be damaged by improper moving. Lift rather than slide, and carry the piece by the lowest load-bearing part.

Chair Care

❖ To make upholstered chairs last longer, use simple seat covers with ties at the corners, sprayed with stain repellent. When the covers get dirty, change them for a new look, or wash them. The chair seats will remain as good as new.

UPHOLSTERED FURNITURE CARE AND MAINTENANCE

Clean Now, Save Later

❖ Embedded dirt can quickly destroy fabric. You can avoid costly in-home professional cleaning or reupholstery charges if you simply vacuum upholstered furniture once a week to remove loose dirt. Even furniture that has been treated with stain repellent is susceptible to ground-in dirt, which will make the piece look dingy over time and wear out the fabric fibers.

Flipping for Dollars

❖ Get the maximum sofa and chair life for your money. Flip upholstered cushions at least once every 4 months, more often if the piece sees a lot of use.

Rehab Recovery

❖ Don't lose the investment you have in a couch simply because the cushions are worn. Most manufacturers will supply replacement cushions and covers. Of course, you'll have to pay for them, but they're probably a whole lot less expensive than buying a new piece of furniture. Call toll-free information at (800) 555-1212 to see if the manufacturer has an 800 number. If it doesn't, try searching the Internet on the manufacturer's name.

Stability for a Long Life

❖ To ensure that your sofa or love seat lasts as long as possible, support the back against a wall so that the piece stays stable, rather than rocking backward, when someone sits down. Constant rocking is one way to effectively separate the back from the foundation.

FRUGAL FORMULAS
THE GREAT MARBLE REMAKE

Don't waste money by throwing away broken marble slabs. Take the broken pieces to a tile shop or stonecutter and have the broken edges cut to match the unbroken ones. Then you can either make a smaller table or shelf or use the small pieces as cutting boards. You'll find a stonecutter at any professional marble contractor; look in the Yellow Pages under Marble Contractors.

BUYING AND MAINTAINING OUTDOOR FURNITURE

Terrific Teak

❖ Hardwood furniture offers some of the best return on investment over the years. Among hardwoods, teak is the most durable. Though expensive, it will stand up to decades of seasonal abuse. So if you're in the market for new outdoor furniture, you may want to splurge on teak, knowing that you're really being frugal in the long run.

❖ Save the cost of oils or finishes. As with most hardwood outdoor furniture, teak weathers to a fine silver gray that fits right in with the natural surroundings. This weathering won't hurt or degrade the wood, however.

❖ Coat the legs of your teak furniture with water repellent (available at hardware and home improvement stores). Apply the repellent 3 inches up the legs, adding a new coat each season. A quick and easy way to coat the legs is to fill a coffee can with repellent and place each leg in the can for a few minutes.

The Metal Alternative

❖ Iron outdoor furniture, which can last decades when it is well-made, can be an excellent investment. Avoid pieces with cracks in the welds or uneven finishes.

❖ Rust can wreak havoc with your iron furniture. Check metal furniture at the beginning and end of each summer for nicks and wear spots where the paint has chipped off. Repaint these areas immediately to prevent rust.

A Good Rubdown

❖ Extend the life of your iron furniture by rubbing it with car wax, applied with a soft cloth, every season. This will protect the metal and prevent rust from developing.

CHAPTER 12

DECORATING ON A BUDGET

*P*art of living the good life is having a nice place to come home to. But you don't have to spend thousands of dollars to hire an interior decorator to make your home beautiful. In fact, you can decorate for less—a lot less—than you may think. The secret is to concentrate on a few key pieces—an area rug or a sofa, for instance—and then to explore inexpensive and eclectic ways to complement them. That's what this chapter is all about.

Here are a few frugal decorating tenets to keep in mind before you get started. First and foremost, choose quality over quantity. When you're decorating on a budget, you may be tempted to divide your available cash among all the purchases—sofa, rug, drapes, lamps—you want to make. The Yankee way is to spend the bulk (but not all) of your cash on a piece of quality furniture—a sofa, say. Generally, when it comes to furniture, you get what you pay for, and a good-quality sofa will last for years, especially with care. That may mean that you'll have less to spend on accessories (don't worry; we have lots of frugal ideas), but as time goes by, you can add more well-made items to your collection.

Second, be neutral. When you shop for that large piece of upholstered furniture, it's best to steer clear of big prints and bright colors. Those may appeal to you now, but how are you going to feel about them a year or two down the road? Can you afford to replace a perfectly good sofa just because you're tired of the design? A thriftier strategy is to choose large pieces of furniture in neutral colors. Then you can liven up the room with bright (and inexpensive) accessories. A year from now, when you're ready for a change, you can rework the entire room by replacing or updating only the accessories.

Enter "Decorating on a Budget." Here's where you'll find ideas for wall accessories, including an attractive and thrifty one using old magazines. Perhaps you're interested in some creative window treatments. No problem; we offer a simple way to make faux stained glass. Heck, we've even found a way to turn empty bottles into decorative objects.

DECORATING BASICS

Neutralize Your Decor

❖ If you already splurged on a bright red or zebra-striped sofa that will seem out of place in the new decorating scheme you want to try, all is not lost. Head to a department store and pick up an inexpensive slipcover—in a neutral color, of course.

Let There Be Light!

❖ Don't underestimate the potential for lighting to affect the look and decor of a room. Lighting is, after all, just about the least expensive accessory at your disposal. You can give your living room an "active" feel with bright light or direct sunlight, or turn it into an intimate conversation area with indirect, subdued lighting and candles. Lighting doesn't have to cost much (perhaps the price of a dimmer switch), but it adds a finishing touch to your decor.

Focus on Your Focal Point

❖ Every room needs a focal point—a spot to which your eye goes immediately when you enter the room. If everything in the room is given the

WORLD-CLASS FRUGALITY

She's the Real Breadwinner

Rosa Patoine of Hardwick, Vermont, is the mother of 16 and knows how to stretch a buck. A few years back, she collected 544 discarded plastic bread bags from the kitchen where she worked, cut them into strips, and wove them into a braided rug. Won first prize at the fair, too.

Create a focal point in a room with a collection of photographs.

same visual weight, the effect can be sloppy. Create a focal point in a room with accessories, lights, color, or furniture arrangements. For instance, you can create a focal point in a square room by hanging a large quilt on one wall or by grouping furniture near it in a conversation nook. Use your imagination: A fireplace is an obvious focal point, but an interesting arrangement of photographs can be one as well.

DECORATING WITH ACCESSORIES

Get Fringe Benefits

❖ Want to give an inexpensive shelving system the glamour of a custom unit? One way to liven up a boring shelf without adding much to the cost is to tack upholstery fringe on it. Fringe and decorative nails are available quite inexpensively at any fabric shop or craft supply store. Choose fringe that complements the rest of your decor—gold and silver are especially rich looking.

Use decorative nails and upholstery fringe to doll up a plain shelf.

To start the fringe, tack it at the side, rear, and front corners. Then use more tacks at regular intervals, about 1 inch apart, to affix the rest.

❖ If you don't like the look of fringe, dress up the edge of your shelves with ribbon, upholstery braid, scraps of fabric, or other bric-a-brac from the notions department of a local fabric store.

This Is Your (Shelf) Life

❖ There's a spot on your wall that needs something, but you're not sure what. And you don't want to hang another picture there. Try this thrifty solution. Make a small shelf out of an old cabinet shelf, a bookshelf, a cutting board, or even a piece of driftwood. It's a neat way to display treasured objects, such as an autographed baseball, a bowling trophy, or even a decorative trivet. Attach your shelf securely to the wall with a decorative wooden bracket, available inexpensively at a lumberyard.

Make a Can-Do Candle Lantern

❖ Back in Granny's day, an aluminum or steel can punched full of holes made a terrific decorative candleholder. Are you thinking what we're thinking? You can duplicate this design. Just remove the label from a clean, empty soup or coffee can and file any sharp edges. Fill the can with water and place it in the freezer until the water is frozen. Meanwhile, draw a design on a piece of paper that will wrap around the can. Remove the can from the freezer and tape the design to the can with masking tape. With a

---

IT WORKED FOR ME

What's Behind Door Number 4?

When I was a kid, my father couldn't stand to see anything thrown away that was still usable. After collecting four doors of approximately the same size, he decided not to toss them but to use them to build an extra closet against an empty wall in our bedroom. He nailed three of the doors together at the  edges and hinged the fourth to the front so that it opened and closed like a normal door. With the addition of an old curtain rod, the doors were transformed into some much-needed closet space. If you attempt this one yourself, remember to remove the nonworking doorknobs first, or you might forget, as I did once, which door is *the* door.

—**Barry Schrager**
New York, New York

In this ingenious equation, four doors equal one closet.

hammer and a sharp nail, punch holes along the outline of the design. (The ice will prevent the can from getting crushed.) Space your holes ¼ to ½ inch apart. When you're done, remove the paper and let the ice melt. Place the can on a pretty saucer or terra-cotta platter, add a candle, and you have a beautiful candleholder.

Trivet-al Pursuit

❖ Need to put down a hot cup or pot without leaving a ring on or taking the finish off your table? You could spend a lot of money at a kitchen shop for a decorative trivet, or you could do it the Yankee way. A tile square, just like the ones on your bathroom or kitchen wall, will work perfectly, and it will look good, too. Visit the local hardware store or home remodeling center and check out the kitchen and

WORLD-CLASS FRUGALITY
Fishnet Fashions

Back in 1935, a 6-foot Cape Cod woman named "Tiny" Worthington started a trend that swept the nation—and it was all because of her thrifty nature. It occurred to her one day while visiting her husband's fish plant in North Truro, Massachusetts, that a pile of creamy white fishnet, which was waiting to be tarred for the traps, would make nice curtains for her pine-paneled home. Some fishermen helped her hang them up, and they approved of the effect. "Now, if an old-time fisherman tells you something looks good," Tiny later said, "you can be sure it does, because they are men of few words." There at the window was the beginning of Cape Cod Fishnet Industries.

It was no great leap to use fishnet for lamp shades, turbans, belts, boleros, capes, scarves, blouses, even an evening gown. Local fishermen's wives sewed Tiny's designs. Within a couple of years, fishnet fashions were featured in *Vogue, Women's Wear Daily, The New Yorker,* and other magazines. Alas, Cape Cod Fishnet Industries is no more, but Tiny's ingenuity should be an inspiration to thrifty folks everywhere.

EIGHT WAYS TO LIVEN UP A PICTURE FRAME

Plain picture frames cost a lot less than fancy ones, so buy a plain one and decorate it yourself. If you have some white household glue or a hot-glue gun, you can attach all kinds of trinkets to the face of most any frame.

1. Lure 'em in. Think that picture of your husband when he caught "the big one" looks great? Imagine how good it would look with the lure he used (or ones like it) displayed along with it, attached to the frame.

2. Who's got the button? Just imagine being able to clean out your button tin and make a beautiful frame at the same time. Carefully glue buttons of the same or varying sizes and colors to the frame.

3. Spin a yarn. Grab your leftover bulky yarn and make stripes or spirals on the frame. It's perfect for a picture of a crafty friend.

4. Make mine mosaic. Tile or glass chips can give a frame a beautiful mosaic finish. Be careful handling sharp edges, though.

5. Cast the first stone. Small pebbles you've picked up in your travels can turn a dull frame into a memento.

6. Play the shell game. Seashells are a natural choice for a nautical-theme picture.

7. Bead mine. When that old string of beads breaks, don't throw it out. Glue the trinkets to a frame to create a jeweled finish.

8. A penny for your thoughts? Interesting domestic or foreign coins can complement a vacation photo. And the best part is that white glue is water soluble, so in a pinch, you can spend the money!

---

bath departments. Individual tiles are inexpensive, many less than a dollar apiece. Glue some small felt pads on the bottom to avoid scratching the table's finish.

❖ But what if you don't have a tile square? Does that mean you're left holding a hot pot? Not at all. Here are some other heat-proof items you might have around the house that would make splendid trivets: a piece of old barn board or driftwood you've picked up on your travels, a horseshoe, a fancy (or not so fancy) carpet remnant, or even a scrap of a caned chair seat.

Love That Loving Cup

❖ If you're tired of putting your cut flowers into the same old vase, give this a try. The old silver trophy cup from that race you won in high school will make an interesting alternative. Check to see that the cup can hold water; if it leaks, you may need to place a small glass or jar inside.

❖ So maybe they don't give out trophies for third place. That doesn't mean you can't display your flowers with pride. An old rubber boot, such as a Wellington, can make a charming vase for long-stemmed flowers. If it leaks, just place a small cup of water inside.

❖ Surely you have an old handbag around, one you were planning to give away anyway. Place a cup inside the bag, fill it with water, and display your flowers there.

❖ If you're looking for something even quirkier, scout around for an old coffeepot, which might look terrific with flowers in it. Or place a cup inside your old sneakers or hiking boots, and they can become planters for the porch.

WHAT'S THE BEST MONEY SAVER?
Let the Buyer Be Wise

You're in a local junk shop looking for an unusual decorative object for your home. You've narrowed your choices down to three items. In the end you choose:

A. An old cast-iron doorstop shaped like a rabbit

B. A small decorative mirror

C. An old desk lamp

If you're wearing your frugal thinking cap, you know that the answer is (A) an old cast-iron doorstop. The reason? It's the most versatile item on the list. In addition to being used as a doorstop, that cast-iron rabbit can move to your bookshelf and become a bookend. Or you can place it on a windowsill as a interesting decoration. It can even serve as a heavy-duty paperweight in your home office.

PICTURES AND PICTURE FRAMES

You've Been Framed

❖ Here's a trick some artists use to make do-it-yourself frames for stretched-canvas paintings. The cheapest piece of lumber in the lumberyard is the furring strip: an 8-foot length costs about a buck. The wood is kind of rough, but with a little sanding and a couple of coats of paint or polyurethane, it can look beautiful. First, sand and paint one 8-foot strip. When it's dry, fit it to the stretcher bar that supports the stretched canvas. Here's the most accurate way to do that. Starting at the top edge of the painting, nail the full-length furring strip carefully into the stretcher bar. Leave ½ inch of the strip overhanging the face of the painting. Saw off the rest of the strip, flush to the corner. Turn the painting and lay the furring strip on the next side, again leaving a ½-inch overhang. Saw off the excess, again flush to the corner. Continue until all four sides are covered and you have a beautiful frame.

❖ For a fancier version, glue wood molding to the face of the frame to dress it up.

Oops . . . I Mean, Sold!

❖ Custom picture framing can be very expensive. Here's a way to get a beautiful custom frame at a considerable discount. Even the best picture framers make mistakes: Sometimes the framer orders the wrong size; sometimes the finish isn't quite right. Of course, that doesn't mean the frame gets tossed. As long as it is sound and usable, it gets put aside. The picture you want framed might just fit into one of those "oops" frames, and the framer will be glad to sell it to you for a lot less than an equivalent non-oops custom-made frame. You may not get the exact frame you had in mind, but the reduced price should add to its attractiveness.

Nail the furring strip to the stretcher bar, making sure ½ inch of the strip overhangs the face of the painting.

❖ To give the frame the "distressed" look of an antique, take it to your backyard or garage and hit it a few times with a scrap of chain, a hammer, or even a sharp rock. (Cover your painting so that it doesn't get damaged.) Then whitewash the frame or stain it. You can tell your friends it's hundreds of years old.

PAINTING IDEAS

Mistints, More Savings

❖ If you've been shopping for paint lately, you know that custom paint colors can set you back a pretty penny. Here's one way to save money on a small paint job. Visit your paint store and ask the manager if he has any cans of mistinted paint (custom-mixed colors that didn't come out quite right and that the customers didn't want). A can of mistinted paint will cost substantially less than another custom color. Ninety-nine percent of the time, though, the paint store will have only one can available, which means you'll need to be painting a small room, such as a bathroom.

❖ If you're painting a larger room and are the type who doesn't mind a little experimentation, try this alternative. Purchase several cans of mistints, bring them home, and blend them together in a 5-gallon bucket. You'll end up with a brand-new custom color to paint a larger room. Here's the important part: Mix, mix, and mix those colors again to be sure they're well-blended.

WALL TREATMENTS

It's Curtains for You

❖ You're getting ready to remodel, and one of your walls needs more work than you're willing to put into it before you can paint it. Don't call a plasterer yet. Rather than painting the wall, hide it with a curtain, which makes a beautiful and interesting room accent. First, box in the perimeter of the wall with the same color paint you're using for the rest of the room. Paint at least a foot in from the corners. When the paint is dry, hang a curtain rod near the ceiling. You may have to visit a lumberyard and buy a long dowel to make an extra-long rod. Choose a fabric that either matches or coordinates with your decor, and dress up the ends of the rod with fancy finials.

FIVE WAYS TO RE-COVER A LAMP SHADE

If your lamp shade has seen better days, check the structure of the frame. If it's sound and only the fabric is worn, you can refurbish it yourself. Here are five inexpensive but attractive techniques anyone can try.

1. String it along. Remove the old fabric from the frame and tie the end of some plain or colored decorative string to the top. Wind the string around the bottom ring and then around the top again, keeping the strands tight together. Keep winding back and forth between the top and bottom rings until the frame is covered. When you need to connect the string ends, tie them on the inside of the shade. Depending on the type of string you choose, you can paint it or leave it unfinished.

2. Use your jewels. For an even more elegant look, prestring beads from old jewelry or a craft supply store onto the string.

3. Re-create the old shade. Carefully remove the old fabric from the shade's frame. Trace the fabric's shape on brown craft paper and use that as a template. Select a new piece of fabric (from the fabric store, or use any other fabric you have around) and use your paper template to cut out a new shade. Wrap the new fabric around the frame, folding the fabric over the top and bottom rings, and attach it with a hot-glue gun. Don't worry if the seam isn't perfect, simply rotate the shade so that the seam side faces the wall.

4. Strap on the old feed bag. Or an old flour sack or any other burlaplike fabric. It will impart a rustic look to a lamp shade.

5. Raise the fabric of your life. Don't throw away that worn pillowcase or tablecloth. Use the scraps to give an old lamp shade a cheery new look. If you're feeling particularly crafty, sew scraps together in a patchwork pattern.

❖ If the idea of hanging a curtain in the middle of a wall doesn't appeal to you, hang a decorative quilt or another piece of fabric artwork there.

❖ This is also a great way to hide an ugly fuse box or a no-longer-used door.

I Know What I Like

❖ Looking for a special work of art for over the sofa? Here's a way to buy "real" art (as opposed to mass-produced prints or posters) for oodles less than you'd spend in a gallery. Contact local art schools and amateur art associations. Look in the Yellow Pages under Art Instruction and Schools or Arts Organizations and Information. Most art schools and amateur art associations regularly present shows of students' or members' work. Have a clear idea of how much you're willing to spend for a piece, and don't be afraid to negotiate. Students and amateurs often have an inflated sense of what their work is worth and suffer separation anxiety over parting with it, so you may have to haggle.

❖ If you like photography, you're in luck, because the same goes for photography institutes and associations.

Sow the Seeds of Decor

❖ If you like the look but not the price of country decor, give this clever idea a try. Next time you buy seeds, carefully slit open the tops of the packets to pour out the seeds. When you have several empty packets, arrange them in a frame to make a nifty decoration for a kitchen or hall wall.

Ad-ditional Artwork

❖ Let's face it, artwork is expensive. And if you're on a limited budget, you might be unwilling or unable to spend much more on your decor. Here's an inexpensive alternative. If you're like most folks, you probably have some old magazines stashed away in the attic or garage. That means you have a source of instant artwork. Thumb through the pages to see if anything catches your eye—the older and odder the better. Advertisements may be especially appealing, as are illustrations and full-page photographs. Scrounge around for an old frame, or purchase one from the local discount store, and frame one or more of your finds. Hang a 1940s ad for toilet paper in the bathroom or a full-page baby food ad in the nursery. Use your imagination and match the theme of the art to the room.

❖ If you don't have any old magazines of your own, head to the thrift store, recycling center, or local garage sales and flea markets.

Traveling Hang-Ups

❖ Do any boating or fishing? What about hiking or camping? If so, you may have some charts or maps around.

EVEN FUNERALS HAVE A BRIGHT SIDE

One of the easiest ways to brighten up a room is with a bouquet of fresh flowers, and getting them for free has to be a good thing, right? When someone dies, you can debate about where the soul goes, but one thing's certain: Most of the flowers sent to funerals end up in the dumpster.

Flowers are purchased fresh and brought or sent to funeral services by mourners. A typical funeral process lasts for 2 or 3 days, but fresh flowers can last for a week or more. When the services end, many of the arrangements stay behind, and by law in most states, funeral homes and florists can't resell or reuse flower arrangements, even if the flowers are still fresh. Consequently, funeral homes throw out dozens and dozens of perfectly good flowers.

Now, we're not proposing that you root through your local funeral home's dumpster. But we do suggest that you inquire as to whether you can stop by occasionally to pick out a bunch of flowers before they're put it the trash. Most funeral homes will be happy to oblige. In fact, many donate these flowers to hospitals and charitable organizations. You may even come home with a free vase and floral arrangement forms, too.

Placed in a frame, a map is a colorful and inexpensive way to dress up a room. Even road maps, especially antique ones, are interesting to look at and make you (and others) think of places you've been or you'd like to go. You might even trace out the route of a favorite trip or several trips to show all the places you've been.

So That's What You Did in the War

❖ We're so used to seeing photographs and pictures on the wall that it's easy to overlook other terrific sources of art. For instance, if members of your family have served in the military, they probably have saved medals or commendations they earned and would be proud to show them off. Place them in a deep picture frame around a picture of your G.I. Joe or Jane.

WINDOW TREATMENTS

Stains Can Be Good

❖ Stained glass has adorned castles and cathedrals for centuries, but if you've shopped for a panel to hang in your home, you know it can be expensive. Not to worry; you can fake stained glass on an ordinary window. First, decide on a pattern. On a piece of sturdy cardboard, draft a geometric or abstract design or a picture. Once you're happy with the design, cut it out, then tape the stencil to the window. Paint your design with acrylic paint; the thinner the coat, the more translucent it will be. The best part is that your design isn't permanent; you can scrape it off with a razor blade.

Make a stencil and use it to create your own stained glass.

Color Your World

❖ Don't waste that sunshine pouring in through your living room window: Use it. The best part? It's free. Fill clear glass bottles, such as milk bottles, with water that you've tinted with food coloring. Place several bottles on a windowsill or a shelf that receives direct sun. When the sunlight hits the bottles, it will cast colored light into the room.

❖ Of course, if you have colored-glass bottles, you can skip the food coloring.

Slick and Tiled

❖ Tired of condensation from under your potted plants ruining the finish on your windowsill? Here's a decorative way to deal with the problem, and it won't require an expensive trip to a home decorating store or a new paint job.

8 FOR UNDER $10

By replacing or spiffing up any or all of these eight items, you can give your room an inexpensive face-lift. If you buy new items, check out local hardware and discount stores for inexpensive replacements. For something a little more impressive, search flea markets and junk shops for bargains.

1. Switch your switch plates— and your outlet plates, too.

2. Look overhead. A new glass dome for the overhead lighting fixture can throw new light on a room. The same goes for a new lamp shade.

3. Plant a rose. You don't have to go overboard with fresh flowers. A single daisy or rose in an inexpensive bud vase will brighten any corner.

4. Ring in a new look. You'd be surprised what new rings or finials can do for a curtain rod (and the whole room). Try them on your shower curtain, too.

5. Turn over a new . . . knob. If your metal or glass doorknobs are dingy, shine them up or replace them.

6. Trim the trim. You don't need to paint an entire room for a whole new look. Invest in a pint of contrasting paint and use it to liven up just the trim.

7. Ask the magic mirror. Hang a decorative mirror on a wall. It will make the room look bigger, too.

8. Give it a clean sweep. Have you replaced your vacuum cleaner bag lately? A new bag will increase the performance of your vacuum and make your upholstery and rugs look a lot brighter.

Head to a tile store or a home supply store and shop for several colorful odd-lot tiles (you'll be able to pick them up very inexpensively). Affix the tiles to the windowsill with some grout. They will protect your windowsill, they're easy to clean, and they're attractive.

❖ Hold it! Before you run out to buy tiles, dig around your garage or basement to find those pretty tiles left over from your bathroom.

MAINTENANCE: TAKING CARE OF WHAT YOU HAVE

Give It a Spit Shine

❖ You've brought home a garage sale painting, and you're sure of two things: Your "find" is not a museum piece, and it needs cleaning. Professional art restoration costs a fortune, but you don't have to be an expert to do it yourself. (If you suspect that your painting is worth anything, have a pro take a look at it first. Most won't charge for a consultation.) You need lots of cotton swabs, several glasses of water, and patience. Moisten a swab in your mouth and use it to brush away the dirt from the paint (your saliva will work as a mild cleanser). Take a drink every so often to keep your mouth moist, and work in small areas. Make sure that no color comes off with the dirt—and be careful not to put a used swab back in your mouth.

CHAPTER 13

FRUGAL LAWN AND GARDEN CARE

*a*vid gardeners are lucky; they're already experiencing the best that frugality has to offer. After all, your hard work and creativity are yielding a vibrant lawn, beautiful flowers, and healthy vegetables. Still, if you suspect that you could be spending less and saving more money on expensive garden tools, seedlings, and books—without sacrificing your garden's natural beauty or its delicious bounty—you're probably right.

The first thing to keep in mind about gardening on a shoestring is that it's a 12-month process. Keeping a sharp eye out during the winter months for tools and supplies will reduce your gardening budget in the summer. That broken hockey stick from last winter will stake your tomato plants this July. That worn-out seat cushion from an old kitchen chair could be a knee pad during planting season. The best gardening accessories—from free plants to free planting ideas—come from the unlikeliest places.

Gardeners know that working with plants keeps them close to the cycle of life. Frugal gardening is even more ecological. Adding coffee grounds to your soil enriches it and helps you avoid chemical fertilizer. Saving your "gray water"—the water from your bathtub and sinks—for use in your garden will not only save money on your water bill, but it will also make you more aware of the types of cleansers you use. That water will feed your vegetables and, ultimately, you.

LOW-COST LAWN AND GARDEN PLANTS

Divide and Multiply

❖ Your own and friends' gardens are cost-free sources of plants. Exchange cuttings with friends, or take cuttings from your own plants and plant them. And don't forget that you can dig up your bulb plants, separate them, and replant them. Don't take a chance by digging up a plant from the woods or a meadow and replanting it in your garden. It could take over your yard.

Red, Gold, and Purple Thumb

❖ If you have limited property and can't decide whether to fill your yard with colorful plants or delicious vegetables, here's good news: You can do both. It's possible to grow vegetables that look as good as they taste. Seed catalogs now sell purple string beans, white eggplants, striped tomatoes, gold beets, and peppers that are crimson, gold, orange, yellow, purple, and, of course, green.

LANDSCAPE DESIGNS

Catalog Your Ideas

❖ There's no need to buy glossy, expensive books on landscaping. Every gardener gets dozens of mail-order catalogs every spring. Instead of throwing them away, look at the pictures. Behind the expensive lawn furniture and fancy tools you don't need are ideas for planting tulips next to Johnny-jump-ups or putting a stone walkway through an herb garden.

Sketch Artist

❖ One of the tools that gardening magazines try to sell you is a garden planner, but if you have some graph paper and maybe a few colored pencils, you can make one for free. Draw your garden to scale on the graph paper (letting one square equal one square foot, for instance). Then sketch an aerial view of your vegetable patch and see how many tomato seedlings you can plant.

Free for All

❖ One of the best sources of free gardening advice is the local horticultural society. You can probably join one for a small fee. Or start your own gardening club by posting a flyer in the library. This will put you in touch with people who want to share ideas, seeds, or cuttings from plants.

FERTILIZERS AND MORE

Something Fishy

❖ If you catch your own fish, you're assured of at least two things: fresh fish and fish parts. If fish head stew doesn't

THE YANKEE MISER RECOMMENDS . . .
Reusing Household Water

I hate to see even a drop of water go down the drain when I could sprinkle it on my grass or plants. Think of all the water you waste waiting for your kitchen or bathroom taps to heat up or cool down. Why not stick a bucket under the faucet or showerhead, catch all that wasted water, and put it to use in your yard?

Don't stop there. Rain is great for outdoor plants, so why not use it to water your indoor plants, too? The next rainy day, stick a bucket or barrel outside and collect some water to use inside. In the winter, collect snow in a bucket or barrel, let it melt, and then use it for your houseplants. How much water drips from your air conditioner? Catch it in a bucket every day during the summer, and you'll probably have enough water for most of your houseplants.

Next time you boil some vegetables, remember that you could also be making dinner for your garden. After the cooking water cools down, pour it and all its nutrients into the soil.

Guano from the Gods

Pigeons might not be considered songbirds, but they did make a major contribution to the music program at the Trinity Episcopal Church in Hartford, Connecticut. Church members bagged and sold as fertilizer the guano that pigeons had been leaving in the bell tower for nearly a century. They sold more than 1,500 pounds of dried droppings in 10 days, raising $30,000 to restore the church's organ.

A few months before the sale, some workmen scraped the guano off the inside walls of the 100-foot tower and stored it in large plastic bags in the church basement while church officials tried to figure out how to dispose of it. Inspired by a novel in which an English priest sells pigeon droppings, the rector recommended that the church go into the fertilizer business. After a state agency tested the dung and found that it contained plenty of nitrogen and no disease-causing organisms, the church held a sale on the parish grounds and marketed its product under the name Sign of the Dove. Suggested but rejected names included God's Guano, Gifts from Above, and Heavenly Droppings.

whet your appetite, use the fish parts as fertilizer. Put the fish in the freezer until it's time to put it in the ground. Make sure it's buried deep enough (at least 6 inches) to keep any stray cats from digging it up. Hey, it worked for the Pilgrims.

Grounds in the Ground

❖ A soil's acidity can determine which plants will grow in it. Many agricultural schools will test the acidity of your soil for free if you take a small sample to them. If your soil is too alkaline—that is, the acid level is too low—for your desired plants, add coffee grounds to it. To find an agricultural school near you, get in touch with your state's department of education or agriculture. You can find both in the government listings of your White Pages.

The Mow the Merrier

❖ When you mow, leave the grass clippings on the lawn. They will hold moisture and reduce the amount of watering required.

All the News That's Fit to Plant

❖ Not only can newspapers dig up dirt, but they can also cover it up. Place dampened newspaper on the ground to help keep the soil moist, just as regular mulch does. The water will keep the newspaper from blowing away, and because the paper is biodegradable, it will eventually dissolve into the ground.

Covering the soil with newspaper also prevents weeds from growing. If you're afraid your garden will look too much like a birdcage with all that newspaper lining it, cover the paper with a thin layer of bark mulch.

Hay Now

❖ An effective, inexpensive way to make sure your perennials bloom each year is to cover the ground with hay or grass clippings in the winter. This cover isn't to keep the bulbs warm; it's to keep the ground frozen. A premature thaw followed by a deep freeze can kill perennials.

Walking on Eggshells

❖ After you have cracked open an egg, you might want to crush the shell and save it. Adding crushed eggshells to the soil is a good way to aerate it.

Homemade Hydraseed

❖ If you want to patch some holes in your lawn, you don't have to spend money on the brand-name products made from grass seed, pulverized newspaper, and green coloring. Instead, if you've already done some gardening and seeding that season, you probably have the ingredients at hand to make your own lawn-patch solution. Just mix equal parts peat moss and grass seed and spread a thin layer over the dirt spots in your lawn. The peat moss will retain water for the seed and promote faster germination. Before spreading the seed solution, be sure to rake the soil to remove any rocks or sticks that will prevent the grass from growing into the ground.

PEST CONTROL

Toad Abodes

❖ No, toads don't give you warts, but they do dine on insects, so they can make friendly neighbors for your garden plants. A good way to make toads feel welcome—

and put otherwise useless items to work—is to place broken terra-cotta pots upside down near your garden. If there are any toads in the area, they'll soon make homes under the pots.

Common Scents

❖ You could buy insect repellents for your garden, but you're more clever than that. For instance, garlic will keep away more than just vampires. Plant it near your roses, and it will deter Japanese beetles. Parsley and basil also will deter bugs and therefore make good companion plants for vegetables. Marigolds are perhaps the most common repellent plants. If possible, plant them around your entire garden, and especially around your tomatoes.

IT WORKED FOR ME

Doggone It

One of the things I liked best about moving out of my apartment and into a house was that the house has a backyard that is small but roomy enough for both my dog, Bunny, and a garden. However, the first year I lived here, I made the mistake of planting along the yard's chain-link fence. No matter how much I scolded Bunny, he insisted on running through the flowers and vegetables, crushing them, even though there was room for him to run in the rest of the yard. I started wondering whether he would have been as obsessed with the garden if I had named him Spot or Rover instead of Bunny.

Anyway, I thought about dividing the yard with another fence, but I didn't want to spend the money, and I didn't want to make the yard seem even smaller than it already was. I eventually figured out that Bunny wasn't interested in the garden at all. He just wanted to be near the fence, where he could get a better look at what was happening on the other side. So the next year and every year since, I have planted away from the fence, and dog and gardener have remained best friends.

—Julie Bean
Venice, California

Wash 'n' Fly

❖ Whiteflies love geraniums, hibiscuses, and dahlias, but they don't like dishwashing liquid. Mix a teaspoon of dishwashing liquid and some water in a spray bottle, and spray those plants every 2 weeks to keep them free of flies.

Adios, Aphids

❖ Aphids are like the teenagers of your garden: If you don't provide them with a good place to hang out, they can cause a lot of trouble. A nasturtium plant will keep aphids from munching on your other plants. And there's a bonus: You can eat nasturtium flowers and leaves—once you rinse off the aphids, of course. Toss them in a salad to add a peppery flavor.

❖ Aphids themselves are a delicacy for ladybugs. To rid your garden of these pests, buy a package of live ladybugs from a garden supply store or through a seed catalog and set them loose amid your aphid-infested plants.

LAWN AND GARDEN TOOLS

Manual Labor

❖ Most of us don't bother to read instruction manuals, let alone save them. Losing or misplacing the manual can be a problem when you need to replace the spark plug in your lawn mower. There are hundreds of different types, and using the wrong one can keep your mower from starting or running smoothly. There is even the risk of damaging a piston by installing the wrong-size plug. A simple solution is to use a permanent marker to write the correct type and size spark plug on the side of the machine. If you own a chain saw, do the same for its spark plug and chain size. And be sure to go over the writing again before it fades.

Wax On, Grass Off

❖ If you spray furniture polish on the undercarriage of your lawn mower, it will help prevent grass clippings from

building up around the blade and allow the mower to work more efficiently. Hose down the undercarriage and let it dry before spraying on the polish.

Have a Wrap Session

❖ Many of the new pruners and hedge shears are equipped with foam rubber handles that slide over the metal arms of the tool. The handles let you get a sure grip, but they tend to slip off the tool. To prevent that from happening, remove the handles and wrap a layer of friction tape around the tool's arms, then slide the handles back over the tape-covered arms.

Two Blades Are Better Than One

❖ If you want to be efficient, buy an extra blade for your lawn mower and keep it sharpened. When one blade becomes dull, you can simply replace it with the sharpened blade and mow your lawn now rather than waiting to have the blade professionally sharpened. When changing the blade, leave the mower on its side or upside down for as short a time as possible to prevent the motor fluids from spilling onto the lawn or pavement or from flooding the engine. To make sure you can change the blade quickly, use a permanent marker to write the size of the wrench required on the side of the mower.

Oil Treatment

❖ A little linseed oil can mean a longer life for your shovels and other wood-handled tools. When a shovel handle snaps, it's usually because the wood has dried out. To prevent that from happening, sand any varnish or splinters off the handle, then pour some linseed oil onto an old rag and rub it into the wood.

Sand and Oil

❖ The best way to make tools last a long time is to clean them properly, even when you're in a hurry. A fast and easy way to clean tools is to grab an old 5-gallon bucket and fill it with builder's sand (available at building supply stores) and enough 10W40 or other lightweight motor oil to make a thick paste. Don't use a vegetable oil; it may entice insects and other visitors you're not eager to attract. At the end of a day of gardening, plunge the business end of each tool into the bucket and stir it around. The sand will scrub away the dirt, and the oil will lubricate the metal and guard against rust.

Day-Glo Spades

❖ One of the costliest mistakes gardeners make is to leave tools outside where they can rust or get caught up in the lawn mower. An easy way to find them in the grass or garden is to paint the handles with oil-based fluorescent craft paint, which is available at any hobby shop. This will make them visible even from a distance.

Cut Your Losses

❖ If you're in the habit of buying $10 sunglasses, chances are you buy quite a few pairs each summer. However, if you were to spend $100 on a pair of sunglasses, you'd be a lot less likely to misplace them. And since they'd be of better quality, they wouldn't break as easily. The same goes for garden tools. You might save money in the long run by buying top-quality items that don't chip or snap under pressure and that won't end up under a set of spinning lawn mower blades or buried in the compost pile.

IMPROVISING IN THE GARDEN

Line of Sight

❖ One problem gardeners have is getting straight rows in the vegetable patch. Here's a cheap way to solve this problem. Get a ball of string and tie the loose end to a wooden stake or the handle of a small shovel. Anchor the tool in the ground at one end of your patch where you want a row. Walk around to the other end with the ball of string

and pull the line tight. It will make a perfectly straight line that you can follow when you sprinkle your seeds.

Screen Out the Bad Stuff

❖ Before you spend money on a soil sifter, check your basement or garage. A screen that's too small for any of your windows won't keep bugs out of the house, but it can remove rocks and other debris from your potting soil.

Egg Plants

❖ Cardboard egg cartons are not only recyclable; they're also reusable. An empty egg carton can make a starter container for a dozen seedlings. Don't overwater the seeds, though, or your pot will become too soggy for the seedlings to thrive.

Got Milk Jugs?

❖ Milk can help you grow big and strong, and the container it comes in can do the same for a seedling. How? By serving as a minigreenhouse. Cut the bottom off a 1-gallon plastic milk jug, remove the cap for ventilation, and place it on the ground over the small plant. The plastic cover will protect the plant from frost and animals.

A Good Break

❖ If you break a rake, you will have lost one garden tool but gained two new ones. The handle can stake a tomato plant, and the head can hold up other garden tools. Fasten the head, teeth facing out, to the wall of your shed, then hang shovels, a spade, or other rakes from the teeth.

Stick 'Em Up!

❖ We've all watched enough TV and seen enough movies to know that some criminals can use nylon stockings to hold up banks. But you can also use them to hold up tomato plants. Because they are soft, flexible, and free, discarded stockings and panty hose are ideal for tying tomato plants to stakes. Just cut the legs into 6-inch lengths, and they're ready to use.

Top-Heavy Tomatoes

❖ An old worn-out bra can still provide plenty of support—for your tomato plants. Use two stakes to tie up each tomato plant and attach the ends of a bra to each stake so that the cups sit under the largest tomatoes. The bra will prevent the plant from sagging and possibly breaking under the weight of the tomatoes.

❖ If you want to get scientific about it, use a black bra before the tomatoes ripen (it will attract more sun) and a white bra after the tomatoes are ripe but before you pick them.

Fore Thought

❖ To save wear and tear on your back and money on chiropractor bills, buy an inexpensive golf shaft protector at a sporting goods store, or head to the garage and grab one of your own. When planting rows of seeds, hold the hollow shaft protector, which is about 3 feet long, over the spot where you want to plant a seed. Then just drop the seed into the top of the shaft.

On the Fence

❖ If you're short on ground space for your garden, try using air space by growing your vegetables up instead of out. A chain-link fence works just as well as a trellis for some vegetables, including peas, beans, cucumbers, tomatoes, even pumpkins and cantaloupes.

❖ The heavier vining fruits will need to be supported, and one of the best ways to do that is with panty hose.

IT WORKED FOR ME
Talk Is Cheap

For a couple of weeks last summer, whenever I walked past one particular yard in my neighborhood, I would hear a transistor radio playing in the garden, but no one was ever around. Finally, one night when I walked past the house, the owner, an elderly man, was in his yard picking some vegetables. I stopped and chatted with him and eventually asked him about the radio. He responded with a smile and then explained that he left the radio on because the sound of the voices kept animals out of his garden. He said he always set the dial on an AM talk radio station rather than an FM station that played music. "I don't want to come out here some night and find the raccoons having a dinner dance," he told me.

—Stephen E. Sickles
Arlington, Massachusetts

When the fruits are small, slip pairs of panty hose or nylon stockings over them, then fasten the hose to the fence. As the fruits grow, the hose will expand and continue to support them.

The Clampdown

❖ In a pinch, a hose clamp—the kind you might find in a car engine holding the radiator hose in place—can hold together a broken shovel or rake handle. The tool won't be as good as new, but it should be strong enough to get you through the task at hand.

Drink Up

❖ Coincidentally and conveniently, the squeeze-top caps on beverage bottles fit perfectly on most 1-pint plastic motor oil containers. When screwed onto a pint of oil, the cap will make it easier to get all the oil into the engine of a lawn mower or other motorized garden machine without using a funnel.

SAVING WATER

Pamper Your Tomatoes

❖ Tomato plants don't require a lot of watering and a lot of space if you have a 5-gallon paint bucket and a pair of disposable diapers. Punch a few holes in the bottom of the bucket for drainage. Remove the absorbent material from the diapers and place it in the bucket. Cover it with soil and plant a plant. When you water the plant, the diaper material will absorb and retain plenty of water for the roots to draw on. You should have to water the plant only twice a week.

IT WORKED FOR ME
A Sharp Idea

My uncle Francis McCarron was a firefighter, and whenever the department bought new hoses, he would keep some of the old hoses for himself and give some to me rather than throw them away. He showed me how I could cut the hose to the length of my chain saw or pruning saw blade and then slide it over the blade as a protective cover.

—**Stephen E. Sickles**
Arlington, Massachusetts

CHAPTER 14

SPENDING LESS AT THE GROCERY STORE

upermarket shopping: Doesn't everything look great? Stroll through the bakery department and breathe in the intoxicating aroma of baking bread and warm cookies straight from the oven. Wander through the produce section and see the bumper crop of fruits and vegetables from all over the world—artfully arranged and glistening as if just picked in the morning dew. The butcher and fishmonger stand tall behind their elaborate refrigerated counters, and for a moment you're transported back to a time when people bought their goods daily from specialty shops.

When you visit each area of the giant superstore, you may find yourself tempted to purchase items you've never tried or normally don't buy. Well, guess what? Those items add up fast and furiously at the cash register. And that's just what the marketing people want you to do—buy, buy, buy—while getting caught up in the ambience of the store. But fear not, frugal spender. In this chapter, we'll let you in on some money-saving strategies for making each shopping trip pay off in the home savings department.

SHOPPING BASICS

Put Your Food Bill on a Diet

❖ Don't know where to start when it comes to trimming your grocery store spending? Set a goal to reduce your total tab by a few percentage points each time you shop. Try to aim to reduce your food bill by 3 to 7 percent. Let's say that 5 percent equals $6. Cut that 5 percent every week, and you'll have an extra $312 at the end of the year.

Make More Meatless

❖ You can reduce the amount of expensive meat and poultry you buy by changing your recipe repertoire to include meatless meals. If you don't want to do without your favorite meats altogether, use them (along with poultry and fish) as flavor enhancers, rather than as the main course. Add chopped meat, chicken, and fish to omelets, pasta, rice dishes, salads, and stews. You won't be skimping on the flavor, only on the budget.

A Substitution for Savings

❖ Uh, oh. You're out of self-rising flour. Does it mean a time- and money-wasting trip to the grocery store? Not if you have a good recipe substitution list handy. That list will help you avoid unnecessary visits to the grocery or (worse) convenience store. Most basic cookbooks include a substitution list; make a copy and attach it to your refrigerator or the inside of a kitchen cupboard door.

Pantry Perfection

❖ Keep a well-stocked larder at all times, and you'll be able to whip up delicious meals effortlessly. Unexpected guests will fare well, as will hungry family members on evenings when you're too tired to think about creative cooking. Keep a supply of pasta and sauces for instance, and anything else your family may especially like. That way, you won't be tempted to call out for a pizza delivery or overspend on take-out fare.

Double Up on Savings

❖ One way to save money at the supermarket is to avoid going too often. So if you're going to the store to buy ingredients for lasagna (or any other casserole or freezable dinner), make sure you buy enough to make one for the table and one for the freezer. That way, you can take advantage of lower unit prices on larger packages of noodles and meat and save a little gas money. The best part? It usually doesn't take much more time to prepare two dinners than it does one.

Be a Listing Agent

❖ In theory, keeping a running grocery list on the refrigerator door is a great idea. And if you can make it work, great. Unfortunately, in many households noncompliance by some members may thwart the effort. Here's an easy way to make sure your list stays current. Attach a small paper or plastic bag to your kitchen waste or recycling receptacle. Tell everyone in your family that you're doing this to keep track of items as they run out. When little Sally finishes the last of the ketchup, she should throw the package (or at least a part of it) in the special bag. When it's time to make the list, you can go through the bag to see what you're out of.

Planning Makes Cents

❖ How many meals will you be responsible for during the week? Take a few minutes to do a little meal planning, and you'll make your journey to the supermarket more efficient and less costly. Count up how many suppers, lunches, and breakfasts you and your family will eat at home or pack. Who will be home for meals in the upcoming week? Cross-reference your list with the supermarket sales circulars and what's in your home larder to come up with recipe ideas.

IT WORKED FOR ME
Pick Your Own

We eat a lot of fruit in our house, and when midsummer comes around, I can't wait to take my young children to the pick-your-own farms. We especially enjoy gathering blueberries, which are far less expensive than the store-bought kind. The kids have a great time and always eat more than what ends up in the bucket. I usually manage to pick at least a dozen or so pints, which gets us through the fall and winter with plenty of blueberry pancakes and muffins. The best part? Those berries supply a sweet reminder of summer in every bite.

—Elissa Barr
Contoocook, New Hampshire

Aisle Be a Savvy Shopper

❖ Want to be the smartest shopper in your neighborhood? Shop only the perimeter of the supermarket. That way, you'll buy healthier groceries. Whole foods, such as produce, meat, and dairy products, are always on the outer edges of the store. Generally, the inside aisles are filled with processed (and more expensive) foods.

Don't Miss This Reduction

❖ Most fish, meat, and produce departments have areas set aside for items that have been reduced due to impending expiration dates. Those items are fine to eat—as long as you do so quickly. If you don't have a meal planned for dinner, wander into your local market; you may luck out and find something delicious at a fraction of the original cost.

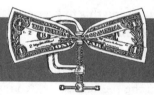

IT WORKED FOR ME
Co-op without Walls

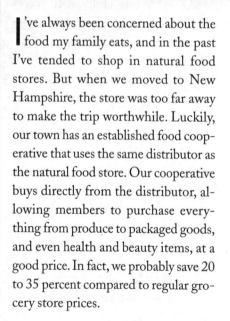

I've always been concerned about the food my family eats, and in the past I've tended to shop in natural food stores. But when we moved to New Hampshire, the store was too far away to make the trip worthwhile. Luckily, our town has an established food cooperative that uses the same distributor as the natural food store. Our cooperative buys directly from the distributor, allowing members to purchase everything from produce to packaged goods, and even health and beauty items, at a good price. In fact, we probably save 20 to 35 percent compared to regular grocery store prices.

Each month, all the members write up their orders and give them to one member, who streamlines the order and places it with the distributor. When the truck comes to town, we take turns unloading it. We have our monthly co-op shopping experience at a local church and give leftover goods to the church's food bank. Our co-op without walls gives us a chance to buy great natural food products at good prices, meet other families with similar interests, and help out a local charity—all at the same time.

—**Liz Warriner**
Henniker, New Hampshire

Superstore: Convenient or Costly?

❖ Many supermarkets now provide customers with services that aren't food-related. Pharmacies, video stores, florists, and banks are cropping up in large markets. Yes, these services are convenient, but be sure to compare prices with their slightly less convenient counterparts.

Scanning for Dollars

❖ Check it out: Many errors are made at the checkout counter. Be a frugal shopper right up until the end of your shopping trip by watching the prices as the items are scanned. Ask the cashier not to start until you have un-loaded your cart, so you can monitor the scanner's prices. If you catch an error, some stores will give you the item free of charge.

Stock Up on Sale Items

❖ Being a frugal shopper sometimes means you have to go overboard on purchases when items you use frequently go on sale. If boneless chicken breast is at a rock-bottom price, buy enough for the next month or two. Just take it home, divide it up, and freeze it. Set aside space in your kitchen or pantry for other items you may want to stock up on during great sales.

Water It Down

❖ Some of the most expensive items in the grocery store come out of the baby goods aisle. Avoid paying a premium price for baby juices simply by diluting regular juices with seltzer or water—as much as you can get away with without turning your kids off.

❖ Make and mash your own baby food with a food mill or processor. A ripe avocado is nature's own perfect baby food—full of nutrition, vitamins, and healthy fats.

❖ Check out diaper prices at buying clubs and discount department stores: The larger the quantity, the less you'll pay per diaper.

Happy Endings

❖ If you need meats, cheeses, or other deli ingredients for salads, soups, and casseroles and don't need them thinly sliced, ask for the end pieces of the large deli packs. You could save as much as 75 percent off the regular price.

Eliminate the Junk

❖ Just say no to junk food. Foods with little or no nutritional value don't belong in a frugal shopping cart. Make your own cookies, pop your own popcorn, and make iced

FRUGAL FORMULAS
STORING THE BERRIES YOU JUST PICKED

Keep fresh berries in the fridge in a shallow, dry container for 2 to 3 days, and don't wash them until you're ready to use them. If you plan to freeze your berries for a midwinter hibernation snack, wash and dry them well. Place them in a single layer on a cookie sheet and put them in the freezer until they're frozen. Once frozen, the berries can go into heavy-duty freezer bags deep in the freezer. Put frozen berries right into dishes you're preparing—no need to wait for them to thaw.

herbal teas and other healthful beverages. Don't buy packaged desserts; eat more fruit, which is a healthier choice and will fill you up faster. Avoid sugar-filled sodas and drink more water—the cheapest and best thirst quencher around.

Bulk Buying? Worth Trying

❖ Most natural food stores offer customers the opportunity to buy goods in bulk. Items typically sold this way include rice, pasta, cereal, granola, flour, sugar, peanut butter, maple syrup, olive oil, nuts, herbs, and spices. Buying in bulk may seem like the most cost-efficient way to make purchases, but you must compare the unit prices of bulk foods to those of non-bulk foods. Organically produced items especially may cost more than their counterparts found at the grocery store.

Souper Saver

❖ Don't you dare pay for high-priced, sodium-saturated soups. Making your own is significantly cheaper and healthier. A whole chicken will provide you with a couple of cans' worth of broth. Put a cooked chicken carcass in a large pot and add enough water to cover the chicken. Add a couple of peeled and quartered onions, a carrot or two, a few peppercorns, some sprigs of fresh herbs (such as sage, thyme, oregano, or basil), a stalk of celery with its leaves, and any other root vegetable you may have hanging around. Bring the water to a boil, then reduce the heat to a simmer and cook for about 2 hours. Let the broth cool completely, then skim off the excess fat and strain out and discard the vegetables. Pour the broth into freezer bags or plastic containers and freeze.

Take a Powder

❖ If you do a lot of baking or cooking with milk, keep an eye out for sales on powdered milk. Many folks don't care for the taste of powdered milk for drinking, but it's fine for cooking and baking. When the milk's on sale, buy it. You'll save money, and you can make only as much as you need.

Keep the Little Ones Occupied

❖ Trying to practice home economics with kids in a busy supermarket can be difficult. Children are targets for food manufacturers, who know that harried parents are likely to succumb to whining kids. But if you make a game out of shopping, it can be a less harrowing—and more frugal—experience. Put older children in charge of using the calculator, adding up the costs of the items as you shop. Give smaller children coupons, and when you're in the appropriate aisle, see if they can find the item that matches each coupon. If your kids are helping you, they're less likely to get fixated on sugary—and costly—cereals and candy.

Cereal Killer

❖ Ah, the dreaded cereal aisle. It's expensive—yet so enticing. Cold cereal is overpriced and overrated. If you have coupons, use them, especially when there's a sale. But the most frugal solution is to get your family hooked on oatmeal; it's more healthful and costs less. Buy the least expensive plain brand and dress it up yourself with raisins, cinnamon, chopped nuts, sliced or dried fruit, or anything else your tastebuds desire.

Personal Pricing Guides

❖ Invest in a small notebook and keep track of the prices of items you buy every week. Compare the prices at all the local supermarkets. You'll likely find that one store sells your favorite flour (or cereal or pasta) for much less than another market. An easy way to start your personal guide is to keep your register receipts so that you can record your item costs. Once you finish your guide, you may find that it will take a little longer to get your shopping done, especially if you're shopping at three different stores, but you'll spend less money in the long run.

Shelf Life

❖ It's a good idea to create extra space around your home for nonperishable items, especially if you're into buying extra items during a sale. Make space in and around your kitchen or in the cellar. Buy sturdy, inexpensive shelving units at a do-it-yourself home store, or use old cabinets or bookcases that you may already have or find at yard sales and flea markets. Then you'll have no excuse for not stocking up when you come across a good deal.

Freezer Facts

❖ Having a spare freezer is great for stocking up on supermarket deals, especially if you use it correctly. When you purchase a freezer, review the manufacturer's energy usage estimate, then check with your power company to find out specifically how much it will cost you to run. You can find the company's telephone number right on the bill.

Smart Shopping Knows No Season

❖ You'll save on your food budget if you buy produce that's in season locally or at least within easy striking distance. For instance, it's a lot cheaper to buy asparagus grown in North America in the spring than it is to buy South American asparagus in December. During the off-season, shipping costs add to the cost of the produce.

❖ You can save even more money by purchasing extra fruits and vegetables in season, then blanching and freezing them for off-season consumption.

Have a Party

❖ Ever wonder what to do with the gallons of berries you've picked? Or how to make homemade sausage or fresh pasta? Hold a cooking party with a few friends. Find one person who knows how to can, make pasta or sausage, or do some other big cooking project, and invite him to show the whole gang. You'll save some money by cooking in bulk, learn a new skill, and have a good time with your friends.

Waste Not, Want Not

❖ Food spoiling in your home is paying the supermarket something for nothing. Avoid rotten eggs and other po-

FIVE MONEY-SAVING SERVICES

Local Cooperative Extension Service offices provide their communities with valuable information about the following subjects. Look for your local office in the county government listings of the White Pages. Live in the city? Check with the agricultural department at a local college or university.

I. What's growing? The extension office can tell you what's available and in season in your area. Remember that locally produced apples are usually less expensive than those shipped in from Fiji.

2. Good for you! The Cooperative Extension Service offers loads of free information about healthful eating for everyone from babies to seniors.

3. Where to get it. Listings of local farmers' markets are available from the extension office. Visit those markets for terrific values on just-picked items and meet the people who produce the ultrafresh vegetables you desire.

4. The truth about canning. Find out what to do with your tomato surplus from the experts at the extension office.

5. Their name is mud. Make sure your garden will grow by having the Cooperative Extension Service perform a soil test. The test can tell you which nutrients your soil lacks, and the extension staff will recommend the right fertilizers to use. This service costs very little but can save you big in the long run.

tential science projects by keeping track of what you have on hand. Stocking up on sale items is one thing, but letting them all go to waste is another.

COUPON TIPS

Do They Help You Save?

❖ The truth about coupons is that many of them are made for expensive, brand-name, processed, foods. A bag of famous-name cookies for which you have a 50-cent coupon may still be more expensive than a bag of store-brand cookies. If you're loyal to certain products, find as many coupons as you can. Check the newspaper recycling bin at your local transfer station for duplicates if you find some you like in your Sunday paper.

❖ Don't be tricked into buying an item you don't need just because you have a coupon for it. Use coupons only for things you normally buy.

The Coupon Connection

❖ Keep your coupons up-to-date and organized, and you'll be more efficient in the supermarket. Some folks like to organize their coupons (and shopping list) in the same order as the store aisles.

Complimentary Savings

❖ If you really love a product, write to the manufacturer expressing your devotion and brand loyalty. You may receive a reply—along with a bunch of coupons.

CHAPTER 15

PREPARING DELICIOUSLY THRIFTY MEALS

*C*ooking inexpensively has always been a great way to pare down the budget. But the rules for saving on cooking have changed dramatically since the days when most households had a full-time wife and mother, thriftily working Spam into a weekday meal and stretching Sunday's pot roast for a fourth dinner.

Most of us don't eat every meal at home anymore, and when we do eat at home, we don't always have the time to marinate that inexpensive cut of meat or cook up one meat, three vegetables, a bread and a dessert (nor do the FDA nutrition guidelines recommend we do so). We also face two foes that our mothers probably didn't face: fast food and convenience food. That oversize fast-food muffin or grease-laden burger and fries cost twice as much as a fresh, light meal prepared at home. Similarly, overpriced, heavily processed convenience foods for the microwave leave us saturated with salt and preservatives—and usually still hungry to boot.

Frugal Yankees know that preparing tastier, healthier, and more satisfying meals at home can save money and make mealtimes more enjoyable. But unlike the old days, the key is not necessarily buying the cheapest stuff you can find. Instead, concentrate on shopping for inexpensive ingredients you will actually use, not the type that will languish in the refrigerator while you call for takeout. And for the sake of the overall food budget, splurge on a special touch here and there—a handful of fresh shrimp, some buttery Boston lettuce, olives for your tacos. Your main goal is to make what you can fix at home preferable to what you can pick up or microwave, and the occasional luxuries will be offset by the savings you realize from not eating out.

There are three other important strategies for preparing thrifty meals. The first is to get organized, so that you can make cooking inexpensive food as easy as possible—whether that means baking one big omelette or freezing batches of browned hamburger. The second is to substitute a less expensive ingredient for a costly one whenever you can without compromising taste or quality. And third, strive to use up what you have, particularly those expensive ingredients, because that's money you've already spent.

But more important than any of these tactics is taking the time to reflect on your good fortune in being able to cook homey, satisfying meals and snacks. In today's frenzied world, home cooking is almost a status symbol and brings unparalleled enjoyment to anyone wise enough to make the time for it.

THE YANKEE MISER RECOMMENDS . . .
Use Your Noodle

One of my favorite dishes to cook for company is lasagna. Almost everyone likes it, and you can make it heavy on the veggies, heavy on the sauce, or with or without meat. I've noticed those "no boil" lasagna noodles at the market. But I don't buy them because they usually cost more and you can't use them for anything but the recipe on the box. I stick with regular lasagna noodles, looking for the ones on sale. But I don't waste time or electricity boiling them. Instead, I add an extra cup of water to my spaghetti sauce and make sure the top layer of noodles is completely covered with sauce and cheese. Also, I cover the lasagna tightly with aluminum foil while it bakes. The noodles get just as tender as precooked or no-boil noodles, but I think they taste even better.

ESSENTIAL EQUIPMENT

Sharpen Your Cooking

❖ It just won't do to hack away with a 20-year-old serrated steak knife when your goal is delicious, appealing stir-fried vegetables, crudités, deli-style sandwiches, minced garlic in butter, or uniform chunks of potato in your salad. So spring for a good, sharp paring knife, even if it costs you $20 (or more) at a cutlery or gourmet store, and pick up a sharpening steel while you're at it. A good-quality knife, kept sharp, will be safer to use (a sharp knife is less likely to slip than a dull one), make your work go faster, and produce better results with less expensive ingredients. It will pay for itself with only a couple of uses.

❖ While you're at that kitchen store, buy a knife with a longer blade for cutting thin slices of lunch meat, cheese, and frozen fish or chicken fillets.

❖ Consider buying one of those not-so-sharp knives (with a heavy blade that extends all the way into the handle) and sharpen it yourself.

The Slow-Motion Solution

❖ If you don't already have one in the garage or attic, buy a slow-cooker, or Crock-Pot, at a thrift store or a discount department store. Use it to stew an inexpensive cut of meat until it's fork-tender, then serve it as an entrée, on hamburger buns, or inside flour tortillas. Try cooking a pork shoulder with a 28-ounce can of pureed tomatoes combined with a cup of molasses, or an

---

𝓕RUGAL 𝓜EMORIES

We All Scream for OJ

In the 1960s and 1970s, like most big families, we ate every meal at home and never left a scrap. My dad was not known as the family cook, but he would occasionally get up early on Sunday and make us all pancakes or oatmeal before we piled in the car for church. And every once in a great while, he would add a tiny scoop of vanilla ice cream to each small glass of orange juice. It probably didn't add up to a pint of ice cream total, but I remember the giddy feeling I had as I bounded downstairs in my church clothes and spotted dad holding that ice cream scoop. It's such a fond memory that it's become a family tradition. Just this year, my own kids and their dad schemed to serve me ice cream in orange juice for my birthday.

—Amy Witsil
Chapel Hill, North Carolina

---

inexpensive roast beef doused with a jar of salsa mixed with a tablespoon of chili powder.

❖ Cook a big batch of dried beans in the slow cooker, especially the types that are expensive to buy canned, such as black beans. No need to soak the beans, just cover them with water, add ½ teaspoon baking soda, and cook on low overnight. In the morning, add your favorite seasonings and continue cooking for 4 to 8 hours more, or until tender. Leftovers? Freeze 'em.

Look—No Hands!

❖ Make an investment in frugal cooking by buying a . . . hands-free phone? This will allow you to spend more time in the kitchen—say, washing lettuce for tomorrow's salad instead of buying a $4 bag—while you return phone calls and chat with friends. Some models cost $20 or less, but even those that cost three times as much can pay off, because you can take the same phone with you while you wash windows, ride your exercise bike, or wind yarn.

IMITATION, NOT DEPRIVATION

Curb the Herbal Cheese Bill

❖ Next time you're at the store, bypass that tiny container of soft herbed cheese and make your own facsimile for a fraction of the cost. Mash 4 ounces light cream cheese and 1 tablespoon butter with a fork, then add 1 tablespoon white wine or a splash of balsamic vinegar. Add 2 cloves minced, mashed garlic and 2 tablespoons finely minced fresh herbs, such as chives, parsley, or basil. Mix up the whole shebang, give it a liberal grinding of black pepper, and let it ripen, covered, in the fridge for a few hours. Then heap it into a decorative bowl and serve.

❖ Fresh out of fresh herbs? Use ½ teaspoon each of dried thyme and oregano.

Son of Sun-Dried Tomatoes

❖ Ever priced a jar of sun-dried tomatoes steeped in olive oil? If so, you probably walked away shaking your head. Instead, try this home-dried version when your garden is in full production. Preheat the oven to 450°F. Halve the tomatoes and seed if you like. Rub the edges with olive oil and sprinkle lightly with salt. Arrange on a rack placed in a lightly oiled jelly roll pan. Put the pan in the oven and immediately reduce the heat to 250°F. Bake for 6 hours.

❖ To store in oil, brush the dried tomatoes with white vinegar, then let stand for 5 minutes. Pack lightly in a screw-top jar and cover with olive or canola oil. Store in the refrigerator for up to a month.

SAVE WITH SHORTCUTS

Pasta Today in Case It's Hot Tamale

❖ Nothing beats pasta for low-priced, home-cooked fast food. But you're even more likely to eat it instead of take-out pizza if you cook a big batch of noodles to last a couple of days. Plus, if it's summer, you'll heat up the kitchen only once. Cook the pasta until it's al dente, or firm-tender, then drain and rinse under cold water. Let cool completely. Mix several batches each with ½ teaspoon olive oil, transfer to plastic containers, and store in the refrigerator. When you're ready to serve the pasta, microwave it in the container on High for 1 to 2 minutes. Add your favorite sauce and serve.

❖ If the pasta is still sitting around after a couple of days, make pasta salad. Just toss it with some Italian dressing, Parmesan cheese, grated carrot, and whatever else appeals to your tastebuds.

The Griddle inside Your Oven

❖ Love homey breakfasts with steaming griddle cakes, but would rather head out to the local pancake house than face half an hour with dripping batter and hot grease? Try one big baked pancake instead. In a 450°F oven, heat 1 tablespoon mild-flavored vegetable oil or light olive oil in a glass pie plate or ovenproof skillet until it is very hot, about 5 minutes. Whisk together 2 eggs and ½ cup milk. Beat in ½ cup all-purpose flour and ¼ teaspoon salt. Don't overbeat; the batter will be lumpy—that's okay. Pour into the heated pan and bake for 18 to 20 minutes. Cut the pancake into wedges to serve.

If You Want to Bake an Omelette . . .

❖ If you've never quite mastered the sleight of hand required to turn out an attractive omelette, don't give up on this thrifty Sunday brunch standard. Instead, make a large baked omelette. (This one requires no skill and can be

SUBSTITUTIONS

One of the easiest ways to derail a baking or cooking project is to discover that you don't have a critical ingredient. Help may be right in your own kitchen, though. Just read on.

If the recipe calls for:	You can use:
Buttermilk (in baking and salad dressing)	Plain or vanilla yogurt
Ricotta (in lasagna)	Small-curd cottage cheese, sour cream, or yogurt
I cup light cream (particularly for soup)	I cup whole milk and a walnut-size piece of butter
I ounce unsweetened baking chocolate	3 tablespoons unsweetened cocoa plus I tablespoon margarine or butter
I cup cake flour	⅞ cup all-purpose flour sifted with 2 tablespoons cornstarch
I tablespoon flour to thicken gravy or stew	½ tablespoon cornstarch or rice flour
I cup honey	I to I¼ cups granulated sugar plus ¼ cup liquid

made with an infinite variety of ingredients to please guests or to use leftover ingredients you have on hand.) Preheat the oven to 350°F. Sauté ½ cup chopped onion in 1 table-spoon margarine. In a bowl, combine 8 eggs, 1 cup milk, ¾ cup grated sharp Cheddar or Swiss cheese, ½ teaspoon salt, pepper to taste, and the onion. Pour into a greased casse-role. Bake for about 40 minutes, until puffed high, and serve right away.

Hot Biscuits? Grate!

❖ Homemade biscuits and pie dough are inexpensive to make and glorious to serve. But a lot of pastry projects are stillborn because it's so, well, messy to cut shortening into flour. Try this instead. Freeze the butter or shortening just until firm, then grate it into the flour. The dough will be a lot easier to work with your fingers or a pastry knife that way.

WORLD-CLASS DESSERTS

Scotch the Prepackaged Pudding

❖ Have you noticed how the price of prepackaged, brand-name pudding keeps creeping up? Treat the kids or some sentimental adults to a homemade caramel pudding that costs less than a dollar for 6 servings. Add ½ cup packed brown sugar to 2 tablespoons butter or margarine in a heavy skillet and cook over low heat for 5 minutes. Add 1½ cups scalded milk and stir until the sugar is dissolved. Slowly add 1 cup cold milk (preferably whole milk) to ¼ cup all-purpose flour, mixing well. Transfer the hot mixture to the top of a double boiler set over simmering water. Add the cold mixture and cook for 15 minutes. Stir in 2 well-beaten eggs and cook for 2 minutes. Spoon into serving dishes and chill.

Who Needs Crust?

❖ When apples are in season or on sale, you don't need to fuss with cantankerous pastry or spend money on the refrigerated kind. Here's a deliciously easy way to make a pie—without a crust. Preheat the oven to 350°F. Lightly butter a pie plate, then peel, core, and slice 6 apples. Put a layer of apple slices in the baking pan, sprinkle with about 2 teaspoons sugar and a shake or two of ground cinnamon. Dot the apples with butter (no more than 3 tablespoons for the whole pie). Continue layering the ingredients until you've used all the apples. To make the topping, blend together ½ cup brown sugar, ¼ cup softened margarine, and ½ cup flour. Flatten little dabs of this mixture into circles (no need to be pretty or exact) and arrange them on top of the apples. Bake for about 30 minutes, or until the apples are soft.

FOUR SPECIAL TOUCHES FOR BRUNCH

You needn't be extravagant to make a brunch or holiday breakfast that's memorable. Instead, serve standard dishes and put a little extra effort (and money) into a few special touches.

1. Basil butter. Flavor a mashed stick of softened butter—or even high-grade margarine—with 3 tablespoons minced basil or 2 tablespoons chives, bruised slightly with the back of a spoon. This is terrific slathered on corn on the cob, potatoes, rolls, or even popcorn.

2. Sugar and spice. Offer vanilla-flavored sugar with coffee—but not the pricey gourmet kind. Make your own by mixing 2 teaspoons vanilla extract with ½ cup granulated sugar, then spreading the mixture on waxed paper to dry completely. Store the flavored sugar at room temperature in an airtight container.

3. Whipped cream, no cherry. Those canisters of whipped cream aren't just for Thanksgiving pumpkin pies. Splurge on a can for your next breakfast gathering and top mugs of hot coffee with mounds of whipped cream. It will melt into the brew to lighten it—if it isn't eaten by the spoonful first. If you're really ambitious, save a couple of quarters by whipping your own cream. Just remember to chill the bowl and mixers in the freezer first.

4. A meal in the Mediterranean. For a Mediterranean flair, sprinkle oregano into your scrambled eggs before they're set.

The Hand That Dips the Chocolate

❖ Hand-dipped chocolates only look complicated. In fact, you can easily make them at home for a special touch after a holiday meal, as a romantic gesture on Valentine's Day, or just because you feel like eating good chocolate without paying through the nose. The process is superbly simple. Melt ¼ cup (½ stick) butter and a 12-ounce package of semisweet chocolate chips in a double boiler or the microwave, taking care not to burn it. Then dip whole strawberries, pear slices, pecans, raisins, tiny pretzels, or whatever into the chocolate, using tongs or tossing them in and then fishing them out with a spoon. Let cool on a foil-covered plate, refrigerate until the chocolate is hard, and enjoy.

USE IT UP

Drink This Tea Gingerly

❖ Seems as if the store always sells pieces of fresh gingerroot that are 8 to 10 times larger than your stir-fry recipe requires. Fret not. You can use the extra ginger to brew some tea. For 2 cups, peel about a 2-inch segment, cover with 2 cups water in a saucepan, and boil for a few minutes. Remove from the heat and let steep for a few minutes. Sweeten with sugar or honey if you like, and serve hot or iced.

❖ Peeling ginger is a breeze if you do it with a spoon.

Bury It with Cranberry

❖ If you serve jellied cranberry sauce at Thanksgiving more for show than because anyone likes it, use the leftovers to make Rosy Meatballs. These are especially good during the "I can't look at any more turkey" period. Rustle up your favorite meatball mixture and brown the meatballs in butter. Then smother them with a can of cranberry sauce (or a cup or so of homemade) mixed with a 4-ounce can of tomato sauce. Simmer for 30 minutes and serve.

Real Men Do Eat Rice Crusts

❖ Had enough rice pudding to last a lifetime? This time, use cold cooked rice to make a crust for your favorite quiche recipe. Preheat the oven to 350°F. Mix 2½ cups cooked rice (long-grain white or brown) with 2 tablespoons melted margarine, 1 beaten egg, and 1 tablespoon all-purpose flour. Consider adding some minced parsley or scallions to the mix for added flavor. Pat the concoction into a lightly buttered pie plate, pressing it with the back of a fork to keep it in place. Bake for 20 minutes, then proceed with your favorite quiche recipe.

Lady and the Tramp Share Breakfast

❖ Hold on! Save those cold spaghetti noodles that look so uninspiring to make a crisp noodle pancake for tomorrow morning's breakfast—or tomorrow evening's supper, with stir-fried vegetables spooned on top. Toss 2 cups cold spaghetti with 1 teaspoon dark sesame oil (if you like the flavor) or vegetable oil. Heat 1 tablespoon vegetable oil in a nonstick skillet with sloped sides and distribute the noodles evenly over the bottom, pressing down with a spatula. Weight down the noodles with foil, a plate, and two 1-pound cans. Cook 8 to 10 minutes or until golden brown. Uncover, turn, reassemble the weights, and cook for 5 minutes more.

AVOID COSTLY MISTAKES

Rubbing Salt in the Stain

❖ Always wipe cast-iron pots and pans clean with a rag and hot water and dry immediately with a clean towel or by placing the pot on the stovetop on low heat. That keeps the seasoned finish ready to seal in juices and cook food uniformly. Cleaning with dishwashing

FRUGAL FORMULAS

MAKE YOUR OWN BROWN SUGAR

Have you run out of brown sugar in the middle of preparing a recipe? Don't fret. Stir 1 tablespoon molasses into 1 cup granulated sugar to make 1 cup light brown sugar. For dark brown sugar, use 2 tablespoons molasses per cup of sugar.

FRUGAL FORMULAS
LET SALSA OUT OF THE JAR

In the thick of tomato season, it's silly to plunk down a couple of dollars for a smallish jar of salsa. Instead, whip up a huge homemade batch using your own tomatoes and about a dollar's worth of jalapeño chile peppers and limes.

Ingredients

1½ pounds (about 6 medium to large) tomatoes
1 small onion
2 jalapeño chile peppers
2 tablespoons freshly squeezed lime juice
2 tablespoons minced fresh cilantro or ½ teaspoon coriander
1 scant teaspoon salt

1. Seed and dice the tomatoes. Place in a medium bowl and grate the onion on top.

2. Peel, seed, and mince the jalapeño peppers and add to the bowl.

3. Add the lime juice and cilantro or coriander. Or try a different flavor by adding 2 minced cloves garlic instead.

4. Stir in the salt. Refrigerate, covered, for a few hours or overnight before serving.

liquid or in the dishwasher will nick and dry out the finish, causing food to stick, burn, or cook unevenly. If you have a baked-on crust or stain that needs to come out, put a bit of salt on a slightly damp rag and scrub the same way you would using scouring powder.

❖ The same goes for commercial aluminum cookware such as Calphalon. Always wash it according to the manufacturer's instructions, and never put it in the dishwasher. Otherwise, you'll destroy the surface—and maybe some expensive ingredients—when food sticks to the pan during cooking.

It's Always Darkest before the Burn

❖ Have you salvaged many a cake with burned edges? Take a good look at your baking pan. Dark pans absorb more heat and make food cook more quickly, resulting in spotty burns, particularly on sweet baked goods. Ideally, bake with lighter stainless steel or glass cake pans and cookie sheets. Or reduce the baking temperature by about 25°F and check frequently.

Traditional Shish Kebabs Are Skewed

❖ Sure, they're picturesque, but those skewers with alternating chunks of meat, cherry tomatoes, pieces of pineapple, and the like can be disastrous. That's because the different ingredients grill on different schedules, so while the chicken breast is drying out, the apple chunk is still hard. Instead, thread each ingredient on its own skewer (as most recipes should recommend). One exception: Small chunks of beef and larger chunks of green pepper and onion can usually be cooked on the same skewer, since the two vegetables don't dry out easily, and if they do, they develop a pleasant "roasted" taste.

Marginal Margarine

❖ Always read the side panel on any margarine or light spread before using it in baking to see if it's recommended for that purpose. Many low-fat spreads will destroy the flavor or texture of a baked good.

❖ The recipe on the side of the margarine box is generally a safe bet, since it's been tested with that brand.

A Tough, Beefy Crowd

❖ Brown beef for stews in small batches, in medium-hot oil. If you throw the entire package in a small pan at once, it will steam and toughen instead of browning, which seals in the juices and makes the meat tender after stewing.

CHAPTER 16

SAVING ON ELECTRONICS AND SMALL APPLIANCES

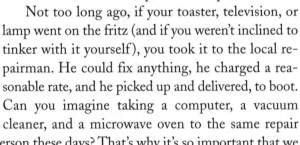

a radio alarm clock gets us out of bed, then an automatic coffeemaker really wakes us up. We spend our days with computers. We talk on the telephone, even when we're not working. We microwave leftovers for lunch and reheat our dinner when we get home late. We nod off to the sounds of the television and switch it off from the bed with the remote control. Our entire day is filled with these and plenty of other electronic gadgets. Many are expensive to buy, and when one breaks down, it can be expensive to repair.

Not too long ago, if your toaster, television, or lamp went on the fritz (and if you weren't inclined to tinker with it yourself), you took it to the local repairman. He could fix anything, he charged a reasonable rate, and he picked up and delivered, to boot. Can you imagine taking a computer, a vacuum cleaner, and a microwave oven to the same repair person these days? That's why it's so important that we frugal Yankees learn not only how to maintain our electronics and small appliances so they last longer but also, whenever possible, how to repair them and replace some of the parts ourselves.

In this chapter, we give you some general rules to follow anytime you're contemplating the purchase of a small appliance or electronic device. We'll show you how to make some simple repairs yourself—repairs that a professional might charge top dollar for. And, naturally, we'll present some frugal solutions to common problems. Your grandmother might have found these solutions useful—if only she had known what a fax machine was.

The most aggressively frugal way to save money when it comes to small appliances and some electronic devices is not to use them. After all, that manual can opener works

THREE WAYS TO SAVE THAT OLD AIR CONDITIONER

Think your air conditioner is ready for the scrap heap? Before you discard one that's not working up to par, try the following tips.

1. Nothing up my sleeve. A clean air conditioner is an efficient one. Open it up by removing the front panel and then the screws (on either side along the bottom) that connect the chassis to the outside sleeve. Leave the sleeve in place and slide the chassis out. Vacuum the dust from around the fan and compressor units.

2. Fin-tastic. Are the soft metal fins on the back of the air conditioner all banged up? This is where the air conditioner exhausts heat removed from the room. If the fins are closed off or bent together, heat can't escape, and that means you need to straighten them. An inexpensive tool called a fin comb is available at your local hardware store, but an old metal or very sturdy plastic hair comb will work just as well. Don some gloves (those fins are sharp)

and draw the comb through the fins to straighten them.

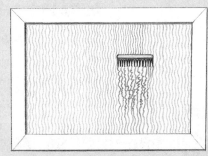

Straighten air conditioner fins with a fin comb.

3. Batting practice. Spend more time in the craft supply store than the hardware store? When it's time to change the filter in your air conditioner, you may already have a replacement on hand. The filter goes on the inside of the removable front panel, and a new one is cut to fit from a larger sheet sold prepackaged at the hardware store. But if you have any polyester batting lying around, you can make a serviceable replacement from that. Just use the old filter as a guide.

just as well now as it did for Grandma 30 years ago, and it doesn't use any power except elbow grease. And is the television so far away that we can't get up and change the channel?

Of course, we can't turn back the hands of time (even this frugal scribe is not planning to return to a manual typewriter), so we might as well learn how to shop wisely and find out what to do when something does go wrong. But should you consider cutting back on using your appliances, remember that the less you use them, the longer they'll last.

REPAIRS AND TROUBLESHOOTING

Switch Plates

❖ One of the most frequent parts of a VCR, TV, or compact disc/cassette player to go on the fritz is the on/off

FRIENDLY SCREEN CLEANER

You don't like to feed your kids fast food, but they just had to have those cute stuffed toy giveaways that come with the kid's meal. And now you have several of the little critters (the toys, not your kids) lying around, and the little ones (the kids, not the toys) have long since lost interest in them.

Why not put those plush toys to work? If they're made of pile, you may have noticed that when you rub them, they get a mild static

Put that old plush toy to good use.

charge (just like you do when you take off a synthetic fleece garment). That makes them just the tool you need to wipe the dust off your computer or television screen.

When your cute new screen cleaners get too dusty, toss them in the wash with the rest of the laundry. Just make sure your kids are through playing with them. If you look as if you're having too much fun, they may want their toys back.

switch because of its heavy use. Before you pack up your machine for the repair shop, try cleaning around the switch with an electronics cleanser or degreaser available at electronics stores for about $5. Once you wipe away any grime, the switch may work just fine—and you'll have saved a hefty repair bill.

(Head)phone Home

❖ Usually, the first parts on a set of headphones to go are the cushions that rest against your ears. But that's okay, because they're the easiest parts to replace yourself. Don't buy the replacement pads that most electronics stores sell. Rather, replace them with scrap materials you probably have around the house. If the old cushion hasn't already fallen off, remove it. If the foam rubber is still in good shape, reuse it. Just re-cover it with a square of thin fabric, such as a swatch cut from an orphaned dress sock. Secure it to the headphones with a rubber band and trim away the excess material.

❖ If the original foam pad is missing, you can replace that, too. Break out that piece of foam packing material you've been saving or a scrap of polyester batting. Cut it to size. If you have enough on hand, double or triple it, depending on how soft you want the pad to be. Re-cover the pad with a swatch of fabric, then secure it to the headphones with a rubber band and trim away any excess material.

Cannibalize It

❖ The next time you're at a yard sale, keep your eyes open for stereo equipment that resembles yours. Even if it's not the exact same model, many types of audio equipment have similar (and salvageable) components. Parts from the old machine, such as small rubber drive belts, springs for cassette doors, and control knobs, may come in handy as replacements for your audio system.

Mend a worn-out headphone with fabric, a rubber band, and packing foam.

Bag of Tricks

❖ If you've ever been stuck with a full vacuum cleaner bag and nary a replacement in sight, you know how hard it is to try to empty the old one through that small hole in the front of the bag. That's because it's fitted with a one-way valve to prevent dirt from falling out. To reuse an old bag, remove it from the machine, then carefully cut a slit in the back of the bag and empty it. To reclose it, fold the open edge in on itself and seal it with some strong tape, such as a high-tack masking tape or duct tape. The capacity of the bag will be a little smaller, but it should work as well as a new one.

IT WORKED FOR ME
The Best Repair I Never Did

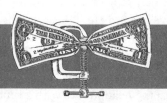

My laptop computer wouldn't hold a charge. The only way to recharge the battery was to plug the adapter into the wall and then plug the battery into the machine. At first I thought the problem was the adapter or the battery (either would have meant a fairly inexpensive replacement), but a simple test administered by the local electronics repair shop (for free) confirmed my worst fear: The problem was deep inside the computer.

When I got home and tried one last time to plug the charger into the machine, the receptacle in the back broke off and tumbled into the casing. I called the nearest authorized service center and described the problem. The technician told me that a major part of the computer needed to be replaced. Worst of all, with parts and labor, the repair would cost half of what I'd paid for the computer 3 years earlier. My wife wanted to junk the machine and buy a new one, but I decided to see whether I could buy the part and replace it myself.

I called the manufacturer and found out that there was a technical recall on that particular model and that the manufacturer would send a box for me to ship it in for a free repair. My small amount of persistence and detective work paid off—and that was the best "do-it-yourself" repair I never did.

—Tom Cavalieri
Astoria, New York

SHOPPING FOR APPLIANCES AND ELECTRONICS

Sometimes You Get What You Pay For

❖ Frugal Yankees know that in the long run, it's best to buy good-quality appliances that will last a long time. They also know, however, that you don't always get the best just by spending more—in other words, low cost doesn't always mean low quality. You may not need all the bells and whistles that are available on many models of electronics. For instance, expensive VCRs come with multiple heads that facilitate features such as tape-to-tape and high-speed recording and ultraslow playback. But if all you're looking to do is play rental movies, you won't use any of those expensive options. Don't buy what you don't want or need.

❖ Power output is another variable that affects cost. For example, when you're shopping for an air conditioner, you don't necessarily want a 20,000 Btu monster to cool an 8-by 12-foot room. Check the box of the model you're considering; it will tell you the dimensions or square footage of the room it can cool.

Shop for Discontinued Savings

❖ Like cars and clothes, electronic equipment and appliance styles go out of fashion. Often a manufacturer discontinues a model because a fashion trend has changed (remember avocado?) and it wants to offer models that are bigger, smaller, or sleeker or that come with new features. Since most consumers want the latest models, stores have to sell off the old ones, usually at a discount, to make room for the current ones. (A smaller dealer may even be willing to negotiate on the price to unload his inventory. It never hurts to ask.) Older model appliances and electronics work perfectly well and come with full manufacturer's warranties. So unless you need the new look or features of the current model, buying the old one is the frugal choice.

Trade Places

❖ Is your VCR or compact disc/cassette player ready to bite the dust? Hang on. Before you rush out to one of those electronics stores (even the discount type), check around with a few friends. Ask whether they are ready to upgrade their equipment, and if so, offer to buy their old stuff. Chances are someone wants to buy up but can't afford to. The money you pay your friend for her old equipment could make that new gizmo affordable for her, and both of you will win.

Make Reparations

❖ Need a new TV, VCR, or compact disc/cassette player, but don't find the price entertaining? Head to your local repair shop and ask whether one of these items has been

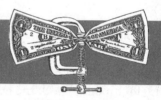

IT WORKED FOR ME
Fantastic Vacuuming

I thought the ceiling fan I installed over the bed was a great way to cool off the room without spending a fortune. That is, until I tried to clean it. Dust collected all over the blades and around the motor, but I couldn't reach the fan without a ladder. And that meant I'd have to move the bed, a major pain in the butt.

I actually could reach the underside of the fan with my vacuum cleaner tubes completely extended, but I wasn't able to reach the ceiling side of the blades, where most of the dust collects. I needed something a lot more flexible, like the vacuum hose,

only at the end of the tube.

My mother had an old vacuum cleaner that she was ready to get rid of, so I confiscated the flexible hose and the brush attachment. I cut an 8-inch section off the hose and fit it over the end of my vacuum's metal tube. I attached the brush attachment to the flexible end and fixed it in place with duct tape. When I held the contraption upright at the end of the tube, it bent into a U shape that fit perfectly between the ceiling and the fan blades.

—Kim Mulhollen
Oneonta, New York

brought in for repair, then abandoned by its owner. (This may happen if an owner moves away, for example.) The shop usually has a standard waiting period, say 6 months, before disposing of such items. If any are available and you decide to purchase one, you'll be responsible only for the cost of the repair, and both you and the shop owner will benefit: You get a machine inexpensively, and the repair shop owner clears out unwanted clutter and collects the cost of the repair.

TAKING CARE OF WHAT YOU HAVE

Steam Cleaning

❖ You know that microwave ovens cook faster than conventional ovens, but did you know that in addition to saving time, they save you money, too? That's because microwaves use less energy than conventional ovens. Did you also know that you can increase the efficiency of your microwave just by keeping it clean? Wipe the inside with a mixture of dishwashing liquid and water after each use; that'll do the job in most cases.

❖ If you forget or don't have time to clean up a spatter and discover a dried-on stain on the inside a day or so later, here's what to do. Bring a mug of water to a boil in the oven, then let it sit for 5 minutes. The steam from the water will moisten and loosen the stain.

Take Care of Your Teeth

❖ Years ago, folks cleaned their teeth with a toothbrush loaded with baking soda. You can clean the teeth of a manual or electric can opener the same way. Make a thick paste of baking soda and water (about 1 tablespoon baking soda and 2 teaspoons warm water) and apply it with an old toothbrush with stiff bristles. Brush around the teeth or the blade that cuts into the can, as well as the teeth of the gear that turns the can.

❖ If the mixture needs a little more oomph, add a drop of dishwashing liquid to the paste.

❖ Out of baking soda? Skip it and just use some toothpaste instead.

Iron Cleaning: Nail It

❖ Melted polyester stuck to the soleplate of an iron can render it useless, meaning a costly replacement. Here's a way to deal with it. Gently scrape off any residue with the corner of a block of wood, a wooden spatula, or half a clothespin. If the stuck-on material won't budge, hit it with a few drops of nail polish remover that contains acetone, then try again with the wood. Make absolutely sure to wipe off all the nail polish remover with a damp cloth before using the iron again.

Some Like It Hot

❖ Leaving water in an iron when it's not being used is a surefire way to clog it up with mineral deposits. That means a shorter life. An easy way to prevent this is to empty the iron immediately after using it. The lingering heat will evaporate the remaining water inside.

Get Tubular

❖ Want to corral all those wires that snake out of the back of your computer or audio system? Don't buy an expensive gizmo to do the job. Just pass them through an old vacuum cleaner tube or a short length of plastic tubing left over from a plumbing job.

Blow Dirt Away

❖ A can of compressed air is handy to blow dust from between the keys on your computer keyboard or from your disk drive. But some simpler, less expensive devices you may already have on hand are a rubber bulb ear syringe, a turkey baster, or a (really, really clean) enema bulb. These devices are great for directing a concentrated blast of air.

Just make sure whatever you use is clean and completely dry first.

A Clean Screen

❖ If you're a frugal Yankee, you already clean your windows with a vinegar and water solution and newspaper. Well, this trick works for computer monitors and television screens as well. Just sprinkle the solution on the bunched-up newspaper (no color sections)—don't spray your screen with vinegar—then wipe the screen. Try not to rub the newspaper against the monitor's case, though, because the ink might come off on the case. If it does, you can remove it with a little rubbing alcohol on a cotton swab or ball.

Wipe Softly

❖ Don't throw out those used fabric softener sheets. After they've been through the dryer once (or twice, if you're like us), they make great wipes for your TV or computer screen.

Unplug for Savings

❖ If you're not planning to use an electric kitchen appliance for a day or longer, unplug it. This is especially true for appliances that have a timer or thermostat—toaster ovens, automatic coffeemakers, and slow cookers, for example. Just because the little red On light isn't glowing doesn't mean the appliance is turned off. It could switch on again without your knowing it. That will waste energy (which costs money), you might burn out a heating element (a potentially costly repair), and you might start a fire (an even bigger problem).

It's Exhausting

❖ Many times an appliance breaks down because it overheats. Generally, appliances compensate for the heat they generate with an exhaust fan or exhaust holes. When these holes get blocked by dust, the machine can't get rid of the excess heat and has a meltdown. To prevent your own China Syndrome, vacuum the air vents.

It's Your Bag

❖ If you have a radio in the kitchen near the stove, you know that it can get covered with grease, which is difficult to remove. The solution? Keep a clear 1- or 2-gallon plastic bag over the radio. Don't seal the bag, or you'll trap moisture inside. Make sure the bag fits loosely, and cut three or four strips, each about ⅛ inch wide, in the back of the bag so that air can circulate around the radio. When the bag gets grimy, you can wash it in warm, soapy water or just throw it away and replace it. This solution works well if you generally keep your radio tuned to the same station and don't fiddle with the knobs.

WHAT'S THE BEST MONEY SAVER?
Cool Savings

It's cooling season. You're comfortable in your air-conditioned room, but you need to go out for an hour or so. You know that every time you turn on the air conditioner, it creates a power surge that you suspect uses more energy than leaving it on full-tilt. Do you:

A. Leave the air conditioner running while you're away

B. Turn it off and back on again when you return

C. Leave it running on the Fan Only setting

You might have guessed (A) or (C), thinking that you'd save the cost of the extra energy required to turn it on. But the answer is (B), and here's why. An air conditioner removes warm air from a room and returns it cooled. The power surges when you turn the air conditioner on and every time the compressor (the part that pumps coolant through the system) turns on. As long as the air conditioner is on, the compressor pumps from time to time as the air in the room warms up. That's extra electricity being used, in addition to what's needed to run the fan.

And speaking of running the fan, remember that the room warms up if the compressor isn't running. By running the air conditioner on Fan Only, all you're doing is blowing around warm air and adding heat to the room by running the motor—and using electricity besides.

The Big Cover-Up

❖ TVs and computers are dust magnets because of the heat and static electricity they generate. There are plenty of plastic covers on the market, but a better, more frugal, and more attractive solution is to use a fabric cover, such as an old pillowcase or bedsheet. Plastic tends to hold in the heat and causes more static electricity to build up, but cloth can be sprayed with an antistatic product (like the one you use on your clothes) and allows the computer to breathe.

It's Dust-Free, Tee-Hee

❖ To keep smaller appliances dust-free and to make them look awfully cute, cover them with an old, child-size T-shirt with the arms and neck sewn closed.

Sack It to 'Em

❖ Everybody has one: a kitchen appliance, such as a popcorn popper or a slow cooker, that's used infrequently and usually needs to be dusted first. Of course, the solution is to keep it covered, but with what? Try an old, decorative case for a throw pillow. A more kitchen-y solution is to cover it with a clean cloth sack that rice or flour comes in.

Weatherproof

❖ Air conditioners are designed to hang out your window or wall, exposed to the elements. But to get the longest life from your air conditioner, take it in during the winter. If you must leave it in its place, you can weatherproof it simply enough. Remove the front panel and the two screws that connect the chassis (the air conditioner's "guts") to the outside sleeve. The screws are usually located on either side, along the bottom. Leave the sleeve in place and slide the chassis out. Cover the exposed fan, compressor, and tubing with a plastic garbage bag, leftover bubble wrap, or plastic grocery bags. Slide the chassis back into the sleeve and replace the screws and front panel. Wrap the plug in a plastic bag or with masking tape, with a note to remind yourself to remove the plastic before using the air conditioner again.

SAVING ON ELECTRONICS AND SMALL APPLIANCES

CHAPTER 17

TRIMMING COSTS IN YOUR HOME OFFICE

*E*ven if you're a nine-to-fiver and commute daily to an office downtown, you also have an office in your home. That home office may be the kitchen table where you pay your bills, the place where your kids do their homework, the pad next to the phone, or the closet where you store the previous years' tax returns. Often work in this office blends seamlessly with the rest of your life—that is, until you need a pen or misplace a bill, and then havoc reigns.

You promise yourself to be more organized and take a long shopping list to the office supply megastore. But you don't need to spend the entire family budget to get your home office in shape. Read on to find out how you can save money on the supplies you need by using items you already have, such as paring down postage costs with a homemade scale. You'll find out how to stay organized without buying an organizer and using a cereal box instead, and in general how to make your office run smoothly and frugally.

SAVING ON SUPPLIES

Damaged? Good!

❖ Buying from office supply megastores is probably the cheapest way to go for some items. One way to make it even more inexpensive is to buy damaged or opened boxes.

Ask the store manager for a discount—10 percent is usual and fair. Most shoppers pass up damaged boxes (but you're not most shoppers; you're frugal), so store managers are left with goods they can't sell. Chances are the damage on the inside of the package is minimal. Who says you can't use a bent envelope?

Their Loss, Your Gain

❖ Keep your eyes peeled in your local newspaper and around town for businesses that are, well, going out of business or moving to a new location. Many will be looking to unload office supplies—desks, chairs, pens, pencils, stationery, staplers, you name it—at rock-bottom prices.

WHAT'S THE BEST MONEY SAVER?
That Depends

What's the least expensive way to organize your desktop?
A. Purchasing a no-name or store-brand three-tier stacking tray set
B. Purchasing a fold-it-yourself cardboard banker's box
C. Rigging up a simple metal baking tray from the kitchen to use as a storage device

None of these options costs much, but the answer we're looking for is "none of the above." That's because the best way to gain space in your office is to eliminate some of the stuff you already have.

We'll bet one stack on your desk has more stuff in it than any other. No matter what you call it—To Do, In, Current, Bills to Be Paid—that stack probably contains a lot of stuff that belongs somewhere else. Here's how to get rid of it and clear some space on your desk.

First, create a place in your file drawers for everything. Bills (paid or unpaid) don't belong on the desk; they belong in a file labeled Bills. The same goes for every other piece of paper that crosses your desk. As soon as you get the mail, open it (don't stack it) and put it away. Try this for a week, and you'll see how much space you gain—and how much money you won't have to spend on elaborate desktop organizing systems.

One Man's Trash . . .

❖ If you work in an office, you may notice that from time to time stationery is updated, desks are replaced, software goes out of date, and used file folders are tossed. Why should all this perfectly good stuff be thrown out with the garbage? Ask your human resources manager who's in charge of those office supplies and offer to take them off their hands.

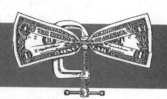

IT WORKED FOR ME
In the Bag

My mother has been a teacher in New York City for years and knows a thing or two about buying (and not buying) stationery supplies. Here are 15 items in Mom's well-stocked home office. Each one cost her less than a dollar; some of them were free. She keeps them all in a gallon-size resealable plastic bag.

1. Glue stick. Great for resealing envelopes and rescued stamps.

2. Child's homework assignment pad. These little spiral-bound books are great for jotting down notes, to-do lists, and the like.

3. Pencil. She brings one home every week from the bowling alley.

4. Pen. She usually has one given to her as a promotional item.

5. Child's pencil sharpener with shavings catcher. Mom has one shaped like a TV, with a picture that changes when you turn it.

6. Pink eraser. Because "those darn pencils from the bowling alley don't already have one."

7. Red marker. What did you expect? She is a teacher, after all.

8. "Little black" address book from the five-and-dime. Of course, she writes in it in pencil.

9. Small merchant giveaway calendar booklet.

10. A few first-class stamps.

11. A few 1- and 2-cent stamps.

12. Mini–letter opener, which she bought at a garage sale.

13. Wooden ruler. "You never know when you'll need to draw a straight line or measure something."

14. Rubber bands salvaged from broccoli and other vegetables.

15. Child's plastic safety scissors to clip coupons.

—**Sue Donnelly**
Flushing, New York

Thanks, Electric Company

❖ These days, you can pay almost any bill by phone or over the Internet. And if you do, good for you. But you still receive your bill in the mail, along with a handy reply envelope in which to enclose your check. Now, if you're a frugal Yankee, you won't throw away that perfectly good envelope. You'll use it to send of mail instead of buying brand-new envelopes. What about window envelopes? Just stick a label over the window and write on it.

SAVING ON POSTAGE

Scale the Heights of Savings

❖ Buying a relatively inexpensive (nonelectronic) postage scale may seem like an unnecessary expense, but it will save you money if you regularly send mail heavier than 1 ounce. Most folks use an additional first-class stamp if they think one stamp isn't enough. But with a postage scale, you'll know exactly how much more postage you need. It could mean a savings of 20 cents or more per letter.

❖ There is a hidden cost in buying a postage scale. As postage rates go up, you may be required to purchase an updated rate indicator card to stay current. Don't buy a scale that can't be updated, or its useful life will be limited. Ask about this feature before you buy.

❖ Of course, you can just update the dial yourself. Use a little typewriter correction fluid on the scale to cover up the old rate, then use a felt-tip pen to write in the new rate.

Scale Down on Postage

❖ You know how much first-class postage will cost, but is that letter you're sending a little too heavy? You could be safe and just add another first-class stamp, but why waste all that extra postage if you don't need to? If this situation doesn't arise often enough for you to buy a postage scale, try this old-fashioned homemade version, using items you already have at hand. First, you need a standard 12-inch ruler. Place a pencil (a six-sided wooden kind is best because it won't roll) on a flat surface such as a desktop. Next, lay the ruler on the pencil so that it crosses the pencil at the 6-inch mark. At one end of the ruler, stack five quarters (which weigh 1 ounce). At the other end, lay the letter in question. If your letter is heavy enough to lift the quarters, it needs more postage.

OFFICE TROUBLESHOOTING

Self-Unstick

❖ Those self-stick stamps are a real time (and tongue) saver—until you put one on an envelope by mistake and need to remove it. In the old days, you fired up the kettle and steamed the stamp off. That doesn't work for these guys. But if you or someone in your household does her nails, you're in luck. Acetone, the main ingredient in some nail polish removers, dissolves the adhesive on the back of the stamp. (You can use nail polish remover that doesn't contain acetone, but you may have to use a little more.) Apply the remover with a cotton swab or ball. Soak the stamp well; the acetone won't hurt it and will evaporate quickly. When the adhesive starts to release, lift a corner and work some of the remover under the stamp, lifting as you go. You should reuse the stamp immediately; just stick it on another envelope while it's still damp and the remaining glue is still tacky. But be sure it stays put. Wait a few minutes until the stamp is completely dry, then see if it's attached. If not, use household glue or a glue stick to adhere it.

Soft Pack

❖ Your friend from out of town was visiting and forgot her watch at your house. You want to mail it to her, but you know you should use a padded mailer. You could buy one, but being the thrifty soul that you are, you decide to make one yourself. All you need to create a padded mailer for any small, delicate item is a paper lunch bag; a small plastic bag; a glue stick; and a couple of layers of felt or batting, some cotton balls, some dryer lint, or the leftover packing material you saved from the last package you received. Cover the inside of the paper bag with glue, and before it dries, line it with whatever padding you've chosen. Place the item in the plastic bag, then put it in your mailer. Fold over the end of the sack and seal it with packing tape. Now mail away with confidence.

TRIMMING COSTS IN YOUR HOME OFFICE

White On

❖ If your little bottle of store-bought correction fluid gets dried out, a few drops of denatured alcohol should get it flowing again. The same goes for the brush built into the cap. Put some alcohol into a small bowl and swirl the brush around in it.

THE YANKEE MISER RECOMMENDS . . .
An Electric Paper Shredder

You wouldn't think this would be the kind of thing I'd have in my office, but sometimes you need to spend a little money to keep from losing money. My paper shredder was inexpensive, but it keeps my credit card and bank information from falling into the wrong hands.

Lately, I've received lots of junk mail offerings for preapproved credit cards. All that mail has my name on it. Then there are the statements for the credit cards I already have and my old bank statements. Those have my name and my account numbers on them, too. I used to tear up all the pages by hand, reveling in the exercise my fingers and wrists were getting, but I realized there was no way to guarantee that I was destroying all the information that could be swiped by an ambitious "dumpster diver."

So now I have an electric paper shredder. Of course, I shopped around for the best price and bought the kind that adjusts to fit any standard-size garbage can. One of the bonuses of owning this contraption is that I never need to buy packing material. I just use all that shredded paper I produce.

FRUGAL ORGANIZING

Office to Go

❖ If you're the type who can never find a clear space on a tabletop to write a check—and can't find the checkbook either—try this inexpensive solution. An old hard-sided attaché case makes a great portable office. You can keep your checkbook, pens, calculator, latest bills, and anything else you need to stay on top of right inside. When you need desk space, close it up, place it on your lap, and write on top of it. When you don't need it, put it away in the closet or slip it under the bed. If you don't already have an old attaché case, you can probably find a suitable one at a thrift store or yard sale for next to nothing.

Desk in a Day

❖ Okay, maybe you can wait more than a day for a spare desk. But don't spend the extra time buying an expensive one. A hollow-core door placed on top of two 2-drawer file cabinets (purchased from a used furniture warehouse) will make a great do-it-yourself desk. An old door, sanded and refinished with polyurethane, is an even more frugal idea. If there's a doorknob hole, you can fit a cup or tin can inside it to hold your pens and pencils. Or you can organize cords for a computer, lamp, or telephone by passing them through the hole.

Save Those Envelopes

❖ So what do you do with all the envelopes and return envelopes that bills and statements (not to mention junk

Not only did humorist Mark Twain write at home, but he often worked in bed. This caused his wife, Livy, some chagrin. Once she came to get him up because a reporter had come to the house to interview him. Twain kept writing and didn't seem very interested in rousing himself or getting dressed. Exasperated, Livy threatened to bring the reporter to the bedroom. "Don't you think it will be a bit embarrassing for him to find you in bed?" she asked.

"Why, if you think so, we could have the other bed made up for him," Twain replied.

mail) come in? If you're frugal, you save them and turn them into scratch pads. Keep a small basket for the discarded envelopes on your desk near the phone. You'll never want for message pads again. Don't forget to keep that little pencil you brought home from the golf course in the basket with them.

Pencils in a Flash

❖ If you're like many folks, your home office may not even have a desk. In fact, you may do all your monthly bill paying on the kitchen table, right there by the refrigerator. If that's the case, we have a neat way to keep pens and pencils close by and instantly available. Buy one of those flashlights that has a built-in magnet for hanging it on metal; any hardware store sells them. Remove the top and put it aside. Hang the body on the side of the fridge and keep your pens and pencils in it. Store the top and bulb housing, as well as some batteries, together so that you can still use it as a flashlight.

❖ Of course, you can use this same flashlight rig even if you do pay your bills at a desk, as long as some part of it or something nearby is metal like a filing cabinet, for instance.

Draw!

❖ Tired of using an old soda can to hold your pens? Here's an interesting alternative. If you know a hunter, militaria collector, or police officer, she may have an old cartridge belt—you know, the kind with loops to hold bullets. Pens and pencils fit into those loops nicely. Hang it near your desk on a decorative hook, and you'll have a new pen holder as well as a conversation starter.

Put Your Mind and Feet at Ease

❖ Here's a cheap storage idea for folks with short legs. Experts recommend that when working at a desk, your knees should be at a 90-degree angle, with your feet flat on the floor. If your legs don't reach the floor, you should use a footrest. But if you hate the idea of putting a piece of furniture under your desk, use one of those inexpensive plastic storage boxes. Choose one about the size of a large shoe box or a small suitcase. The best part is you can use it to store office supplies or old records and receipts, too.

*Turn a cereal box
into magazine
organizers.*

Breakfast Reading

❖ One major source of desk clutter is that pile of magazines you've been meaning to read. If you want to save entire magazines (as opposed to keeping a clippings file), you have a few choices. You can buy a plastic magazine rack at the stationery store (boo!), you can stack them up on a corner of your desk (double boo!), or you can make your own magazine holder (yea!). Grab an empty economy-size cereal box and cut it in half diagonally from the top left corner, across the front and back, to the lower right corner. Voilà! An upright magazine storage box. If you cut carefully, you can get two holders from each cereal box. Now that's frugal.

❖ If you don't want Cap'n Crunch or whoever is on the most recent Wheaties box staring at you all day, cover the outside with contact paper.

Can the Stamps

❖ Stamps from a vending machine often come in a roll, and some folks find them hard to manage. You could buy a desktop dispenser, or you can make one yourself from a plastic film canister. You'll need a very sharp craft knife and a steady hand. With the knife, cut a slit an inch long down the side of the can, starting at the open end. Make the slit wide enough for a stamp to pass through easily. In the side of the cap, cut a small notch to match. Drop the loose stamp coil into the can, so that a stamp comes through the slit. Pop on the lid, lining up the notch with the slit, and unroll your stamps one by one.

Carefully cut a slit in an old film canister to make a stamp dispenser.

One from Column A

❖ We spotted this clever way to keep a few pens and pencils ready on the counter of a Chinese restaurant. Fill a small container (like the kind take-out soup comes in) with uncooked white rice. Place your pens and pencils upright in the rice, which anchors them. When the rice gets dingy, just replace it.

❖ If you don't like the idea of wasting perfectly good rice, use sand instead.

Quart Storage

❖ Do you have 3½-inch computer disks lying around? If you need a place to store them, try using a quart-size milk or orange juice carton to make a dandy disk holder. Make sure the carton is totally clean and dry, then cut off one long side and the entire folding top.

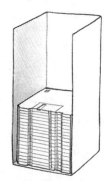

A clean quart-size carton is perfect for storing 3½-inch computer disks.

CHAPTER 18

CUTTING TRANSPORTATION COSTS

*T*he costs of commuting rank right up there with food costs and other major expenses. In fact, transportation spending often eats up as much as 30 percent of the home budget. And there seems to be no way to escape these expenses. In most cases, you absolutely have to get where you're going—such as work or school—and you usually have limited ways to get there.

But that doesn't mean you can't make the most of your commuting dollars. All it takes is finding creative ways to (sometimes significantly) cut your transportation costs. Whether you're traveling by car, bus, train, or subway, you can choose from a bounty of cost-cutting measures to ensure that you're not paying a dollar more than is absolutely necessary.

For most people, this means cutting the costs associated with driving their cars. The U.S. Department of Transportation estimates that the average car costs about 31 cents per mile to keep on the road. This includes a wide range of expenses—from the necessary protection of insurance, to filling the tank with gas, to keeping your car running safely. You can find ways in every one of these areas to save a buck when you get behind the wheel. One of the best is carpooling.

For many people, mass transit is often the most economical (or only) means of commuting, but you can save money even on this thrifty alternative. Regardless of the method you choose, getting from here to there does not need to break the bank.

THE LEAST EXPENSIVE ROUTE

The Two-Wheel Alternative

❖ Sometimes the best solutions are the simplest. When it comes to transportation, the most cost-efficient way to get around is a bike. Although this solution is far from ideal if you're commuting 20 miles to work, you can use a bike for around-town errands. The savings pile up quickly when you consider that maintaining a car costs an average of about 31 cents per mile. Riding a bike is also cheaper than any form of mass transit. Last but not least, biking is a great way to get plenty of fresh air and aerobic exercise. If you use your bike regularly, it should pay for itself in less than a year.

MASS TRANSIT FOR LESS

Strength in Numbers

❖ Save commuting costs by ganging up. You can take advantage of volume discounts for train and bus passes by organizing a large group of fellow employees or friends who commute regularly. You usually need 10 or more people buying the same type of commuter pass. You can expect to save 5 to 10 percent by buying transit passes in bulk, and you'll be a hero to everyone else in the group. Inquire about group rates by contacting your local transit authority (look in the city government listings of your White Pages).

Schedule Savings

❖ Take 20 to 30 percent off your train fares by adjusting the hours during which you travel. Ask your employer if you can work flextime by coming in and leaving early or late so that you can commute during off-peak hours. Off-peak rates are often at least 15 percent lower than peak rates, and the trains are less crowded, too.

It Counts to Discount

❖ Don't be shy about taking advantage of cost savings offered by transit authorities. Most mass transit agencies offer discounts that are not widely advertised. These include lower rates for senior citizens, students, children, and people with disabilities. You may be able to take advantage of the student discount even if you just attend a night school class after work. Discount policies are usually listed on schedules, on separate flyers that you can pick up at ticket windows or fare booths, and on route maps.

CARPOOLING

The Numbers Game

❖ Where carpooling is concerned, the more, the merrier (and the cheaper). Carpooling with one other person cuts your commuting costs by 50 percent. Add just one more person, and you'll reduce those costs by an additional 20 percent or more. If you're going to carpool, seek as many partners as possible.

The Employer Break

❖ Start your car pool savings by talking to your employer. Many states offer deductions on business income taxes to companies that subsidize employees who commute efficiently. Ask your human resources director about any programs your employer offers to underwrite company-based car pools. Suggest that the company start such a program if none is already in place.

Insurance Relief

❖ If you're thinking of forming a car pool, look for insurance savings as just one more benefit. Most automotive insurance policy prices are calculated based on usage. If you're carpooling, theoretically you're using your car half as much (or even less if there are more than two people in the pool). Contact your insurance agent and inquire about a rate reduction due to the lower number of miles traveled.

Car Pool Jr.

❖ Work is not the only place you can save money with carpooling. Get other parents on the bandwagon by forming a neighborhood car pool to take kids back and forth to school. Trade off with other parents by picking up a carload of kids and delivering them to school or bringing them home. If the school is fairly far from your home, the savings can be substantial.

SAVING ON INSURANCE

How Low Can You Go?

❖ Completing a driver and traffic safety education course is a nearly painless way to get an insurance discount—sometimes up to 10 percent annually. High schools and community colleges offer these programs for a small fee and a minor investment of time (30 hours in some cases). Browse through those community college bulletins you get in the mail or call your local university or college (listed in the Yellow Pages under Schools). If you don't get the bulletins in the mail, drop by the local library, which will have copies of the most recent public mailings.

Cut the Fat

❖ Cut costs on coverage that doesn't make fiscal sense. Some coverage is duplicated by other insurance, as with medical coverage already included in your work medical policy. Other coverage is used so infrequently that the odds are you would save more by paying the costs outright than paying extra for a policy that covers them. These include car rental expense coverage and towing coverage.

United You Save

❖ Look to achieve lower rates by consolidating your insurance policies. Many insurance companies offer discounts when you take out multiple policies, such as home, life, and auto. For this reason, you should begin your insurance shopping with your own life insurance or home owner insurance company. You also should realize a significant dis-

SIX RULES FOR CAR POOLS

Setting up a car pool can be one of the biggest money-saving ventures you will ever tackle. The trick is setting good ground rules and clearing up any potential problems before you start carpooling. Following are questions you need to answer with any potential car pool partners.

1. Driving duties. Do you like to drive most of the time? All of the time? If you don't mind doing most of the driving, you can accept carpool members who don't have a car or who own a motorcycle or small car. Of course, any arrangement other than an equal sharing of driving will mean that you have to work out how much people will chip in for gas and maintenance.

2. Smoker status. Will you allow smoking?

3. Fuel costs. Even if everyone in the car pool does an equal amount of driving, different cars get different mileage. Will everyone pay for his own car, or will fuel costs be divided equally?

4. Late rules. It's important that everyone understand how long the car pool driver will wait for members. Set the rules in advance, including what it takes to get kicked out of the car pool.

5. Rules of the road. What constitutes dangerous or poor driving habits? Everyone has a different opinion, but basic rules regarding speeding, erratic driving, and unlawful practices will keep members on the same page.

6. Radio waves. What will people listen to on the way to work? Who decides?

count if you insure more than one vehicle with the same company.

Raise Your Hand

❖ Get hidden discounts just by asking. Many insurance companies do not volunteer the discounts they offer for nonsmokers, safe drivers, antitheft devices, and even good school grades among younger drivers. Ask and save. And when you're comparing rates among insurance companies, make sure to ask specifically about each of these discounts.

Bet on Your Good Skills

❖ Increase your deductible to decrease your premiums. A low deductible can increase the cost of insurance from 10 to 50 percent. The savings in a year can often cover the cost of the deductible. Unless you're a bad driver or extremely unlucky, you are not likely to pay the deductible more than once over the life of your car.

Just Say No

❖ To rental car insurance, that is. Rental car companies offer insurance for their cars, often accompanied by scare tactics. Although the fee does pay for coverage, it usually includes a markup for the rental company. In most cases, this insurance duplicates coverage you already have. Usually, you are insured by your own car policy, and many major credit cards offer rental car insurance as part of their member benefits. Check your existing auto policy or credit card brochure before renting. If the rental company requires you to accept its insurance, go to another company.

Take the Hit

❖ Prevent increases in your premiums by avoiding small claims. If you have a fender bender and the cost to fix it is just slightly more than your deductible, pay for the repair yourself. If you process a claim through your insurance company, the company will likely raise your rates, regardless of how little it actually had to pay out.

CUTTING TRANSPORTATION COSTS

Un-Coverage

❖ Save a considerable amount of money by dropping your comprehensive and collision coverage when it no longer makes sense to keep it. When your car ages past a certain point—marked by a large drop in its blue book value—the insurance company will most likely total it in the event of an accident. This means the company will pay you a small amount of money rather than pay for the repairs. Generally, you should consider dropping comprehensive and collision coverage if the true market value of your car drops below the $2,500 to $3,000 range.

STRETCHING YOUR FUEL DOLLARS

Put a Miser in Your Tank

❖ Easy does it on the gas pedal. A consistent speed saves fuel and money—that's where cruise control pays off. And don't speed up and slow down repeatedly—that's the biggest waste of fuel going. A moderate, controlled speed will also save you the cost of a speeding ticket.

Shoot That Breeze

❖ Catching a breeze can be costly, so drive with the windows closed when you're driving at highway speeds (and at all other times, too). Open windows radically affect the dynamics of a car, causing wind drag and slowing the car. This can add up to 10 percent to your fuel bill. The same rules apply to sunroofs.

Be Clean

❖ To get the most mileage for your gas dollar, clean your air filter regularly. For the most savings, perform this simple task once a month. Remove the filter and tap it on a hard surface to remove dirt and other contaminants (don't try to wash the air filter, or you'll ruin it). Clean the filter housing with a rag moistened with a little gasoline or a dab of mechanic's hand cleaner, then replace the filter in a different position than you found it (if your filter allows this). Your car will run cleaner and more efficiently.

Your Tank Overflows

❖ We know it's tempting to top off your gas tank to get to a whole dollar amount, but it's a bad idea. Most of the extra gas will evaporate or wind up on the street. Most cars theses days are equipped with a gas overflow tube. If your filler tube is full of gas, it will evaporate or drain out the overflow as the car moves around during driving, taking your money with it.

FOUR WAYS TO DETECT CAR PROBLEMS

You'll save a lot of money on major repairs by keeping your eyes and ears open for small signs of trouble in your car.

1. Proper planning. Read your owner's manual to understand the gauges and warning lights on your dashboard. The manual will usually recommend actions to take as soon as the gauges or lights indicate problems.

2. Getting an earful. New noises are the first indicators of trouble. Take action as soon as you hear something odd, such as a whistling, clanking, or grinding sound.

3. The eye exam. Inspect the car at least once a week. Look for leaking fluids, low tires, turn signals and headlights that don't work, and other potential problems. Also be aware while you are driving. Is steam coming from the front of the car (overheated radiator)? Are you exhausting a lot of white or black smoke (rings, head gasket, valve problems)?

4. Keeping in touch. Often the first sign of trouble is that the car doesn't feel right. Even if you can't immediately identify the problem, don't ignore this. You may be feeling a vibration through the steering wheel, signaling poor wheel balance and leading to premature tire wear. Or the car may pull slightly to one side, a sign of bad alignment or improper tire inflation. You may even feel a vibration through the seat (possible universal joint problems). Don't be shy about asking your mechanic to inspect the car when you have a bad feeling.

Inflation Is Good

❖ Stretch your fuel dollars by simply inflating your tires to the recommended pressure. The more surface area exposed to the pavement, the more fuel needed to move the car, which is why flatter tires raise fuel consumption. This quick check can save $5 to $10 per month, depending on how much you commute. However, don't go crazy and overinflate the tires. This will cause uneven wear, and you'll spend all the money you saved on gas replacing your tires before their time.

A GUIDE TO SERVICING YOUR CAR

The three ways to head off problems with your car are maintenance, maintenance, and maintenance. Although you can learn to do many of these simple procedures yourself, even paying someone to do them will save you money on repairs in the long run.

Every 3,000 Miles or 3 Months, Whichever Comes First

1. Change the engine oil and filter.
2. Lubricate the chassis.
3. Check the fluids and tire pressure.
4. Check all the belts and hoses.

Once a Year or Every 10,000 to 12,000 Miles, Whichever Comes First

1. Replace all the filters, including air and fuel.
2. Rotate the tires.
3. Check the brakes for excessive wear.
4. Tune up the ignition system. This includes changing the plugs and checking the rotor and rotor cap.
5. Inspect the cooling system hoses.
6. Check the temperature of the engine thermostat.
7. Check the vehicle for leaks and other problems.

Every 2 Years or 20,000 Miles, Whichever Comes First

1. Bleed the brakes to renew the fluid and remove contamination from normal wear and tear.
2. Flush and fill the cooling system. Add distilled water (to prevent scale buildup) and coolant as specified by the owner's manual. Also add an over-the-counter corrosion protectant. These can be found at most auto parts stores.
3. Replace the automatic transmission fluid and filter.
4. Replace the pollution control valve.

❖ Check the pressure once a month or so, when the tires are cold.

Lose Weight, Gain Money

❖ Removing 200 pounds from your car (check the trunk—that's the trouble area for most of us) will increase its fuel efficiency by 1 percent or more. That can amount to considerable savings if you drive every day.

Rack Up Savings

❖ Don't drag down your fuel economy with a roof rack or bicycle rack. These racks add drag to the car, lowering the miles per gallon you get. Don't think it's much? You can save up to 5 percent of the gas in your tank by simply removing the racks when you're not using them.

Minute by Minute

❖ Remember the simple minute rule. If you are going to be stopped for more than 1 minute, turn your car off, because you'll use less fuel to start it back up than to continue idling. Keep in mind that this rule doesn't apply in traffic or at stoplights, where stopping and starting your car can create a safety hazard.

I'm Warm Already!

❖ Avoid wasteful warm-ups. The electronic ignitions and engines in most cars today don't need to warm up extensively, and idling while they do just wastes fuel. If you need to check your mirrors or adjust your seat, do it before you start your car. This is true even in cold weather.

Spare the AC

❖ Air-conditioning is one of the biggest drags on fuel economy because your engine has to work much harder to drive the high-pressure pump in the air-conditioning unit. Use your AC sparingly and opt for internal air vents whenever possible. At highway speeds, the fresh air often will cool you down almost as well.

What a Drag

❖ Spend less on gas for a pickup truck by simply removing the rear gate. This gate creates a great deal of wind drag and can cut your gas mileage by more than 10 percent. If you need a gate, consider using a cargo net instead.

Pump Pricing

❖ Buy gas from the cheapest gas station you can find, even if it's an independent operator. The government regulates gas regardless of the seller or brand. It monitors gas quality and how much detergent it contains, as well as the fuel's octane level.

Ride the Right Route

❖ Plan ahead. Gas prices vary quite a bit from one area to another, even from one city or town to the next. If you commute 10 to 20 miles each day, look for the places that have the best gas prices and make those regular stops on your commute.

SAVING ON CAR COSTS

Safe and Saving

❖ Avoid the cost and turmoil of a crash. Statistically, speeders and reckless drivers roam the far left lane, and that lane is the one where most accidents occur. Stay to the right and let others go as fast as they dare. You'll also save on gas by sticking to the slow lane, and you'll avoid unwanted attention from police.

Half to Keep Your Car Whole

❖ Make it a regular practice to keep your gas tank half-full, and you will keep your car running at its best. By keeping the gas level above the halfway mark, you'll ensure that contaminants and water condensation fall to the bottom of the tank, below the filter screen. You'll also avoid running out of gas.

Go Black for More Green

❖ When you have a choice, choose black-wall tires. White-wall tires are normally more expensive, and you won't get any better performance for your money.

Slam the Scam

❖ Don't fall prey to the alignment sale. Unscrupulous tire shops will try to sell you an alignment with every tire change. If your tires have worn evenly and have lasted as long as you could reasonably expect, there is nothing wrong with your alignment, and you shouldn't pay to have the car realigned.

Working around Warranties

❖ Although many warranties are worded to make you think you have to use the dealer for basic servicing such as oil changes, you don't. You can save up to half the cost of an oil change or tune-up by taking your car to a shop specializing in those services.

It's about Time

❖ Timing belt replacement is one of the best investments you can make in the longevity of your car. Most manufac-

CUTTING TRANSPORTATION COSTS

THE NOSE KNOWS

Noticing the smells associated with your car is extremely important because it is not only a way of detecting possible problems, but it also can prevent dangerous situations. Here are some of the odors you need to be aware of.

I. If you smell exhaust fumes, your muffler may be damaged, or your tailpipe or exhaust manifold may be cracked. If either is leaking exhaust fumes through the floorboards, you are inhaling carbon monoxide, and that can be fatal.

2. A sweet smell could signal leaking antifreeze.

3. A sulfurlike odor (rotten eggs) could indicate emissions problems.

4. Overheated wiring may produce a burning, caustic odor.

turers recommend replacing the timing belt between 60,000 and 100,000 miles. The replacement usually runs $200 to $500, whereas the damage from a broken timing belt can easily run into the thousands and may even render an older car worthless.

Fender Funds

❖ If you've had a minor fender bender, save the money a body shop would charge to fix the damage. Instead, take your car to a vocational school or community college (look under Schools in the Yellow Pages). The students will get a chance to hone their skills (under the watchful eye of the teacher), and you'll save on labor costs.

Put the Brakes on Spending

❖ Save hundreds of dollars by having your disc brake pads replaced before the rotors need to be turned. This means bringing the car in before you hear the metallic squeal of the safety tab wearing a groove in the rotors. Have your brakes checked every 3 months or whenever you have your oil changed (your mechanic should check the wear for free; have the pads replaced when they are down to about 5 percent). Rotors can be turned only twice before they have to be replaced, and the cost of turning them can easily be a third or more of a brake job. If the repair shop insists that the rotors need to be turned, get a second opinion.

Salvage Your Own Repair Bill

❖ Your mechanic doesn't shop for the best deal on replacement auto parts, but you can. With just a little time and effort, you can save hundreds of dollars. For instance, if you need a transmission, call around to junkyards and salvage yards (operations that buy or tow wrecked cars, disassemble them, and then sell the perfectly good parts). Once you find an acceptable part, you'll need to buy it and bring it to your mechanic, but you'll have saved a bundle. Find salvaged parts in the Yellow Pages under Junk Dealers or Automobile Parts and Supplies—Used and Rebuilt. Keep in mind that some garages, because of liability issues, won't install junkyard parts, so call ahead before you purchase anything.

Written Repairs

❖ Avoid paying more for a repair than you expected. Most states require automotive repair shops to provide you with a written estimate prior to doing the repair. The facility cannot charge you more than that estimate unless it has your authorization to proceed with a higher-cost repair. If you are surprised by an inflated bill, you are obligated to pay only the amount on the written estimate. Never sign a blank service order form before the garage figures out what's wrong. If you do, you will be authorizing an open-ended service charge.

Tread Wisely

❖ Replacing your worn conventional tires with radial tires can save you money in the long run. Radial tires not only increase your gas mileage, but they also last longer than conventional tires. Just be sure that you don't mix conventional and radial tires on the same car, which can put your alignment and safety at risk.

Shifting Wear and Tear

❖ Avoid costly manual transmission repairs by simply keeping your hand off the gearshift when cruising. Resting your hand on the shift can cause early and excessive wear of the devices that synchronize the gears and allow them to shift smoothly. A rebuilt transmission can cost hundreds of dollars.

Adjusting Payback

❖ Extend the life of your rear brakes by using your emergency brake. When you engage the emergency brake, it automatically adjusts the rear brakes, making your front and rear brakes wear more slowly.

CHAPTER 19

SAVING ON CARS, OLD AND NEW

A car is more than just a means to an end. It's like a child. You take pride and joy in it, especially just after bringing it home. And similar to a child, a car requires continual cash payout. The Yankee way is to minimize these expenditures. From the initial purchase to yearly maintenance, we'll show you how to take control of your driving budget.

The first step is getting the best buy on a vehicle. Begin by determining a budget, then execute a list of must-haves. You may think that you need a new car, but you can get a used car—one that's almost like new—for a fraction of the cost. Keep an open mind and envision what a detailed cleaning and a few enhancements will do for that old jalopy. Besides the appeal of a lower purchase price, a used car means lower insurance costs and taxes and slower depreciation. Who could ask for more?

When buying new, you'll have other fees besides the purchase price—financing (if you need it), taxes, registration, licensing, and so on. Don't get caught short at the table: Know the exact figures up front.

Staying informed will provide you with more confidence when shopping and negotiating. Do your homework. There's a wealth of information available in newspapers and magazines and on the Internet. You can even find out the frequency of repairs used models have. And don't forget about the Better Business Bureau for verifying a used car company's reputation and complaint assessment.

Above all, get a comprehensive written agreement when buying a car so that both parties, buyer and seller, know exactly what's expected. One last thing: Whether a car is purchased from a dealer or privately, and whether it's new or used, make sure the gas tank has been topped off before you drive away.

BEFORE YOU SHOP

"I See a Rebuilt Engine in Your Future"

❖ If you have a mechanic you trust, ask him how much longer your car will last without a major repair or how much it would cost to get your car in shape. Compare this cost, combined with tune-ups, new tires, and so on, to the first-year costs of purchasing a new car.

I Can Afford It, as Long as I Don't Drive It

❖ Before you consider buying a new car, find out how much insurance will cost compared to your current vehicle. The added cost might just cool your passion for that new car—and new car loan.

Go by the (Blue) Book

❖ Before you consider buying a new or used car, estimate your current car's value by looking it up in the blue

THREE THINGS NOT TO KEEP IN YOUR TRUNK

I. Flashlight. Keep it accessible. Place it in your glove box or under the passenger's seat. If you have to leave your car on a dark night, you should be instantly visible, not rooting around in your trunk.

2. Ice scraper. Put it inside your car, too. It's of little use to you in a frozen-shut trunk.

3. Lock deicer. Don't even keep this in the car. Instead, keep it on your key chain in frosty weather.

book at your local library. But don't stop there. Find out how much value you are likely to lose if you hold on to the vehicle for another year, 2 years, or 5 years. Is this year's blue book value substantially different from last year's? Does it differ from what it was 5 or 10 years ago? In general, at what age does your particular model, or similar makes or models, lose a substantial amount of its value? And how long does your make or model normally last before it becomes substantially less valuable than it is right now?

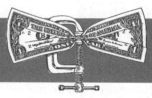

IT WORKED FOR ME
The Lath Resort

Years ago I worked on construction sites in New York City, and I witnessed many obstacles overcome by man and machine. What impressed me most, however, was how those brawny construction guys got their cars out of mud and snow. They carried strips of masonry lath in the backs of their vans or trucks. The lath is made of a rigid mesh-like wire. It comes in sheets and has a treadlike pattern. The workers would pick up old pieces of leftover lath from job sites and cut them into strips 1 foot wide and 3 or 4 feet long. When a van was stuck in the snow or mud, they would wedge a strip in front of the stuck tire and extend it straight out. I watched this dozens of times, all successful.

Lathing creates traction.

The lath creates great traction because it's both metal and pliable. The tires are able to grip the lath because it's perforated and treadlike itself. It's made of a coated metal, which makes it virtually rustproof, and it's available at contractor supply warehouses and lumberyards. A word of caution: Don't let anyone stand directly behind the stuck tire. The lath could shoot out from under the tire.

—Tom Donnelly
Flushing, New York

SHOPPING FOR CARS: USED AND NEW

Runt of the Litter

❖ Check out the slow seller on a dealer's lot. If a car has been around for more than 90 days, the dealer may be eager to move it. Remember that the sales cycle varies for some cars. A convertible may sit on a lot during the winter, and a four-wheel-drive vehicle may sit around during the summer. Some dealerships lose money each day a car doesn't sell, which gives you the upper hand. Research the dealer invoice price (a guide to what the dealer paid) of a prospective car at the library. *Edmund's Automobile Buyers Guide* offers that information; ask the librarian to help you find it. The invoice price will be lower than the inflated sticker price you're expected to pay. Then take the dealer invoice price and subtract any manufacturer incentives and rebates (also found at the library) to get a low-end number to begin negotiations.

Dealer Dialogue

❖ At the dealership, don't mix your figures when discussing warranties, service contracts, and financing. Discuss these costs separately from the purchase price. Your goal is to get the absolute lowest purchase price, because you'll benefit from residual savings: lower monthly payments, taxes, and interest.

Saying Yes to Options

❖ Don't discount all options as frivolous add-ons. Some features that initially take money out of your pocket will eventually put money back in later. If you plan to resell your car, consider laying out for options such as air-conditioning, a radio and cassette player, a central locking system, and power windows, which will add to the car's resale value.

❖ Other items that add to the car's resale value include a six-cylinder engine (when it's an option over a four-cylinder one); an automatic transmission; an antitheft device or alarm system; a sunroof; a navigation system; cruise control; high-end tires; leather seats, shift knobs, or steering wheel; body side molding; additional stereo speakers; and illuminated vanity mirrors. Whew!

Insure More Savings

❖ We know, you're trying to subtract dollars from the purchase price, but bear with us on this one. The following features may cost you more up front, but they will save you money later on when you reap those annual insurance discounts: antilock brakes, an antitheft device, daytime running lights, passive restraint (automatic seat belts or air bags, including side air bags), and traction control.

Saying No to Options

❖ Just as there are options you'll want to spring for, others aren't worth the cost. What options can you safely skip? Stain repellent is one. Applying a fabric protector to your seats is cheaper and more reliable.

❖ Rust-proofing is another option you can decline if you maintain a regular regimen of washing and waxing. (See if it's covered under the factory warranty.) Most cars today are more resistant to corrosion than they were years ago.

❖ An extended warranty, which can cost up to a thousand bucks, is usually a waste of money, especially on used cars.

Number Crunching

❖ Take your time before signing an agreement. Don't be too eager to grab the dealer's cash-back option—it may not save you the most money in the long run. You can't go wrong if the offer is 0 percent interest; that's basically free money. However, if the options are $2,500 cash back or a 5-year loan at 3 percent interest, the answer isn't obvious. Any reputable salesperson will help you calculate which option is better based on the actual purchase price, the fees involved, and how much money you can afford to put down. Make sure you fully understand the calculations, and remember that it's in the salesperson's best interest to find you the most affordable alternative so that she can close the deal and collect her commission.

❖ Always mark on the sales agreement "subject to buyer approval on delivery." This allows you to back out of the agreement if you go to pick up the car and something has changed—like the dealership has replaced the original tires with cheaper ones. Before you sign for delivery, take the car for a quick test drive to make sure there are no obvious problems. If there are, refuse to take delivery until those problems are fixed.

SHOPPING FOR USED CARS ONLY

The Cream of the Crop

❖ Old rental cars aren't put out to pasture once they've gone to seed. They're sold to the public or auctioned off. What's the advantage of buying a used rental car? You are guaranteed a late-model, fully equipped, well-maintained vehicle at a good price—a minimum of $1,000 to $2,000 below what a dealer would charge. Since rental car companies buy the vehicles new, you'll have the car's life history (including any manufacturer warranties that still apply), with up-to-date service records. (Each time a car comes back from a rental, it is cleaned and serviced.) Call a local rental agent or the company's toll-free number (both of which you'll find in the Yellow Pages under Automobile Renting) for a list of locations near you where cars are sold. Companies will vary in their policies on quoting prices over the phone, available financing, and trade-ins.

❖ Some folks drive rental cars much more roughly than they do their own. It's a good idea to have a mechanic check the car and its service records for any evidence that the car has been mistreated. If it has, that means more repairs for you down the road.

A Tool for the Supersleuth

❖ If you're suspicious about a used car's history—if you think it may have been in an accident, for example—there's an easy way to check to see if the original parts have been replaced or repaired with cheap plastic body filler. Hold a small magnet around the seams of the doors, wheel coverings, hood, trunk, or any area in question. If the magnet doesn't stick, that means metal isn't underneath the paint. Plastic body filler is often used for repairs or to fill in dents,

10 HINTS FOR BUYING A USED CAR

Despite what your mother always told you about not being able to judge a book by its cover, when you're buying a car, sometimes you can. It's just as important to scour the exterior of your prospective purchase as it is to see what's making it tick on the inside.

1. Look for any cosmetic flaws that could spell trouble—a streaky, mismatched paint job or scratches, for example.

2. Find out what warranties are available: "As is" condition means all expenses will be out-of-pocket—your pocket. Consider only warranties that are offered by the dealership; many are third-party products that are shoddy at best.

3. Ask how long the car has been on the lot or in the owner's possession.

4. Make sure an inflated spare tire is included, as well as a jack.

5. Find out whether a set of snow tires is included.

6. Check to see if the upholstery is worn. Check under the floor mats. Also check the gas and brake pedals. If the odometer says 35,000 miles and the pedals are heavily worn, the odometer has probably been tampered with.

7. Check all mechanical and electrical parts, such as the headlights and interior lamps.

8. Have your mechanic inspect the vehicle.

9. Test-drive the car in as many different situations as possible—traffic, hills, highway, and so on.

10. Ask to see the service record. Also ask whether a new service contract will be available.

then smoothed over before a fresh coat of paint is applied. It's an undesirable alternative, since plastic lacks the durability of metal and can crack over time. A magnet won't stick to plastic, so it's a great way to uncover what's being covered up by a new paint job.

Legitimate Steals

❖ If you know a thing or two about cars, you can save thousands at a car auction. In the past, auctions were open only to dealers, but now many are open to the public. Keep a lookout in newspapers (especially the classified section), or do some research at your local library or on the Internet (search on the keywords "public auto auctions"). But remember, what you see is what you get.

❖ If you don't know a thing or two about cars, try to talk a car-savvy friend into going to the auction with you. Or better yet, make friends with a local mechanic and ask him to go along with you.

DO-IT-YOURSELF REPAIRS AND MAINTENANCE

Puddle Talk

❖ If you notice a puddle of fluid on the ground beneath your car, you should investigate it before visiting the car doctor. The leaky-fluid color palette is as follows: Oil is brown, gasoline is clear (you'll recognize the odor), brake fluid is a very light brown (almost clear), power steering fluid is usually red, transmission fluid is pinkish red, and coolant is often a bright bluish green.

Retiring Tires

❖ Worn tires not only cost you money in fuel, but they're also dangerous. Do you have to pull into the repair shop to get a checkup? Not at all. You can perform your own at-home examination for tire tread wear that will cost just a penny—and it's refundable. Insert the penny into a tire groove, with Abe's head facing down into the tread. If you can still see his head over the top of the tread, it's time for a trip to the tire store.

❖ To maximize tire efficiency, always keep your tires well-inflated and rotate them every 5,000 miles or so. Rotating your tires will increase their life expectancy, since tires wear unevenly.

Make a Custom-Fit Washing Mitt

❖ Making your own car-washing mitt is a breeze. The only materials you need are two plain 100 percent cotton washcloths, a needle, and some sturdy thread. To begin, place one washcloth on top of the other in perfect alignment. Securely stitch all but one side together. Leave one side open just enough for your hand to fit comfortably through. Remember, you want the fit to be snug enough that the newfangled mitt doesn't come off when you lower your hand into the wash bucket.

Stitch two wash-cloths together to make a car-washing mitt.

Squeaky Clean

❖ Don't wait until a downpour to discover that your windshield wipers need to be replaced. Replace your wiper blades every 6 to 12 months for maximum effectiveness, but don't call on the dealer for this task. Purchase inexpensive refills and change the blades yourself. Instead of paying $20 to $30 for a pair of blades, you may find the same blades for $5 to $10 at a discount auto parts store. Just think of the cumulative savings! You can use that extra money to buy a fun car accessory or some new compact discs.

On the Mend

❖ Having the dealer repair your upholstery can be a costly investment, so do it yourself. Iron-on patches are just the solution for small fabric upholstery tears. Look for matching pieces or swatches in a fabric or discount store (heck, check your sewing box; you may find some there). For small cuts or holes in leather, try some of the fillers available at auto parts and furniture stores. Vinyl repair kits also are available to repair minor cuts in the dashboard.

❖ To prevent tears in leather upholstery, apply a thin coat of baby oil periodically.

A Dangerous Bucket of Suds

❖ It's hard to believe, but you should resist reaching for your favorite dishwashing liquid when making a bucket of homemade car wash. The soap could damage your paint job. After all, dishwashing detergent is designed to cut

WORLD-CLASS FRUGALITY
The Anti-Chrysler

I don't believe in taking any car to a mechanic—not when it's so easy to make even the most serious repairs at home. So when my nephew complained that his old Chrysler wouldn't budge, I promised to fix it. Never mind that this meant rebuilding the engine block and using an old manual that had diagrams but no written instructions. I was pretty darned proud when I delivered the car to my nephew. It ran like a top.

That is, until it blew up. Actually, he left the car running while he went into his local video store, and the engine ignited. No one was hurt—unless you count my pride when I had the car towed back to my house to try again.

Unfortunately, I didn't get to it right away. It took more than a year to rebuild the engine again. By then, a family of mice had moved into the car. Dozens of them lived, procreated, and died there. They nibbled on and nested in the seats, and you can't imagine the stench they left. In the end, I had to replace the seats and douse the entire car with chemical deodorizer.

As car repairs go, this probably wasn't my best bargain, but ultimately I prevailed. The new engine works perfectly—although I won't be quitting my day job to become a full-time mechanic anytime soon.

—TJ Wilson
Monticello, Illinois

grease. Lurking in those seemingly benign bubbles could be killers waiting to attack that protective layer of wax. As an alternative, purchase a bottle of car wash soap at an auto parts store. A little will go a long way, and the cost is just a few cents per wash.

❖ To remove bugs and bird droppings, gently rub with an old plastic scrubbing pad.

Isn't Best Better?

❖ Are you casting pearls before swine? We don't mean to insult your vehicle, but you may be doing just that by pumping premium-grade gasoline into your car. That's because not all cars require the most expensive grade. Some even run better on lower-grade gas. How can you know? Just consult your owner's manual and rely on your own experience. Give your car the least expensive gasoline your manual recommends and evaluate its performance. Does it seem to suffer any negative consequences? Do you hear any unpleasant engine noises? If there are no problems, you can fill 'er up with the lowest-grade gasoline available.

WHAT'S THE BEST MONEY SAVER?

It's a Wash

When is the best time to wash your car?

A. On a clear, bright, sunny day
B. Immediately following a snowstorm or rainstorm

You may have chosen (A), thinking that a snow or rainstorm gives you a reprieve from car-washing duty. But that's incorrect. The most important time to wash your car is (B) immediately following a snowstorm or rainstorm. Why? Acid rain. Even though the rain evaporates, the acid is left behind and will eat away your car's finish, requiring a new paint job down the line. Generally, the best defense is to wash your car regularly and to wax it every 6 months. Your car's "skin," like yours, will benefit from a facial and a high SPF.

❖ Generally, people buy either supreme or regular gas. That means the middle grade sits there forever, going stale and mixing with water from condensation. Dirty gas can mess up your engine, leading to a pricey tune-up. So to be safe, choose either the most or the least expensive gas.

BEING PREPARED ON THE ROAD

Do the Shag

❖ Looking for a reason to hang on to those old carpet scraps? Here's how to put those purple, deep-shag, Riunite-stained remnants of the Nixon years to good use. Cut them into strips measuring 1 by 4 feet and use them when your car gets stuck in the snow. Just jam a strip down in front of each stuck tire.

❖ Store the strips flat, over the spare tire area, and use them as a buffer when you carry things on your roof.

Car-ifornia Dreamin'

❖ You've accidentally shut the car door (it's locked, of course), and your keys are still in the ignition. Perhaps the car is running—of course it's running—and now you'll have to try that old clothes hanger trick or find a locksmith. By the time you actually find one, the car will have run out of gas. And because you were listening to an old Mamas and the Papas tape, you're draining the battery, too. If only you had another set of keys. But you don't need another set of keys—you need only one key, the door key. Keep a copy of it tucked inside your wallet, and you'll never have to worry about being locked out again. The key will take up almost no room—certainly no more than the credit card you'll need for that locksmith.

❖ Keep a spare ignition key hidden in the trunk. That way, if you're out and lose all your keys, all you'll have to do is open your wallet, then the trunk, and away you'll go.

CHAPTER 20

THRIFTY WAYS TO DRESS WELL

*C*lothes make the man, they say. Every closet contains one or two blasts from the past that make you feel good or seem to bring you luck when you wear them. You get compliments rather than comments on their age, and you handle them with loving care.

We can all be a little crazy when it comes to our favorite pieces of clothing. How did we get them? Why do we keep them? Maybe, with your first paycheck, you sprang for an off-the-rack quality coat, figuring the investment would pay off in time—and it did. And how did you live without that no-brainer blazer found at the church rummage sale that looks terrific with everything from blue jeans to jewels?

Whether your wardrobe is straight off the fashion show runway or warrants a visit from the fashion police, looking stylish on a shoestring can be a simple matter of how you select and care for your clothes. A well-made garment—one that has been cut and sewn with care and is tended to after each use—guarantees a polished image and a long life regardless of its price tag. And knowing how to make minor repairs can turn any piece of clothing into an heirloom.

In this chapter, we'll take a look at keeping clothes spiffy and consider several tips for selecting quality clothing at bargain-basement prices. We'll explore the upkeep and repair of the cast of supporting characters such as shoes and socks, including the secrets of spit polishing from a soldier and darning how-tos from a mother of seven. Along the way, we'll air our dirty laundry and spin through nifty ways to give your old duds a new life.

SPOTTING WELL-MADE CLOTHING

Inside Information

❖ As any frugal Yankee knows, it's more important to have a few well-made garments than a closet full of poorly made ones. You can quickly tell from just a few details whether you should purchase or pass. Loose threads are a sure sign of sloppy overall workmanship. Seams should lie flat and not pucker. Hems should be even and not curl. The stitching on the seams should be even, too—no skips or breaks. Check the topstitching; it should be perfectly straight, with no backstitching or breaks.

Built to Last

❖ Let's say you're shopping for a jacket, and you want to make sure you get the best, most frugal buy. What exactly do you look for? An unlined jacket should have finished seams around the shoulders, sides, sleeves, armholes, hems, and facings. That means no fraying edges. On jackets made from light and middle-weight fabrics, the seam edges should be turned under and stitched. For medium to heavy fabrics, the seam edges should be covered with a bias binding, or they should be finished with zigzag stitching. They shouldn't curl.

Liner Notes

❖ If you're shopping for a jacket and you have a choice between a lined and an unlined one, go with the one that's lined. A lining can extend the life of a jacket. In addition, a lining around the shoulders can enhance the fit.

❖ When you try on a lined garment, concentrate on the lining. Is it too big or small? Do you even notice the lining? It should provide silent support.

Closing Comments

❖ Yet another way to tell whether a garment is well-made is to examine the zipper. It should be of the appropriate weight for the fabric. A nylon zipper will curl on a heavy fabric (such as denim), and one that's too heavy—either metal or nylon—will look clunky on a lightweight fabric. The right zipper also will keep the gap closed, not explode from stress. A heavy-duty zipper is necessary for frequent closure. In other words, a dress zipper doesn't have to be as sturdy as one for a jacket.

WORLD-CLASS FRUGALITY
Holy Spit!

What does it take to muster a brutal attack on the boots and feet of a foot soldier?

"Cloth diapers, honest to God," says Major Peter L. Fitzgibbons, a chaplain in the U.S. Army Reserve. "Everyone has his own little trick. That's mine."

Off base, in a parish posting, old cotton T-shirts are the best medium to apply a lubricating paste polish to a pair of 9-year-old jungle boots. "Father Fitz," a frugal Yankee from Warwick, Rhode Island, and a veteran of the Gulf War, says that the polish is essential protection against moisture, especially on the seams of the boot, where rot first occurs. Floor polish cracks as it dries, so its immediate shine doesn't merit its use.

What about the "spit" part of the polish? Just water. "Spit polishing" calls for using your basic paste polish with water sprinkled on as the polish is applied in a circular motion. (This is in contrast to a buff shine, which is made when the polish is applied and then brushed with a dry shoe brush.) The water helps the polish penetrate the crinkles in the leather, especially where the toes join the foot. The leather lasts longer in boots that are treated with the polish.

Then there is the question of what to wear inside the boot to prevent chafing on, say, a 12-mile training march. For Father Fitz, it's always 100 percent wool socks—black, of course. Some soldiers recommend wearing women's knee-high nylon stockings underneath, but so far, he says, he hasn't tried that.

Check Out the Buttons

❖ You can tell the quality of a garment by looking at the buttons and buttonholes. They may be a small part of the overall item, but the way they're attached and constructed can tell you a lot about the overall quality of the piece. What should you look for? The buttons should line up directly under the buttonholes. When all the buttons are buttoned, there should be no gaps or pulls. And the buttons should be sewn so that the direction of the shank corresponds with the direction of the buttonhole: vertical shanks with vertical buttonholes, horizontal shanks with horizontal holes.

❖ Buttonholes should lie flat, and there should be no frayed fabric showing through the stitching of the hole. On items such as suit jackets and coats and on delicate fabrics, the buttonholes should be bound—that is, encased in fabric, not sewn by topstitching.

TAKING CARE OF WHAT YOU HAVE

A Stitch in Time

❖ Think you're just imagining that holes in your clothes get bigger the longer you ignore them? All that agitating in the washer and dryer worsens the damage to the fabric, which can mean early retirement for your clothes. Keep a pincushion of sewing needles threaded with assorted colors in the laundry room for fast repairs. A 12-inch length of thread will usually service two or three tears.

Spot Check

❖ Tired of losing your favorite shirts to stains you forgot about? Fill a small squirt bottle (recycle the one that comes with a box of hair coloring, or use a travel-size shampoo bottle) with liquid laundry detergent and keep it in the bathroom. Apply it to spots you notice on your clothes as you undress. Rinse the spot and set the piece aside to dry, then throw it in with the dirty laundry.

Hang 'Em High

❖ Confess it; you'll squeeze another day out of a shirt or dress you have to send to the dry cleaner just to save on the bill. Keep an over-the-door triangular hanger unit on a closet shelf so that you can air out the garment as you take it off. Make sure it hangs freely so that it won't wrinkle on the bottom. You can buy these metal hangers in the laundry center of any hardware store or discount store.

Attention, Marathon Runners

❖ Give panty hose a life after death. You've paid enough for them; wouldn't it be nice to have them serve double duty? Cut off the panty part and braid the legs around a metal clothes hanger. Now you have a tender holder for a fragile blouse—one that will prevent stains and pulls from rusted or thorny spots on the metal. The nylon also will dry quickly, so you can hang a damp item on it.

IT WORKED FOR ME

Fairy Godmother Logic: It Doesn't Hurt to Ask

It started as an effort to clean out my closets and turned into a real Cinderella story.

I knew that even consignment shops wouldn't take my collection of "lovely" mint-condition bridesmaid's dresses. The shops I called already had too much custom-made bridal party couture. Brainstorming with my mother, an assistant principal at a Manhattan high school, I decided to offer the gowns (and matching accessories) to students for the upcoming spring prom. Mom knew that not all the girls could afford new clothes and approached the prom director with the once-worn offerings.

When word got out among the students, the demand was overwhelming, and a raffle was planned to fairly disperse the booty. I sent an e-mail requesting other closet-bound formal treasures from my coworkers so that even more girls could attend the ball.

—**Lynn Naliboff**
Stamford, Connecticut

GIVING OLD CLOTHES NEW LIFE

A Victorian Secret

❖ Just because the cuffs on that blouse have started to fray doesn't mean it's time to throw it away. Instead, give it a new lease on life. To hide those rough edges or stains on a jacket or blouse, add a touch of lace. Attach some lace seam binding to a pocket, cuff, lapel, or collar. Your friends will ask where you bought your new outfit.

It's the Pits

❖ Have a favorite shirt or blouse that you can't wear anymore because of the stains under the arms? Don't spend money on a new one. Rather, give the old one a day in the summer sun by turning it into a tank top. Use one of your existing tanks as a pattern and cut off the sleeves, allowing ½ inch for a hem. Turn under the edges and sew the hem on the machine or by hand.

Every Good Turn . . .

❖ Just because the collar of a blouse or shirt is frayed doesn't mean its life is over. If the collar isn't laundry-marked on the underside, use a needle or seam ripper to carefully cut the stitching that attaches the collar to the shirt. Turn the collar, pin it to the shirt, and restitch it with a machine or by hand.

❖ If there are laundry marks on a blouse, consider turning it into a boat neck. Cut off the collar entirely, trimming the neckline evenly so that it scoops the shoulders. (Use an existing blouse for a pattern.) The results will seem like a whole new garment. To prevent this problem in the future, if you patronize one laundry, have it mark the yokes of your shirts instead of the collars.

Tracks of Our Tears

❖ If a good old patch is the way to save a torn garment, there's no reason to hesitate. For the best fit, imagine the tear to be a round spot or a rectangle and cut a piece of matching fabric about ½ inch larger on all sides. (You may need to take a swatch from the lining, seam, or underside of the hem or collar of the afflicted item.) Baste under the

IT WORKED FOR ME
Darn!

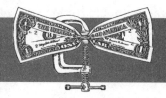

Darning is something of a lost art. Most folks don't think to mend socks these days. After all, socks are practically disposable, right? Many are, but if you've ever been brokenhearted to see a hole forming in a pair of expensive woolen socks, you'll want to know how to perform this small miracle. As a mother of seven, I learned early the value of darning.

Use a wooden darning egg—available at sewing or knitting stores—for a sock (or other knitted garment) and an embroidery hoop for a flat piece of woven fabric.

Darn under a good light. Use a fine (not thick) needle.

Darn with like material—cotton with cotton, wool with wool—and use the same thickness of thread as in the

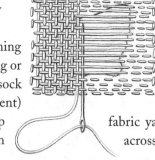

Make side-by-side stiches (top), then weave across the stitches at right angles (bottom).

rest of the garment. If possible, use a thread from the inside seam or a scrap of fabric.

Always keep the stitch tension even and not too tight. Pulling the stitches too taut can cause puckering.

To get started, work on the right side of the fabric. Take a tiny back-stitch near the edge of the hole to anchor the thread, but don't knot it. Then make small running stitches around the hole in a rectangle and fill it in with side-by-side stitches running parallel to the fabric yarn or thread. Next, weave across these stitches at right angles, keeping the woven patch as flat and even as possible. Keep working until you've finished off the hole or fray.

—Dorothy Johnson
Statesville, North Carolina

edges of the patch and sew it in place with tiny stitches, sewing only on the turned-under edges; not through the patch, where the stitching will show.

Prayer Meeting

❖ So you've been putting in extra time seeking divine intervention. No one would know if it wasn't for those shiny spots on the knees of your trousers and the elbows and wrists of your jacket. Sponge the telltale patches with a solution of 1 tablespoon ammonia and 1 cup water. Rinse, dry, and give thanks.

CLOTHING FROM UNUSUAL SOURCES

Wedding Bell Blues

❖ Is your dream day turning into a nightmare to organize and finance? Take the stress out of decision making by going antique—for the dress, that is. The supply of old wedding dresses exceeds the demand, so in this arena, you're a winner. You'll find antique shops listed in the Yellow Pages under Antiques—Dealers.

❖ Consignment shops and your local newspaper's classified ad section are terrific places to look for a wedding dress, too.

❖ You can buy a plain, well-fitting dress at a department store, then go to a fabric store to get the decorative elements—lace, beads, train, veil, and headpiece—you need to complement your eclectic taste and artist's budget.

Swap 'til You Drop

❖ Wouldn't you love a whole new wardrobe every year—without spending an arm and a leg? Would you believe that you can have one—for nothing? It's not a miracle, only a clothing swap. Here's how it works. Invite some friends over and ask them to bring along all the clothes they're tired of. For every garment someone puts in, she can take one out. Include the accoutrements—shoes, ties, hats, jackets, purses, and pocketbooks—if you like. One of the best things about a clothing swap is that if you do it with friends who live close by, your clothes won't be lost forever. If you decide you'd like to wear that maroon blouse again, you can probably get it back.

THRIFTY CLOTHING REPAIR

Pencil It In

❖ Fix sticking metal zippers by rubbing the tip of a graphite pencil over the teeth. For nylon zippers, use an appropriate-colored wax candle. Pull the slide up and down to spread the good news.

Seeking Closure

❖ So you've blown out a zipper. In lieu of paying for a replacement, pull the slide up beyond the broken teeth. Pull the slide back and forth over the remaining teeth, test to see that they align smoothly, and stitch by hand or machine to create a block of thread over the bottom few teeth, making a new base.

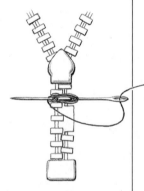

A broken zipper is easy to repair with a needle and thread.

❖ If the zipper is on a bag or a jacket, consider using Velcro, which will secure an opening that's not subject to intense stress. Use a razor blade to remove the old zipper, then sew Velcro strips onto each side of the opening. You can purchase Velcro at any sewing supply store.

Pearls before . . . Burns

❖ Has your favorite blouse suffered a nasty burn? Don't fret—and certainly don't buy a new blouse. Cover up the burn. Trim the burned portion off the fabric and sew a patch over the hole. If the patch is too noticeable, cover it with lace, pearls, sequins, or an appliqué. A flower boutonniere, scarf, or piece of jewelry also can be called into service.

Torch Song Soliloquy

❖ You thought that scorch mark was irreparable? Not to worry. To treat scorch marks on washable items, gently rub the mark under cold running water using another piece of fabric—not your fingers. Soak the cloth in 1 tablespoon borax dissolved in 2 cups cold water. Rinse well and launder as usual.

❖ For scorch stains on nonwashable fabrics, apply a solution of equal parts glycerin (available at any drugstore) and warm water. Let sit for 2 hours, then sponge with warm water. Get the item to the dry cleaner as soon as possible.

Give It a Little Room

❖ It doesn't take a tailor's eye to notice when buttons squeeze the line of a jacket or coat instead of simply sliding into place. The solution to excess pressure? A thread shank that allows a little extra room for give. Place a bobby pin, match, toothpick, or straight pin under a button when attaching it so that it will not be too tight against the fabric and the buttonhole can fit over it.

❖ Sew four-hole buttons by stitching two holes at a time, then finish off the thread before doing the other two holes. This way, the buttons will not fall off, even if they become loose or one of the stitches breaks.

REMOVING STAINS

Stain-Removing Fundamentals

❖ Just because you've stained a favorite piece of clothing doesn't mean you have to replace it. If the stain is not greasy and the garment is washable, loosen the stain by soaking the whole garment in a mixture of enzymatic laundry detergent (no special type is necessary—just find the least expensive brand that lists enzymes as an ingredient) and cold water. Do not soak dyed silk, moiré fabrics, or wool.

Place a match under a button when you attach it to keep it a little loose.

Set in Its Ways

❖ When you find a stain on a garment, your first instinct may be to douse it with hot water. After all, you wash yourself with hot water when you're dirty, right? Unfortunately, in the case of stains, the opposite is true. Hot water actually sets stains, so turn on the cold water instead.

Whiten Socks . . . In the Dishwasher?

❖ Dingy socks? Don't toss 'em. Use dishwasher detergent to whiten them. Add about 2 teaspoons to the washing machine and wash as usual.

Pen Pal

❖ Saturate a ballpoint pen stain with milk, or rub it with the cut side of a tomato. Since milk and tomatoes can leave their own stains, soak the whole garment in a mixture of enzymatic laundry detergent and cold water, then launder as usual.

It's a Little Rusty

❖ For rust stains, hold a white absorbent pad, such as a clean white washcloth, under the stain and rub the stain with the cut side of a lemon. Sprinkle the stain thickly with salt and let dry. Rinse off and launder as usual.

Is There Nothing Lemon Can't Do?

❖ Rub fruit juice and cola stains with the cut side of a lemon, then rinse and launder as usual.

Painted In

❖ If your van Gogh routine has gotten a little messy, here's help. For best results, treat oil-based paint stains while they're wet. Treat the stains with paint

WORLD-CLASS FRUGALITY
Save Money on Pajamas

Lawyer Clarence Darrow took on some of the most controversial cases of his time, and he was known as a workaholic. As his fame grew, reporters would sometimes tease him about his rumpled clothes. Such a clever and renowned attorney should try to look his best, they teased. Darrow always replied that he bought his suits from a very reputable tailor and that he probably spent more money on his clothes than any reporter he met. "The difference between us," he said, "is that you probably don't sleep in yours."

thinner, turpentine, or rubbing alcohol until the paint is soft, then wash in heavy-duty laundry detergent.

Allergic to Yellow?

❖ To remove pollen, turmeric, or curry stains on washable fabrics, apply a solution of one part hydrogen peroxide and six parts warm water, then launder as usual. Sponge fresh stains on unwashables with cold water (do not soak) and then with the peroxide mixture. Dab with cold water and dry-clean as usual.

Egg 'Em On—And Out

❖ Egg, which is protein-based, makes for pretty tough stains. If you treat them immediately, though, they'll come right out. Mix ½ teaspoon salt with about 1 teaspoon water—enough to make a thin paste that will cover about a square inch. Rub the paste into the stain in a circular motion, then sponge the stain with water and blot with a soft cloth—an old cotton T-shirt is ideal. Before washing, smear the stain with liquid laundry detergent.

❖ For older egg stains, sponge them with warm—not hot—salt water. If you have a soda water siphon, spray the stain and blot it, or pour plain soda water on the stain and blot. Dab the stain with liquid laundry detergent, then launder as usual.

Water Is Thinner Than Blood

❖ Cut on your finger? Even if the blood has migrated to your shirt, there's nothing to worry about. Soak blood-stained clothing in a pail of cold water containing a handful of salt for 15 minutes. Then wash the garment in an enzymatic laundry detergent.

CHAPTER 21

SPENDING LESS ON HOBBIES AND SPORTS

*D*oes this sound familiar? You work too much and play too little, and you would like nothing better than to shift that balance so that you're working less and playing more. But if the things you do for leisure—the sports you play, the recreational activities you participate in, or the crafts and hobbies you pursue—carry a hefty price tag, you have to put in extra hours on the job just to fund your fun.

Crafts and other creative hobbies would seem to represent the very essence of frugality: You make at home what you could buy at the store. The fact is, however, that what you could buy premade in the store often costs less than the supplies that you purchased to do it yourself. You might spend $100 on wool yarn to make a sweater that you could buy for half that price.

You can make your hobby more practical and more affordable by not wasting money on unnecessary accessories such as a $15 needlecraft kit when a 50-cent disposable plastic sandwich container will do. If you do spend $100 making a sweater or a quilt, you don't have to spend more money on dry-cleaning bills when you can do just as good a job cleaning it at home with some common items.

Hobbies and crafts can be expensive, but if you play sports, you probably feel an even stronger tug on your wallet. Americans spend $45 million a year on sporting goods, which is about equivalent to the combined annual salary of the New York Yankees starting lineup. Sometimes it may seem as though you need a professional athlete's salary to afford the equipment required for your favorite sport—unless you know where and when to buy. For example, bikes and fishing rods are much cheaper in the fall than in the spring, and you can outfit yourself for a game of hockey or a round of golf far more affordably if you don't mind purchasing used equipment. If you take the time to look, you'll find many ways to play for a lot less.

FRUGAL IDEAS FOR YOUR HOBBY SUPPLIES

Through Thick and Thinner

❖ If your hobby involves painting with oil-based paints, you're going to have to buy some paint thinner to clean your brushes—but not too much. Paint thinner is reusable. After you finish painting, pour a cup of thinner into a glass jar and rinse the brushes. Cover the jar, and in a week or two, the paint remnants will settle to the bottom of the thinner and solidify. When that happens, pour the thinner back into the original container and use it again and again to clean your brushes (but not to thin paint).

Put the Squeeze on Paint

❖ Instead of buying a foam paintbrush for hard-to-reach or very precise spots on your craft project, you can make your own out of a discarded sponge. First, thoroughly clean the sponge with soap and water. Then cut it to a size that suits your purpose and trim one of the edges into a bevel shape. If it's a thin slice of sponge, attach a clothespin to one end to use as a handle. If your homemade brush is more than a couple of inches wide, use two clothespins side by side for the handle.

Bevel the edge of a sponge to make a painting tool.

It's in the Bag

❖ If you're working with acrylic or oil-based paint, it's possible to take a lunch break from a painting project without having to clean your brushes. When you want to stop painting for a while, just place each brush in a plastic sandwich bag. The bag will keep the paint from drying out and keep the bristles pliable for at least a couple of hours. Note

WORLD-CLASS FRUGALITY
The Little Train Club That Could

It wasn't easy being a charter member of the Moscow Railroad Fan Club. Members had to have ingenuity and persistence as well as model-building skills.

A small group of model train buffs formed the club in 1969, when there were no Soviet companies making model railroads and no hobby shops where you could buy supplies to build your own miniature locomotives, railroad cars, rails, and train stations. Members crafted trains out of discarded Plexiglas and scrap metal. They scrounged for plastic glue substitutes—including a solvent used to clean ink off the plates of printing presses—to hold the parts together. They bartered at automobile factories for buckets of auto paint because no stores sold model paint. One member collected moss to use as bushes for his layouts.

Supplies weren't readily available, but there was no shortage of national security—related paranoia, which proved to be just as much trouble for club members. During one of the club's early informal meetings in front of a Moscow toy store, a member had his model smashed by a policeman who suspected him of a capitalist offense. The member was proudly showing off his work to his fellow members, but the cop thought he was trying to sell the train, which was illegal without a permit.

Club members couldn't design their minitrains from blueprints of the real railroads because they weren't available. Any information about the country's infrastructure was a closely guarded government secret. So the model railroad buffs used to go to the railroad yards with their rulers and notepads and take measurements—after they convinced the railroad workers that they weren't spies.

that this trick doesn't work with latex paint, which tends to form a skinlike coating on the bristles when the brush is in a plastic bag.

Wet Your Palette

❖ If you're planning a long painting session, there's a simple, inexpensive way to keep the acrylic paints on your palette from drying out or forming a puddinglike skin before you have finished the project. Instead of using a plastic or paper palette, squirt the paint on a few layers of moist paper towels. The moisture will prevent the paint from drying out without watering them down.

Pinot and Needles

❖ The next time you have an inexpensive table wine with dinner, don't drop the carafe in the recycling bin. It's tall, heavy, and wide enough to hold your supply of knitting needles. The needles will be positioned upright, making it easy to read the numbers on the heads and select the size you want.

Frame Work

❖ That wooden picture frame with the smashed glass can't hold photos anymore, but it can hold your needlepoint project in place while you work on it. People who do needlepoint recommend that you tack your canvas to a wooden frame while you work on it to keep it from getting tugged out of shape. But rather than buy a frame from a craft supply shop, you can use a discarded picture frame if it's the right size.

GOOD BUYS ON SPORTS EQUIPMENT

Don't Pass on Outlets

❖ Many sports shoe companies have their own factory outlet stores, which are worth checking out. You'll find great prices on sneakers that are in fine condition except for a slight blemish. Typically, sneaker factory outlet shelves are filled with last year's models. The only thing wrong with the sneakers is that they're a couple of months out of fashion.

Firm Footing

❖ If you're buying football shoes for your child, you might be able to save some money if he is still growing. Football shoes are made with either permanent cleats (similar to soccer shoes) or replaceable cleats that screw onto the soles of the shoes. Shoes made with replaceable cleats tend to be more expensive but also more durable, because the cleats can be replaced when they wear down. So if the player is going to outgrow the shoes in one season, it makes more sense to buy the less expensive permanent-cleat shoes. He will need a new pair of shoes before the cleats wear out.

❖ The same goes for hockey skates. There isn't much sense in paying hundreds of dollars for top-of-the-line skates if the player is going to wear them for only one year. And the younger the player, the less difference the quality of the equipment will make in her performance.

The Hockey Exchange

❖ Many youth hockey programs hold preseason used equipment sales or exchanges as fund-raisers. Parents can bring skates, helmets, shoulder pads, and other equipment that their kids have outgrown and sell them to other parents looking for an inexpensive way to equip their children. Often the equipment has been used for only one

---

IT WORKED FOR ME

A Good Deed Rewarded

I used to do some volunteer work at a nursing home, and as an unexpected perk, I ended up learning how to crochet. I visited the home one or two times a week and spent an hour or so visiting some of the residents. A couple of the women were always crocheting when I arrived, so one day, just to make conversation, I casually asked, "How do you do that?" They sat me right down and gave me an introductory lesson. When I returned the next week, I got another lesson, and then another. A month later, I finished my first afghan.

—Julie Bean
Venice, California

season, so it's still in great shape. The prices are usually a fraction of the cost of new equipment, and the proceeds from the sale are split between the sellers and the youth hockey organization. Contact the youth hockey programs in your area to find out if any such sales are planned.

Après-Ski Season

❖ Visiting a ski area's equipment shop at the end of the season could pay off. Many shops want to sell their rental equipment to make room for next year's models, so they offer the old equipment at huge discounts.

❖ If you know a professional skier or snowboarder, ask him to purchase your equipment for you. Manufacturers offer great discounts to the pros.

❖ Don't be afraid to buy last year's model of skis if you find them in a store. Chances are they will be drastically reduced in price, but they will be only slightly different from the high-priced current models. Sometimes manufacturers change nothing more than the graphics painted on the skis.

It's All Downhill

❖ When equipping a child with ski equipment, especially boots and bindings, it might be wiser to rent than to buy. For the amount of use he might get out of the boots before he outgrows them, renting might be cheaper. However, if you have more than one child, buying might be more cost-efficient than renting, as the younger child could benefit from hand-me-downs. If you do decide to rent ski equipment, it might be cheaper to rent it at a suburban ski shop than at the ski area rental shop. A package of skis, boots, and poles can cost nearly half as much off-site as on-site.

The First Resort

❖ A good place to find great prices on ski equipment and other outdoor equipment is the sporting goods shops located in ski resort towns. Often those shops sell used equipment on consignment. It's not always in the best condition, but if you search for good equipment, you may find some. Of course, if the equipment is critical to your safety, such as climbing rope, crampons, an ice ax, or other rock-climbing or mountaineering gear, don't take any chances.

(On)lining Up a Putt

❖ A number of Web sites selling golf equipment have popped up in the past few years, and some of them offer much better prices than those at golf shops. Some sites offer golfing tips and golfing news, too, but the products on these sites tend to have a heftier price tag. Generally, the better-looking the site, the higher the prices are. Be aware that with most sites, the buyer bears the shipping costs, and you don't have the chance to test-drive (or test-putt) the equipment before you purchase it. So know exactly what you want before you buy.

Hand-Me-Downs for Hackers

❖ If you're looking for a set of golf clubs or maybe just a putter or an iron, check with the private and public courses in your area. Often the pro shops at those courses sell used clubs that are in good shape for a good price. According to golfing lore, Gary Player won the first of his three British Open titles playing with a used putter.

❖ If you're just beginning to play golf, your best bet might be to visit a discount department store such as Wal-Mart or Kmart. There's no sense paying top dollar for top-notch equipment when you have bargain-basement skills.

Falling Prices

❖ The best time to buy a new bicycle is in late September or early October, just after the industry's largest trade show. Retailers will have placed their orders for next year's models and will want to clear their shops of this year's. The best way to do that is to reduce prices.

❖ Similarly, the best time to buy fishing equipment is at the end of the fall, when the fishing season has ended. That's when retailers are looking to unload stock from this year before filling their shelves with new equipment for next season.

❖ If you're looking for a good price on a kayak or canoe, head to the stores in September, when retailers are trying to sell off their summer products to make room for ski equipment.

Wheeling and Dealing

❖ When you go shopping for a new bicycle, don't be afraid to barter. See if the dealer will throw a few extras into the bargain, such as a water bottle, a helmet, or toe clips. In that sense, buying a bicycle is not much different from buying a car.

❖ If you find two similar models with similar prices, buy the bicycle with fewer features. The construction of the essential equipment, such as the brakes and gears, may be of higher quality on the stripped-down bike.

The Way the Ball Bounces

❖ Before you buy a basketball, consider what kind of court you're going to play on. The more expensive leather balls are designed for indoor wooden courts and quickly get scuffed and ruined on an outdoor asphalt court. If you intend to play outside, buy a less expensive rubber ball or one made of synthetic leather, both of which are designed to be used on hard, abrasive surfaces.

𝓕RUGAL 𝓜EMORIES

A Round of Lost and Found

When I'm playing a round of golf, I usually walk to my ball along the side of the fairway—which is where my tee shots usually wind up anyway—and pick up a couple of lost balls on the way. I've also found that a few minutes at a water hazard with some type of ball retriever can yield a nice collection of uncut and well-cursed Titleists and Maxflis. At one club, I was often met on the course by a couple of scruffy, wet-haired kids carrying diving masks. For a very reasonable price, they would sell me golf balls they had found by diving in one of the course's water hazards.

—Jack Falla
Natick, Massachusetts

HOBBY LESSONS FOR LESS

Craft Course

❖ Check with local hobby shops or yarn shops to see whether they're offering any free or low-cost instructional courses. It makes sense for them to do so because courses can be an effective way to lure people into the shops, entice them to buy the materials they'll need for the lessons, and get them to keep coming back for more.

SPORTS LESSONS FOR LESS

Camp Counseling

❖ Sports camps can be expensive, but you might be able to cut the cost if you've been to the same camp two or three times. Contact the camp director and ask if, in exchange for tuition—or maybe even for a paycheck—you could serve as an instructor. At a hockey camp, for example, this would be a cost-free way of getting some valuable ice time, which is a major expense for any hockey player—or any hockey player's parents.

Two's Company; Three's Even Cheaper

❖ Rather than sign up for private golf or tennis lessons, get a friend or two at the same skill level to enroll with you. Semiprivate lessons are much less expensive than private ones. Group lessons cost even less, although the more people there are in the group, the less individual instruction each one will receive.

MAINTAINING YOUR BOARD GAMES

You Can Still Pass Go

❖ If you're missing pieces from your favorite board game, a number of common household items can serve as substitutes. Thimbles, poker chips, and bingo chips and markers can all be used to mark your spot on the board. Coins also can be used in a pinch. But if you really want that silver racing car that's missing from your Monopoly game, visit yard sales, flea markets, church bazaars, and thrift shops. For a fraction of the cost of a new game, you can purchase an entire set of replacement pieces.

MAINTAINING YOUR NEEDLECRAFT GEAR

Needles to Say

❖ When working with needlecrafts, never leave the needle and thread on the fabric work surface or leave the fabric in the embroidery hoop for an extended period of time. Needles can leave rust stains on the fabric, and hoop ring impressions can be difficult to iron or steam out.

Iron It Out

❖ If your embroidered or counted cross-stitch item is wrinkled, place it facedown on a towel and press a hot iron against the back of the needle-work. Just pressing the iron against the fabric should remove any wrinkles, but if you have to move the iron back and forth, do so gently.

Dyeing and Bleeding

❖ To prevent the dyes in a newly made quilt from bleeding, soak it in a mixture of cold water and salt (about ½ cup salt per 1 gallon water) for a couple of hours.

❖ You can remove a spot from a white section of a quilt by mixing cream of tartar and bleach into a paste and dab-

IT WORKED FOR ME

Quilt Grafting

I once repaired an antique quilt for someone by removing the entire row of outside blocks and securing the second row of blocks to a new backing. I salvaged as many of the outside blocks as I could and used them to replace the quilt's torn blocks. But sometimes items are best left unrepaired. Someone once told me that nothing can do more damage to a quilt, afghan, or sweater than a human termite with the best of intentions.

—Robin Stroot
Hastings, Nebraska

bing it on the quilt. Allow it to dry to a powder, then brush it off.

An Organizing Mesh

❖ If you use yarn, ribbon, or twine for decorative gift wrapping, you probably have trouble keeping it untangled when you store it. If you own a mesh shopping bag, you have the solution. Place your yarn and ribbon in the bag and pass a strand from each roll or skein through the mesh. Then draw whatever lengths you need from the roll.

Thread Bearer

❖ A narrow piece of cardboard is all you need to keep your embroidery thread organized. Cut a series of grooves along the top and bottom of the cardboard, then wrap different-colored thread around the cardboard and in the grooves.

Waxing Practically

❖ You don't want to work with dirty knitting needles because the dirt could stain the yarn. To clean them, simply

WORLD-CLASS FRUGALITY
Home Ice Advantage

The parents of most NHL stars spent lots of money on their children's sport, especially for ice time. But for all the skating Wayne Gretzky did as a child, much of it didn't cost his father, Walter, anything other than some higher-than-usual water bills. That's because Walter built a homemade rink in the backyard of their home in Brantford, Ontario.

Mr. Gretzky did have to buy his son hockey equipment, and he made sure Wayne appreciated the value of that equipment. Every night, he watered the ice with a lawn sprinkler so that a new surface would await Wayne in the morning. If the boy had left his stick and pads on the ice the previous night, he would find his equipment frozen in the next day, and he wouldn't be able to use it until it thawed out.

wipe them with a damp cloth. But after you have cleaned the needles, the yarn might stick to them, which makes it very difficult to knit. You can remedy that situation by vigorously rubbing the needles with heavy waxed paper. If your steel needles have rusted, clean them with a rag dipped in kerosene before you wash them. Rinse them well before drying them and rubbing them with waxed paper.

Brush Down

❖ If you want to extend the life of your watercolor brushes, store them on their sides after cleaning them. Never store them upright in a jar or can because water can seep into the ferrule—the metal part that attaches the bristles to the handle—causing mold to grow or the handle to warp.

MAINTAINING YOUR HOCKEY GEAR

Keeping Your Edge

❖ Each time you have your ice skates professionally sharpened, it will cost you at least $5 to $10. So the less often you need to have your edges touched up, the more money you will save. The best way to keep your blades from getting dull is to keep them off your feet unless you're on a soft rubber surface or the ice. Always dry off the blades after you have finished skating to prevent them from rusting.

Glove Is Forever

❖ The first—and usually only—parts of a pair of hockey gloves that wear out are the leather palms. But they can be

Frugal Memories

Coming Unglued

I once bought a pair of top-of-the-line hockey skates for $300 and remembered reading somewhere that if you soaked your skates in water and then wore them for an hour or so, the leather boots would mold to your feet and fit like a glove. But I made the mistake of using very hot water instead of warm water. The next day, my brand-new skates were literally falling apart because the hot water had loosened the glue that held them together. The moral of the story? If you want your skates to last a long time, keep them on ice and out of hot water.

—Adam Frattasio
Needham, Massachusetts

replaced for about half the cost of a new pair of gloves. Many sporting goods stores will repair the gloves for you, or you can look for companies advertising glove-repalming services in hockey publications such as *The Hockey News.* Not only will repalming save you money, but it also will save you some mishandled pucks and bad passes while you try to break in a new pair of gloves.

WORLD-CLASS FRUGALITY
Page Protectors

NHL Hall of Famers Gordie Howe and Milt Schmidt were among the kids growing up during the 1920s and 1930s who, when they played ice hockey, taped Sears Roebuck catalogs around their legs and used them as makeshift (but effective) shin guards.

A wine cork makes a terrific fishhook holder.

MAINTAINING YOUR FISHING GEAR
Reel Life

❖ Salt water will quickly corrode many metals, including the ones used to make fishing reels and tackle. To fend off corrosion, be sure to rinse your reel, rod, and tackle with fresh water after a day of ocean fishing.

❖ To extend the life of your nylon fishing line, keep it out of direct sunlight when you're not fishing. The sun's heat will break down the line's elasticity, making it easier for a fish to snap it.

A Corker of a Tip

❖ A good way to prevent your fishhooks, lures, and flies from doing any unintentional damage to your clothing or skin (and to keep them together in one place) is to stick them into wine corks when you're not using them.

MAINTAINING YOUR CAMPING GEAR
Hung Out to Dry

❖ Don't make roughing it any rougher than necessary. Before you store your tent, hang it on a clothesline and make sure it is thoroughly dry and will stay dry. Otherwise, the scent of pine needles and fresh air will be overpowered by the odor of mildew the next time you go camping.

MAINTAINING YOUR GOLF GEAR

Brush after Your Tee

❖ An old toothbrush makes a dandy tool for cleaning the faces of your golf irons. By brushing the dirt and grime out of the grooves after each use, you will prevent the irons from pitting and corroding and give them a longer life.

MAINTAINING YOUR BASEBALL GEAR

Crack of the Bat

❖ Baseball purists will point to many reasons why wooden bats are better than aluminum ones, but aluminum bats don't break as frequently as wooden ones do. The rubber handles tend to tear, but they can be replaced with new handles or with some cloth tape, though the tape doesn't absorb the bat's vibration as well as the thicker rubber handles so. If you prefer wooden bats, rub them regularly with linseed oil to keep them from becoming dry and brittle, making them more susceptible to cracking.

*F*RUGAL *M*EMORIES

Butter Up

You can use a number of oil-based household products to condition and soften a new baseball glove, including petroleum jelly, mineral oil, neat's-foot oil, and even butter. But go easy on the butter.

I remember when I was young, this kid in my neighborhood, Peter, decided to use the butter in his re-frigerator to soften his glove rather than buy a special oil from the sporting goods store. He figured that if a little butter was good, a whole lotta butter was better. So one night he covered his glove with butter, stuck a baseball in the pocket, and wrapped it tight with an elastic band. Not only did he use too much butter, but he neglected to wipe off the excess before he went out to play.

In the middle of our game the next day, Peter, who was playing right field, came running in from the outfield in a panic and nearly in tears. By the time he got to the pitcher's mound, we figured out why he was in such a hurry: Right behind him was a swarm of hungry yellow jackets, trying to get a taste of his glove.

—Stephen E. Sickles
Arlington, Massachusetts

CHAPTER 22

CUTTING PET COSTS

*P*et owners looking to save money on their four-legged, finned, or winged friends should take a closer look at how they're spending it. Consider that the average dog owner—more than 30 million Americans share their homes with at least one dog—spend $550 a year on veterinary bills, grooming, and food, and some dog owners pay more than $1,000 just for food. And before they incur these costs, they buy a dog for an average of nearly $200. In fact, many pet owners spend more than they have to acquiring, feeding, entertaining, and caring for their pets.

You can start saving money immediately by adopting rather than buying a pet, and you can continue to save if you put some forethought into the adoption. Some pets are less expensive to own than others. For instance, goldfish are always going to be cheaper than dogs, but some dog breeds are more suitable than others for the frugal-minded. A small, short-haired dog, for example, eats less, costs less at the vet, and needs infrequent if any grooming. Suppose you settle on a goldfish as your pet. It's inexpensive to purchase and feed, and couldn't that large floor vase collecting dust in the garage serve as a fish tank? And wouldn't that old marble collection make just as colorful a liner for the bottom of the tank as the dyed rocks you could buy at the pet shop?

Americans spent $23 billion on pet products, food, and services in 1997. By using common sense and a little imagination, you can contribute far less to that sizable kitty for your kitty.

PAYING LESS FOR PETS

A Breed Apart

❖ If you would like to adopt a specific dog or cat breed but can't afford to buy a puppy or kitten, contact a breed rescue group. The groups, with names such as Just Pugs and Love a Lab, recover adult dogs and cats from people who can no longer care for them or, in the case of retired greyhounds, animals that are no longer of any use to their owners. The adoption costs can be a bit higher than those at a pound—from $60 to $100—but the animals have been treated as if they were family pets while waiting to be adopted. Contact the American Kennel Club or the Cat Fanciers' Association on the Internet for information on local breed rescue groups. Keep in mind that some rescue groups have very stringent adoption requirements, such as a fenced yard and the assurance that the animal will not be left alone for long periods of time.

Low Mileage and Lots of Meows

❖ Not only can you find a great deal on a 1978 Chevy Nova in your local newspaper's classified ads, but you might also discover a free furry friend. The classified section is a common means for pet owners to give away unexpected litters or animals they can no longer keep.

Dropout Dogs

❖ Not every Lab or golden retriever that trains to be a Seeing Eye dog makes the grade. Although these animals may not be able to navigate a crosswalk, they can make wonderful, well-behaved pets, and they need homes. Contact your

---

IT WORKED FOR ME

Hold the Hot Wax

Sandy, my family's golden retriever, always used to get in the way whenever I tried to wash my car. I got an idea: If Sandy liked playing in the water and suds, then why not give him a bath while I was washing the car? So from then on, whenever I washed my car, I would do it with both car-washing detergent and a bottle of dog shampoo handy. It was much cheaper than taking Sandy to the groomer, and since we were outside, I didn't have to clean up afterward.

—Brian Gaffey
Arlington, Massachusetts

---

local animal shelter or association for the blind to find out how to adopt one of these training school dropouts. Shelters are listed in the Yellow Pages under Animal Shelters or in the government listings of the White Pages.

WHAT'S THE BEST MONEY SAVER?
Health Risk

You've just adopted a kitten, and you live in a state where pet insurance is available. Before you take your new pet to the vet, you can decide between two options.

A. Pay the vet bills for each visit
B. Buy pet insurance

Pet insurance is no different from human health insurance in that it pays off when you have to treat a serious illness. With advances in veterinary science, more and more serious animal injuries are treatable.

The lowest-priced pet insurance policy costs nearly $100 a year and covers $1,000 per incident and $5,000 per year. The most expensive plan costs about $300 a year and covers $4,000 per incident and as much as $18,000 per year. Most policies don't cover routine care such as vaccinations, dental cleaning, or parasite treatment. They also don't cover preexisting conditions such as cancer, diabetes, and allergies.

A dog or cat owner can expect to pay $100 to $250 a year in vet fees, but most of those fees are for treatments not covered by insurance policies. That means that you might pay as much as $300 for an insurance policy and then spend nearly as much on vet visits—not a very frugal action. However, if your pet has a tumor, the fee to remove it could be as much as $2,000. Now the insurance policy pays dividends.

Ultimately, whether pet insurance is prudent depends on how you view your pet: as a family member or as a possession. If your pet is a family member, you might feel like the Annapolis, Maryland, couple who spent $20,000 on their cocker spaniel's cancer treatment. They were willing to pay any amount to keep their dog alive. Had they purchased an insurance policy, their devotion would not have been so costly.

If your pet is just a possession, you might treat her like a VCR, which gets replaced rather than repaired because it's more cost-efficient to do so. If euthanasia is your first choice when a pet becomes seriously ill, pet insurance doesn't make much sense.

Join the Clubs

❖ There are a number of tropical fish and bird clubs whose members include breeders. By joining such a club and attending its meetings, you should be able to get some good advice and good deals on pets from other members. The Federation of American Aquarium Societies has chapters in most large cities. To find other local bird or fish clubs, contact a pet shop or a veterinarian who specializes in birds or fish.

A Walk in the Park

❖ If your city has dog parks, visit them when you're looking to adopt a dog. Many parks feature bulletin boards that have notices from dog owners who are seeking new homes for their pets.

SAVING MONEY ON PET CARE

Keep It Short

❖ The best way to save money on grooming is to buy or adopt a dog or cat with short hair—a pet that never needs a haircut.

❖ If your dog or cat has long hair and you choose to groom it at home, keep a bottle of mineral oil handy. A drop or two of oil will loosen any mats in your pet's coat.

Take a Dip

❖ Some humane societies or even some feed stores in your area may sponsor low-cost flea dip days. Check with your local animal shelter (listed in the Yellow Pages under Animal Shelters) or pet food source to find out if and when any dip days are scheduled.

Make Some Flea Tea

❖ Rosemary works as a natural flea repellent. Steep a couple of teaspoons of dried rosemary in boiling water. Let the water cool down, then rub it on your pet's fur. Repeat as necessary after the aroma gets faint.

Pawing the Pavement

❖ If you're a city dweller, you can avoid the often tensive chore of clipping your dog's nails or the expense of having a groomer do it. Walk your dog regularly, and the city's concrete sidewalks will serve as one big emery board.

Bowwow Bathhouses

❖ Just as you can save money at a do-it-yourself car wash, in some cities you can take your dog to a self-service dog wash and pay only half of what you would pay at a grooming salon. These dog-washing shops provide you with a huge tub, shampoo, and a blow-dryer. Best of all, you can clean your dog without messing up your bathroom or kitchen. To find a self-service dog wash, check the Yellow Pages under Pet Grooming.

Alternative Medicine

❖ Homeopathic care is catching on among pet owners. Office visits to homeopaths tend to be cheaper than visits

FISH NET WORTH

Pets that also serve as pet food, such as white mice, can be very inexpensive to purchase. But as with other pocket pets, in addition to buying the animal, you have to buy a cage and other amenities. You can obtain a cat or dog at the pound for a minimal cost, but then you have to feed the animal and take it to the vet at least once a year. Chickens are cheap to buy, will eat vegetable left-overs, and can make nice meals if you get tired of taking care of them. But they require space and some type of domicile.

The ultimate low-cost pet is a goldfish. Fish may not be cuddly or offer the best companionship, but they certainly are cheap to buy and to keep. You'll spend less than $10 a year on food, and goldfish can live for decades.

to veterinarians, and many of the prescribed remedies, such as echinacea, can be purchased at health food stores at a cheaper price than veterinary pharmaceuticals go for. To find a homeopathic vet, check the Yellow Pages under Veterinarians.

Tail and Hammer

❖ Baking soda is not only good for keeping human teeth clean, but it can also help keep your dog's teeth bright, shiny, and free of tartar, which can lead to tooth decay. At least once a week, use either a toothbrush, a piece of cotton, or a damp cloth dipped in baking soda to go over your dog's teeth. Don't use human toothpaste; it contains ingredients that are harmful to dogs.

You Say Tomato, I Say Peroxide

❖ Contrary to popular belief, a tomato juice bath is not the only, and certainly not the best, solution if your dog or cat gets sprayed by a skunk. Even after being bathed in tomato juice, pets still tend to smell like skunk, especially when their fur gets wet. And if you have a white-haired dog or cat, tomato juice might turn his fur pink. A better way to get rid of the smell is to bathe your pet in a mixture of peroxide, baking soda, and soap, which will neutralize the offensive chemicals in the skunk spray. A cat-size recipe includes 1 quart hydrogen peroxide (3 percent), ¼ cup baking soda, and 1 teaspoon liquid soap. Triple those amounts for a large dog. *Caution:* Don't store the mixture, because it might explode. Also be aware that the peroxide might bleach your pet's fur.

SAVING MONEY ON PET FOOD

Eat Your Vegetables

❖ If your dog has to shed a few pounds, reduce the amount of canned dog food you normally feed her and make up the difference by mixing in some cooked green beans or carrots.

The vegetables will add bulk to the meal without adding any fat or many calories.

❖ Also, instead of feeding your pet dog biscuits, let him chew on raw baby carrots. Dogs like the sweet taste of carrots, and they are a much healthier treat than biscuits, which are often loaded with fat and calories. Because they are crunchy, carrots are as good as biscuits for a dog's dental health.

Hold the Lox

❖ If you want to make a sterilized bone even more of a treat for your dog, fill it with peanut butter or cream cheese. Your pet will treat the snack as you would an Oreo: He'll lick the inside, then chew on the outside.

Woofs for Hoofs

❖ If you live near a farm where there are horses, those animals are walking around with some dog treats on their feet. Dogs love to nibble on horse and cow hoof trimmings.

WHAT'S THE BEST MONEY SAVER?
Insurance Salesman Puts the Bite on Dog Owners

You want to get a dog, but you don't want the pet to cost you a lot of money. You have two choices.
A. Buy a collie for $500
B. Adopt a chow from a neighbor for free

In the long run, it might be cheaper to (A) buy a collie. In 1996, insurance companies paid $250 million in dog bite claims. Now some insurers are questioning home owners more closely about their dogs, and some may refuse to insure homes that include particular breeds. The Centers for Disease Control and Prevention has a list of the highest-risk breeds. They include Akitas, Alaskan malamutes, chows, Doberman pinschers, German shepherds, Great Danes, huskies, pit bulls, rottweilers, and Saint Bernards.

Pet stores sell the trimmings as dog treats, but if you know a farmer, you might be able to get them directly from her—for free.

SAVING MONEY ON PET TOYS

Puppy Love

❖ If you're a tennis player, don't discard your balls after they have lost their bounce. Your dog will have more fun chasing or chewing on the dead balls than you had chasing them around the court.

❖ Don't use racquetball or squash balls as dog toys, especially for larger dogs. Although in one sense they are better than tennis balls because they are made of hard rubber and will last longer, their size and smoother surface make them potentially dangerous because they could get swallowed or lodged in a dog's throat.

Elastic Demand

❖ To put a little bounce into an old cat toy, attach it to a doorknob with a long rubber band. The toy will bob around when the cat paws at it, similar to the way fishing rod–type toys do.

In a Roll

❖ The cardboard cylinders from paper towel and toilet paper rolls make excellent toys for pocket pets such as gerbils and mice. They'll spend hours—even days—running through the rolls, and when they get bored with that, they'll chew on the rolls, which will promote healthy teeth.

Watch the Birdy

❖ If you want to provide your cat with some live entertainment without spending an arm and a leg, create a butterfly garden or put up a bird feeder within sight of her favorite windowsill. Plants that attract butterflies include butterfly bush (buddleia), butterfly weed (asclepias), and purple coneflower (echinacea).

SAVING MONEY ON TRAINING AND INSTRUCTION

Shake, Rattle, and Silence

❖ One way to get a dog to stop barking is to place a dozen or so pebbles in an empty coffee can and shake the can when your dog starts to bark. The noise will startle and silence the dog, perhaps because it will annoy him as much as his barking annoys you. Remember, you need to be consistent for any training to have an effect.

Toil and Vinegar

❖ Once a dog relieves herself in a particular spot, chances are she will return to the scene of the crime and commit another offense. One way to prevent this is to spray the spot with a solution of vinegar and water. The smell will mask the scent and discourage her from returning to that spot.

A Cat's Bark

❖ If you have an outdoor cat, furniture scratching probably isn't a problem. That's because outdoor cats have access to trees. Rather than spend money at a pet store on a carpeted scratching post, go to the forest and find a fallen tree branch. Cut the branch down to about 2 feet and nail some plywood to the bottom to serve as a base. Now you have a homemade, natural scratching post.

Can You Dig It?

❖ Some dog breeds are more prone to digging holes than others. In fact, the word *terrier* is derived from the Latin word for earth, *terra*, because these dogs were originally bred to dig in pursuit of small animals. Now dogs usually dig because they're bored, and they tend to dig in the same spots. If you want your dog to stop digging and you don't have time to provide him with stimulating entertainment or scintillating conversation, place chicken wire or rocks in the holes before you refill them. This will discourage digging in those spots. To encourage the dog to dig in a more acceptable spot, dig a hole, fill it with sand, and bury some dog biscuits or bones in the sand. Repeat this (consistency is the key) until your pet learns to dig in that spot only.

Spray It, Don't Say It

❖ If you have a spray-top water bottle or a water gun, you have an excellent—and frugal—cat-training device. A quick spritz from the bottle is one of the most effective ways of telling a cat that she's misbehaving.

❖ A loud noise is another deterrent. A sharp bang on an aluminum pan will get your cat to stop what he's doing.

WHAT'S THE BEST MONEY SAVER?
Room Service for Rover

You own a Labrador retriever, and you've accumulated enough frequent flier miles to take a weeklong trip and stay at a luxury hotel. There are three things you can do with your Lab. Which do you choose?

A. Put him in a kennel for a week
B. Hire a dog-sitter to visit him twice a day
C. Take him with you on the trip

Depending on which hotel you're staying in, the most inexpensive choice might be (C). A kennel may charge as much as $15 to $20 a day to board a dog as large as a Lab, and a pet-visiting service may charge $10 to $20 per visit. However, the Four Seasons hotel chain, which welcomes pets, says that its guests who bring pets usually spend about $12 a day on pet-related services. Those services may include a room service order of chopped filet mignon, an on-site grooming, a walk with the concierge, or a visit from the hotel's on-call vet. Of course, none of this includes the cost of taking your dog on an airplane—either in a carry-on case or as cargo. That will run you another $50 or so, plus the cost of a kennel, if you need one.

CHAPTER 23

REDUCING CHILD CARE COSTS

What's the best way to save money on children? Some folks will tell you not to have them. But guess what? Raising kids doesn't have to be expensive. Keeping them well-dressed, busy with inexpensive toys and projects, and involved with outside activities doesn't have to break the bank.

How can that be? Well, you have to take a kid's-eye view of the challenge: Reach for your imagination instead of your wallet. For instance, you can cut babysitting costs dramatically by trading child care responsibilities with friends. Instead of shelling out your money to pay for games and toys at the toy store, make your own—from wooden blocks to board games. Forget expensive arcades; kids love to visit pet stores and flower shops. These tips and more will help you enjoy good times with children without going broke.

SAVING ON CHILD CARE

Try Group Therapy

❖ Can't seem to find a minute—let alone an hour—to spend with adults because there is no one to care for your child? Join a social group that offers free child care—through your church or town recreation department, for example, or perhaps an informal group of adults who discuss literature or share some other hobby. You and your child will make new friends, and it won't cost you a dime. (This is an especially good idea if you have moved to a new town.)

Invest in the Tot Exchange

❖ Sitters cost a lot more than they did when you were doing the babysitting, and you can't be sure of the quality of care your kids are getting. So make arrangements to swap babysitting services with a friend on a regular basis. For instance, you watch your friend's children every Monday morning, and your friend watches yours every Wednesday afternoon. Or you watch your friend's kids one Friday night a month, and he takes yours another Friday night. You'll not only save a bundle on child care, but you'll be a lot more relaxed during your time away from your kids.

Hire the Mother of All Helpers

❖ Nighttime babysitters can run up your child care bill pretty quickly, and maybe you're not comfortable leaving your child after dark. Check with friends and neighbors to see whether any of their older kids (ages 10 to 13, say) is interested in being a mother's helper. You may need some help one afternoon a week for 2 hours, or maybe a couple of days a week during the summer. A mother's helper can play with your child in your home while you get a few chores done—laundry, gardening, vacuuming. Helpers usually charge less than sitters because you're still around to supervise. Your child will enjoy the attention, and you'll get something accomplished.

FRUGAL FORMULAS
MAKING COLORED SAND

Children love to play with colored sand, but when you buy it at the store, you can feel your money sifting right through your fingers. It's easy to make your own. Buy a large container of salt at the supermarket. Find an empty jar with a lid (such as a peanut butter or mayonnaise jar) and fill it about two-thirds full of salt. Then squeeze a few drops of food coloring into the salt, screw on the lid, and shake the jar to color the salt. Repeat with as many jars and as many colors as you want.

SAVING ON CLOTHES

Homespun Swap Meets

❖ Just because your kids need some new items of clothing or some toys doesn't mean you have to run off to the retail store. If you have friends and acquaintances with children older and younger than your own, hold a swap meet. Invite your friends and ask them to bring clothes, toys, sports equipment, footwear, and other good-quality items no longer useful to them. Trade items for keeps or just temporarily.

WORLD-CLASS FRUGALITY
Use a Little Co-op(eration)

Dinner and a movie used to be an inexpensive night out, but after factoring in child care costs, you may as well settle on renting a movie and popping your own corn (a good idea even if you do go out to the movies). But I learned how to save big on time away from my young children. A group of local families started a babysitting co-op that enables parents to exchange babysitting services. Here's how you can do the same thing in your area.

You need at least 10 and no more than 20 families. The group appoints a president and a treasurer. Each family contributes $5 in annual dues, which pays for tokens, postage, and paper costs. The treasurer allots each family 40 tokens. One token is worth one child for ½ hour. The treasurer sends out a quarterly statement to each family so that everyone can get a snapshot of which families need to earn tokens and the availability of sitting services.

Let's say you have two kids and you need a sitter for 4 hours. You check your list of members and find someone to care for your children. Total cost to you: 16 tokens, which you pay to the co-op sitter.

Co-ops don't work well for full-time day care coverage, but they are great for errands and weekend dates. It's also a terrific way for children and parents to meet new people—and save money.

—Janet Schwalm
Northborough, Massachusetts

What Clothes Around Comes Around

❖ You've figured out that children's clothes can cost more than your own, but you don't have time to comb consignment shops and yard sales. Try setting up a "library" of children's clothes with friends or neighbors. When your child outgrows his or her clothes, wash, fold, and store the ones that are in good condition in a clearly labeled box or drawer. (Put the size and season of the clothes on the label.) Have your friends do the same. When your child moves up to the next size, call around to see who has clothes of the size you need. Borrow them from the library for as long as you need them. If they are still in good condition when you are through, wash, fold, and store them in a box, ready for the next person to use. This way, you'll have easy access to good-quality, in-style clothing that's the right size—without making a single trip to the mall.

FRUGAL TOYS AND OTHER FUN

Color My World

❖ Summertime fun doesn't have to be costly or elaborate. Here's one idea that lets you use your own backyard or local park as an enormous playroom. Pick daisies or Queen Anne's lace and place them in a container of water. Add food coloring and watch the flowers turn colors.

More Than Books

❖ You already know that the public library is a great source of kids' books. But check it out for children's books on tape and for videos, both of which cost plenty to buy. Books on tape (free, of course) are great activities for young children during nap time or quiet time; they're lifesavers during long car rides. You can borrow videos from many libraries for the same period of time you'd rent them from a video store and pay either nothing or a very small fee—maybe 50 cents or a dollar.

Just Remember This

❖ Kids love games, but you can't use Monopoly money to buy them at the store. One favorite among the young set is any version of "memory," and it's easy to make your own. Make at least 20 cards using construction paper, oak tag paper, cardboard, or any heavy-duty paper. Each card must have a duplicate, but you can design your pairs of cards however you (and your child) want. When your cards are complete, shuffle them and place them facedown on the table or floor. Children take turns choosing one card and then trying to find its mate. If a player chooses correctly, he takes another turn. The player with the most correct matches wins. Your kids will love this game, and your purse will, too.

She's a Doll

❖ Paper dolls are an old-time favorite among children, but prices for premade ones at the store are anything but quaint. You and your child can still indulge in this pastime for free by making your own paper dolls. Gather up a stack

SUMMER FUN: FIVE GREAT WAYS TO SPEND THOSE SUMMER DAYS

Summer is fun, but it sure can get expensive if you take the kids to theme parks, arcades, or even movies. Here are five great ideas for having just as much fun and spending little or nothing.

1. Go for a treasure hunt along the beach at the ocean or a lake. Look for shells, sea glass, rocks, bark, driftwood, crabs, and so forth.

2. Head out for a nature walk in a local park or public forest. If the site has trails, you can usually find a map near the entrance.

3. Visit a local science or learning center that offers free days. Check your local newspaper for listings.

4. Join a public lake or pool. Fees at these sites are considerably lower than those for private clubs and beaches.

5. Have a sprinkler party in your yard. Invite your kids' friends to bring their bathing suits and towels, then turn on the spray!

of catalogs and magazines and cut out the people you and your child like. Glue each figure to a piece of cardboard, then cut the cardboard to the shape of the figure. Create a stand by cutting a ½-slit in the base of the figure and inserting a rectangle of cardboard into the slit, perpendicular to the figure.

Play House

❖ Kids love to play in their own little clubhouses, but you'd almost have to take out a mortgage to buy one of the premade ones at the store. You (and your kids) can make your own for nothing more than the cost of a few decorations. Ask for an empty box at an appliance store (boxes from refrigerators, washing machines, and stoves are great). Haul it home and set it up in the basement or driveway, then let the kids decorate it with crayons, markers, stickers, whatever. They'll have a great time decorating and living in their own home, and your pocketbook won't suffer a bit.

Play Hide-and-Shriek

❖ Here's a twist on the old hide-and-seek game that young kids love—and it's free. Once it's dark outside, find a flashlight. Choose one person to be "it" and send the others off to hide. Then turn off all the lights in the house or in the area where you're playing. After counting to a certain number, the "it" player turns on the flashlight and searches for the hidden players. When the flashlight beam hits a hidden player, that person is "found." Be prepared for lots of squealing and shrieking when the flashlight beam locates a player.

Turn Outside In

❖ It's raining or snowing outside, and the kids are bored. But you don't want to haul them off to one of those expensive indoor arcades or movie theaters. Stay put and have an indoor picnic. Prepare a picnic lunch—sandwiches, lemonade, whatever you can find in the cupboard—and pack it in a picnic basket. Then spread out a blanket, gather the kids around, and enjoy your indoor feast.

❖ Alternatively, have a make-believe slumber party. Put the kids in their pajamas, get out sleeping bags or blankets, make some popcorn and other snacks, and snuggle down to read books, play games, tell ghost stories, and so forth. The hours will pass quickly, and the children will love their party.

Reading, Writing, and Crafting

❖ Fed up with expensive toys and entertainment? Call your local library or bookstore. Both may have free activities such as story or craft hours, readings or performances by local authors, or events celebrating holidays. Both places will welcome you and your children— and you won't have to spend a dime.

Hunt-and-Pack

❖ Kids love searching for treasures. If you're at the beach, build a sand castle and hide shells or pebbles in it. Then let the kids dig into the castle to find their prizes. If you're at home, take an empty dishpan; a large, coated cardboard box; or even a plastic sled and fill it with rice

---

IT WORKED FOR ME

A Sweet Solution

My daughter built a house in less than an hour—and it cost me pennies. When I was planning my daughter's seventh birthday party, I was wracking my brain trying to think of a craft that the kids would enjoy—but wouldn't break my birthday budget. Then I remembered something my daughter had done in kindergarten. I picked up a bag of miniature marshmallows and a couple of boxes of toothpicks. I poured both into bowls on a big table and let the party guests go to work.

Using marshmallows and toothpicks, they built all kinds of structures—one made a barn, another a house, still others fanciful sculptures. This kept a dozen 7-year-olds busy and quiet for over an hour, and I hadn't bought a single craft supply.

—Laurie Zwaan
Exeter, New Hampshire

ear's a terrific story about a town that created a library of Halloween costumes. Each year, families donated outgrown costumes, then borrowed their "new" selections from the collection. That way, the costumes were recycled many times, and the children had their choice of different costumes every year—for free.

or dried beans. Then bury marbles, pennies, or action figures for the kids to find. (Keep in mind that small treasures like this should be reserved for children over age 3. Use larger items for toddlers.) Either let the kids keep their prizes or pack them away for another day.

Rescue the Sock That's Not Missing

❖ Save the sock that lost its partner in the wash and turn it into a puppet. Sew on buttons for eyes and nose, glue or stitch on cut pieces of felt for ears and mouth, and add a few strands of yarn for hair. If you're not crafty, just draw the features on with magic markers. You can make a whole family of puppets from your family's stray socks. Create a puppet theater from a large cardboard box. Cut out half of the flat bottom for the opening. It should fold easily for storage. Have everyone do a little painting or drawing to spruce up the theater.

Roll the Dice

❖ Here's a great game to play anytime you're stuck waiting—at a restaurant, in a doctor's office, or riding in a car, plane, or train. Carry a pair of dice in your pocket or purse and roll them to play math games. Have young children count the dots on one or both dice. Older kids can add, subtract, multiply, or divide the number of dots on each die. Or you can get really creative and have kids figure out special dates (a seven and a four could be the Fourth of

July; a six and a three could be June 3, Mom's birthday). Once they get into the swing of things, the kids will start creating their own dice games.

❖ Alternatively, have each player write the numbers 2 through 12 on a sheet of paper. Players then take turns rolling the dice, adding the numbers that land faceup, and crossing the total off the playing sheet. (For example, if the numbers 2 and 4 land faceup, cross off the number 6 on your sheet.) The first player to cross off all the numbers on his sheet wins.

Make Contact

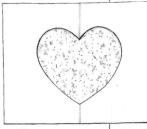

❖ Kids of all ages love craft projects, but you could spend a mint at the craft supply store. Here's an easy and frugal project to try. Fold a sheet of construction paper in half, then cut out a simple shape, such as a heart or star, starting at the fold and working outward. Unfold the sheet so that you can see the cutout shape in its entirety. Peel the backing off a piece of clear contact paper and adhere it to the back of the construction paper, covering the hole. Then turn the construction paper over and let the kids sprinkle colored sand, glitter, sequins, or whatever they like on the sticky portion of the cutout. They'll have a charming picture when they're finished, and you hardly spent a cent. To make the design more permanent, cover the front with another sheet of clear contact paper.

Sprinkle glitter and such on the sticky side of the contact paper for a fun project.

Dig In

❖ Children love to garden, whether they live in the country or the city, and it's an activity that's dirt cheap. Get the kids to help you dig holes and plant bulbs or flowers. If possible, offer them their own garden patch. If you don't have enough space for a garden, buy an inexpensive terracotta flowerpot and a flat of marigolds or impatiens for each child, then let your kids go to work.

Play Clothes

❖ Got a rainy day with nothing to do? Let the kids dress up and put on a play. You can even call a couple of your friends to join you in the audience. But how do you put together a collection of dress-up clothes without buying expensive ones at the store? Easy. Search your closet, your friends' closets, and your relatives' closets (with their permission, of course) for items you no longer need or want. Favorites among kids include old uniforms, prom and bridesmaid's gowns, shoes, costume jewelry, hats, purses, and other accessories. (Kids don't care if the items are adult-size.) Ask for a large empty box at the grocery store and let your kids decorate it. Then toss all the dress-up items in the box, and you're ready for hours of free fun. And who knows, maybe you'll be encouraging a budding actor.

Appoint Artists in Residence

❖ Here's another way to pass the time on a rainy day. Read a story out loud to the children (or have an older child read the story), then let the kids make drawings, paintings, or collages based on the tale. This project can occupy them for quite a while, and your wallet won't become an open book.

Your Number's Up

❖ Got an empty egg carton and a pair of dice? If so, you have a game. Number the egg compartments 1 to 12. Each player rolls the dice and moves a stone or button to that number in the egg carton. You can go around as many times as you want without declaring a winner. Or you can decide on the

REDUCING CHILD CARE COSTS

IT WORKED FOR ME

The Grandparent's Survival Kit

I love having my young granddaughter, Nina, visit me. But after several hours of play, I need a rest. So to keep Nina occupied while I put up my feet, I have a box filled with treasures any 4-year-old girl would adore.

Inside are pictures of us from when she was here before, stickers and small toys I find on sale, odd notions, costume jewelry and silky scarves I no longer wear, pictures I cut out of magazines, doilies, a new set of crayons, and just about anything I think she'll be tickled over. I keep the box nearby when she's not here so that I can fill it with new treasures as I find them. It's also a constant reminder of how much I love and miss her.

—Carolyn Muller
Rockport, Massachusetts

number of laps each player must make, declaring the first one to complete them all the winner. This is a good activity for young children who need to practice counting.

Movie Madness

❖ We all know how much kids love videos, and most families end up with an extensive home video library. Unfortunately, kids tend to watch one movie several times until they—and their parents—get tired of it. Here's an easy way to save on movies. Instead of going to the video rental store or purchasing new movies, simply trade movies you already own with other families. Do it monthly at a play group or other gathering. When you get a little more organized, you and the other families can decide which new movies you want to buy and split the cost.

Free Fun Is Good Fun

❖ Pour a container of salt onto a cookie sheet, and what do you have? An instant doodle pad. Or fill a cookie sheet with shaving cream and add a few drops of food coloring to make a rainbow of fun. All it takes is a little finger and an imagination to create artwork again and again. The best part of these ideas is that you'll avoid buying expensive toys and games that provide the same entertainment as your homemade toys.

THE YANKEE MISER RECOMMENDS . . .

Planning Ahead

I really look up to people who plan ahead. I know a pair of grandparents who stashed away some of their own children's special toys—wooden blocks, pull toys, a tricycle, and a wagon—and brought them out again when their grandchildren were born. The grandkids loved them, and the grown-up children went misty-eyed at the memories. Those smart grandparents got two generations' worth of play out of the toys.

FRUGAL FORMULAS
SAVE DOUGH: MAKE YOUR OWN

Here's a very inexpensive way to make great imitation Play-Doh, and it actually lasts longer than the commercial brand. You also can make vibrant colors that aren't available in stores.

Ingredients

1	cup all-purpose flour
¼	cup salt
2	tablespoons cream of tartar
1	cup water
1-2	teaspoons food coloring
1	tablespoon vegetable oil

1. In a medium saucepan, combine the flour, salt, and cream of tartar. Add the water, food coloring, and vegetable oil.

2. Stir over medium heat for 3 to 5 minutes. When the mixture forms a ball, remove from the heat and knead gently on a floured surface. (Place waxed paper or parchment paper on the surface for quicker cleanup.)

3. Store in an airtight container or resealable plastic bag.

More Than Books

❖ Did you know that most public libraries have passes to local museums that you can borrow for free? And if you've been hemming and hawing about purchasing a personal computer, send your kids to the library. Most town libraries have computers with Internet access.

To the Dump Dump Dump!

❖ The ultimate bargain is the town dump—now often referred to as the recycling center or transfer station. Some more elaborate town dumps even have an area for high-quality items, which usually go quite fast. Swing sets, plastic outdoor gear, board games, you name it—it's probably been there at one time or another. Avoid scooping up items that have a lot of fabric (hard to clean) or that may be unsafe (car seats, strollers, and playpens, for instance). Make sure that what you take can be scrubbed down thoroughly when you get it home.

CHAPTER 24

SPENDING LESS
FOR QUALITY HEALTH CARE

othing is more valuable than your health. Perhaps that's why health care costs so much. As with so many kinds of repairs, an ounce of prevention is much less expensive than a pound of cure. Taking care to eat properly and exercise regularly can cut health care costs considerably by eliminating ailments such as fatigue, headaches, and colds.

In this chapter, you'll learn how to go beyond that and heal minor ailments at home using products from your own medicine chest (and kitchen cabinet). You'll find that vinegar soothes a host of ailments ranging from athlete's foot to sunburn and that yogurt is an international traveler's best friend. You'll learn how to prevent air sickness with ginger tea and eliminate warts with castor oil.

But what about the costs you can't reduce or eliminate just by taking good care of yourself? How can you save money on doctor's visits, hospital bills, and alternative care? Health care really is one of those professions in which time is money. The less time you spend in the doctor's (or specialist's) office, the more money you save. And you don't have to make a trip to the pharmacy to get your prescriptions; you can save time and money by having them delivered to you.

By taking a little time to research your ailments and your choices of treatments and doctors, you can keep yourself healthy without spending a fortune.

INEXPENSIVE HOME REMEDIES

Cast Off Warts

❖ To get rid of unsightly warts or corns, you could invest in an expensive over-the-counter medication, or you could use castor oil, a natural conditioner that softens the skin. Rub the oil into a wart several times a day to shrink it.

❖ Or rub it into a corn to soften the skin so that you can remove the corn with a pumice stone.

Chase the Blues Away

❖ When you have a bit of a headache or upset stomach or you are suffering from the blahs, it's tempting to take some kind of pain reliever. A cheaper solution is to take a 20- to 30-minute walk around the neighborhood. Moving gets the body's natural endorphins flowing. Not only will they relieve most minor pains, but they also will lift your mood.

Take Two Glasses and Call Me in the Morning

❖ One common cause of headaches is dehydration, particularly in warmer months and following exercise. Dehydration is one of the leading causes of hangovers, too. The best and cheapest way to get rid of that pounding is to skip the aspirin and drink a full glass or two of water.

Give Your Aspirin a Jolt

❖ If your usual pain reliever isn't working, give it a boost by having a cup of coffee. Caffeine is a natural stimulant that will enhance the effectiveness of your painkiller.

Dampen Cramps

❖ Menstrual cramps are no fun, especially when you go to the drugstore and find out how much those special pain relievers cost. You'll need those pills less often if you make sure you take a multivitamin with iron every day the week before your cycle. The vitamin will replace any iron or vitamin B that your body might crave.

❖ You can also use a heating pad to warm and soothe your midsection. This will relieve any cramping and associated backaches.

Loosen Up

❖ Most people control arthritis pain with aspirin. When that doesn't seem to be enough, take fish oil pills or any omega-3 oil to lubricate the joints.

❖ Control arthritis pain by dressing in layers. This will keep the joints warm, which will keep them from stiffening.

❖ One of the many uses of vinegar is to ease swelling in joints. Mix a tablespoon of cider vinegar in a glass of water and drink it twice a day. The vinegar will help dissolve calcium deposits in the joints and reduce swelling.

COLDS

Old Salty

❖ Mom was right. When you have a sore throat, you should gargle with warm salt water. Dissolve a teaspoon of salt in a cup of warm water.

Old Vinegary

❖ Don't like the taste of salt? Then make a concoction of one part vinegar and one part water and gargle with that morning and night. It will soothe your throat and kill the nasty bacteria that are causing the irritation.

Mineral Power

❖ More and more people are realizing that zinc helps prevent colds. That's why the drugstores are filled with zinc tablets and lozenges—all of which are a bit pricey. What they don't tell you is that your multivitamin may have enough zinc to battle a cold before it starts. Fifteen milligrams is the recommended daily allowance of zinc.

Swish the Pain Away

❖ One unpleasant side effect of a winter cold is a sore spot in your mouth. The doctor can prescribe an expensive remedy to relieve the pain, or you could buy something over the counter, but chances are you already have a remedy in your medicine cabinet. Milk of magnesia will numb the area quickly and give it a protective coating. Take a swig and swish it around in your mouth, but don't swallow it (remember, it's a laxative). It will help that sore spot heal.

❖ You can also rinse your mouth with equal parts hydrogen peroxide and water. Don't swallow that, either, or it will burn your stomach.

BURNS

Sweeten the Burn

❖ You have a minor burn and know enough to wash the area gently with soapy water. But what if you're out of that

---

FIVE WAYS TO COOL OFF IN A FLASH

One of the most uncomfortable aspects of menopause is the hot flashes that come with it. Here are some simple ways to lessen their effects.

1. Wear layers. You can control your body temperature by adding or removing layers as you need them.

2. Bring wet wipes. Most hot flashes occur from the waist up. If you carry wet wipes with you, you can wipe your face and neck with a cool cloth.

3. Drink water. It will help regulate your body temperature.

4. Eat light. Small meals every couple of hours will help regulate your blood sugar level, which in turn will help control your body temperature.

5. Apply vinegar. Prepare a solution of 2 tablespoons cider vinegar and 1 cup water. Use this solution to make cool compresses. It will provide more cooling power than straight water.

handy antibacterial cream? No problem. Spread honey on a burn to seal the wound against infection. In fact, honey is a natural healer that can act as a mild pain killer, and it will reduce tissue damage to the area.

❖ If you don't happen to have any honey, you can use vinegar to take the sting out of a minor burn. It also reduces the likelihood of infection because of its natural antibacterial properties. Cider vinegar works best. Apply it straight, without diluting it.

DECIPHERING A HOSPITAL BILL: HOW IT COULD SAVE YOU BIG BUCKS

Here are some tips to help you reduce your hospital bills—before and after you receive them.

1. Get an estimate. If you're going into the hospital for a procedure ordered by your doctor, he should be able to give you some idea of the cost of the procedure, including the number of days you'll be in the hospital and the amount of medication you'll need. Get this in writing so that you'll have a comparison statement.

2. Take notes. If you can, keep a notebook of what medicines you actually take while you're in the hospital and which doctors actually speak to you.

3. Demand a detailed bill. Hospitals love to send bills that summarize your expenses. Only a line-by-line bill will show you that the

oxygen tank your roommate used for 4 days was charged to your account, or that the tests performed on you were billed twice by mistake.

4. Make noise. If possible, look at the bill before you leave the hospital. If there is a discrepancy, go straight to the hospital administrator. Usually, you can get satisfaction before going home.

5. Demand a discount. Some HMOs negotiate secret discounts with insurance agencies. The HMO sends you the full bill, and you pay your percentage, but it sends your insurer (which pays only the portion that you don't) the discounted bill. That's a crime punishable by law. Demand a list from the hospital of what the insurer has paid. Your portion of the bill should be calculated after the discount.

❖ If you happen to have some used tea bags sitting around, they can help reduce the swelling of a minor burn, just as they reduce the swelling under your eyes. Lay one or more bags across the burn and let the skin soak up the tannin.

Chill Out

❖ If you don't have an over-the-counter sunburn medication, use chilled yogurt to cool the burn. Leave it on for 10 minutes, then rinse it off with cool water. Don't wipe it off, because that will irritate the skin.

❖ As with other minor burns, you can use cider vinegar to relieve the sting of a sunburn. If the sunburn is too severe, the vinegar might provide a little of its own sting. If this happens, just cut it with an equal amount of water.

When You Burn, Baby, Burn

❖ If your sunburn has some blistering or is more serious than usual, spread honey on it. Honey is a natural antibacterial that will relieve the pain and reduce the inflammation and tissue damage of minor burns.

❖ The worst thing you can do for a serious sunburn is to scratch it, although it will probably itch quite a bit. Relieve the itch and the burn with an oatmeal bath. Sprinkle 2 cups oatmeal into a lukewarm bath (don't use hot water; that will sting) and soak for 20 minutes.

A Dollop of Prevention . . .

❖ If you know you burn easily in the sun, you may want to start using sunblock a few days before your big trip to the beach. Studies show that if you apply sunblock routinely, your skin will have more resistance to burning. Try applying a sunblock with a fairly high SPF, such as 30, 2 to 3 days before you go to the beach.

❖ You can boost your skin's natural protection factor by taking 2,000 milligrams of vitamin C and 1,000 milligrams of vitamin E in the morning before heading out to the beach. You can find inexpensive vitamins, even chewable ones, in almost any drugstore.

INSECT BITES

Extinguish the Itch of Mosquito Bites

❖ You could go out and buy a special medication to take the sting and swelling out of mosquito bites, but once you

THE YANKEE MISER RECOMMENDS . . .
Take a Nap

Millions of people suffer from chronic tension headaches. They go from one dose of painkiller to the next. Rather than spending all that money on taking the pain away for a couple of hours, think about other remedies that will take it away for longer or prevent it from starting at all.

1. Take a hot shower. Heat applied to the head and neck will soothe the muscles and relax them; that will help relieve your headache.

2. Take a nap. Fatigue is a major contributor to all kinds of headaches. Sometimes lying down for just 10 to 20 minutes will refresh your system and clear your head.

3. Exercise. Even a brisk walk for 30 minutes every day will help relax you and your muscles. It will also help you sleep better at night—as long as

you don't take that walk right before bedtime. Studies show that exercising less than 3 hours before you turn in can interfere with sleep.

4. Drink some water. Mild dehydration is a common cause of many headaches.

5. Take vitamins. When you're under a lot of stress, your system runs out of some nutrients, such as vitamin B and magnesium. Replenish what you're missing, and your system will be less likely to stay out of whack.

6. Avoid certain foods. Ripened cheese, chocolate, monosodium glutamate (MSG), nuts, yeast, and alcohol can cause mild allergic reactions that result in headaches. Experiment through elimination to see whether any of these could be causing your problem.

know that the main ingredient in those products is ammonia, you won't have to. Simply dab a few drops of ammonia on the bite, and it will stop itching right away.

Take the Bite Out of Bee Stings

❖ The trouble with bee stings is that they keep on stinging long after the bee is gone. Take care of a sting by washing it with warm, soapy water, or give it a swipe with a wet wipe. Then hold an ice cube on the sting to take away the pain and keep down the swelling.

❖ As an alternative, make a paste by adding a few drops of cold water to some baking soda. Dab it onto the sting to take away the pain.

SWIMMER'S EAR

Wet behind the Ears—And inside Them

❖ If you love to swim but hate the earaches that follow, there's a simple solution. Combine equal parts rubbing alcohol and vinegar, then pour the mixture into the ear that's clogged with water. The trouble with water trapped in the ear is that it softens the tissue of the inner ear and makes it vulnerable to infection. The alcohol will help dry up the water, while the vinegar will kill any bacteria.

MINOR ACCIDENTS

The Hot and Cold Shoulder

❖ There aren't many cures for bruises, but one way to ease them is to use the cure that professional athletes favor. They apply ice packs and cold water to a bruise during the first 24 to 36 hours. This will stop the internal bleeding and reduce the swelling. After the bleeding has stopped, they use hot water and a heating pad to help the body reabsorb the dried blood under the skin.

Improvised Support

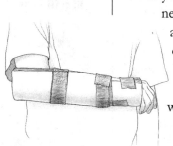

❖ If you've suffered a bad sprain or a broken bone, you need to secure the injury before you go to the doctor, as further jostling can make it worse. To do this, you can use a couple of magazines or a thin phone book as a splint. Wrap it around your injury and secure it with duct tape. This will give you extra support while you travel to the emergency room for x-rays.

In a pinch, you can improvise a splint with some magazines and duct tape.

POISON IVY
When in Doubt, Wipe It Out

❖ You're out gardening or hiking, and after a couple of hours you realize that you've been frolicking in a patch of poison ivy. Now what? Don't worry. You can lessen the effects of the rash before it develops by swabbing the area with rubbing alcohol. Poison ivy attacks the skin by leaving a toxic oil on it as you rub against the leaves. The alcohol will cut through the oil and dilute it. Then wash the area with soap and water to get rid of the rash before it starts.

Healing Tonic

❖ If the rash has already started, help soothe it with a mixture of equal parts cider vinegar and water. Apply it to your skin liberally and let it dry. The vinegar will help alleviate the itch and will guard against any infection that might come with too much scratching.

TRAVELER'S TROUBLES
Drink Up (in the Sky)

❖ Nothing will dehydrate you faster than sitting in an airplane for a few hours. Not only will this give you chapped lips, fatigue, and perhaps a headache, but it also will increase any jet lag you might feel on the other end of the trip. Fight dehydration by packing a water bottle and perhaps a bottle of your favorite sports drink to keep you refreshed. On average, you should drink 8 ounces of water for every hour of flight time.

❖ Get rid of chapped lips by applying a little vitamin E oil from time to time.

Look Out Below!

❖ Sometimes international travel can make a disaster area out of your digestive tract. The easiest solution for this is to eat yogurt—and plenty of it. Make sure the yogurt you buy

FRUGAL FORMULAS
VINEGAR HEALS ALL WOUNDS

If you have no other item in your home first-aid kit, make sure you have gallons of cider vinegar on hand. It can perform all kinds of healing miracles, curing everything from athlete's foot to arthritis. Be sure to use cider vinegar, which contains more nutrients than the white distilled kind. Here are some of the other things vinegar can be used as.

I. Antifungal. Use it to disinfect everything from insect bites to dog bites. It's also a great cure for athlete's foot, ringworm, and any other fungus. After you wash, douse the affected area with vinegar, then rinse and dry well.

2. Douche. Equal parts vinegar and water will fight yeast infections by restoring a healthy balance of bacteria.

3. Palliative for sunburn. Use it straight to ease the sting of sunburn.

4. Treatment for heat exhaustion. Mix a tablespoon in a glass of water. The naturally high potassium will refresh your system. Add honey to sweeten the mixture and provide even more potassium.

5. Soothing mixture for the stomach. Vinegar even helps fight food poisoning by acting as an antibacterial in the stomach. Dilute I to 2 tablespoons in a glass of water.

6. Sore throat remedy. Mix 3 tablespoons in I cup water and add a pinch of cayenne pepper. This mixture will act as an antibacterial and loosen up the sinuses as well.

7. Relief for poison ivy. Vinegar restores the pH balance of the skin and soothes the itch.

has active cultures (it will be indicated on the label). They will take the place of the bad bacteria that are trying to set up shop in your system. Eat 1 cup a day for 3 days before you leave for vacation. Then eat a cup a day during your trip to prevent Montezuma's revenge.

Teatime

❖ Some people get so dizzy and sick when they fly that they don't leave the ground without a healthy dose of Dramamine. If you don't suffer that much but feel a little uncomfortable during plane trips, you can forgo the drugstore cures in favor of something much simpler and cheaper. Ginger has long been known to soothe the stomach. You can take advantage of this fact by brewing a cup of ginger tea. One tablespoon of powdered ginger in a cup of hot water is enough. Drink this 30 minutes before you get on the plane, and it will give you a much more pleasant ride.

❖ You can also find ginger tablets or capsules at most health food stores.

SAVING MONEY ON MEDICINE

Try before You Buy

❖ One of the surest ways to save money on medications is to get freebies. When your doctor writes your prescription, ask whether she has any samples to share. Most doctors have sample packets—as much as a month's worth of a particular medication—given to them by pharmaceutical salespeople and are more than happy to share these with patients.

❖ Using samples also gives you the chance to try out a medication to see if it causes any stomach upset or side effects that you don't like. Once you buy the prescription, you can't return the unused portion, so it's better to find out if the pills agree with your system before you buy them.

Medicine by Mail

❖ If you take only one or two prescription medicines and can purchase them in advance, you might try ordering them by mail. Several organizations, including the American Association of Retired Persons (AARP), offer services that fill your prescriptions by mail. You can call them and set up an account, then send in your prescriptions. They'll confirm the information with your doctor, then fill the prescriptions and send them back, along with your bill. Since these organizations order medications wholesale, they can offer drugs at a significant discount. Ask your doctor about such programs or contact the AARP (call toll-free directory assistance at 800-555-1212).

SAVING MONEY ON GLASSES

I Can See Clearly Now

❖ When it's time to get new glasses, you could order them from your eye doctor, who knows your prescription well, or you could go to a discount service that will have the glasses done in an hour. It's tempting to think that your doctor will do a better job, but that may not be true. If your prescription is very strong or unusual, your doctor knows best. Otherwise, there's no reason not to go to a discount service. These places often run specials, take coupons, and give extra pairs of glasses for free because they need to do a high volume of business to make money. Why not take advantage of that and get as much for your dollar as you can.

Glasses off the Rack

❖ A small number of people are lucky enough to have the same prescription in both eyes. These people also have no astigmatism, a disorder that alters the shape of the eye and requires special lenses. If you're one of the lucky ones, then you don't need to buy your glasses from an optometrist. You can probably get them at your local discount store in the sewing and knitting section. That's where you'll find glasses for needleworkers who want a little magnification as they work. Sometimes these glasses sell for less than $10, and they come in different strengths. Ask your doctor whether these glasses are safe for you.

SAVING MONEY AT THE DOCTOR'S OFFICE

Go to Medical School

❖ If you live near a medical school, then you live near a discount clinic. Student dentists and ophthalmologists who work in these clinics either are about to graduate or have just graduated. They are carefully supervised and do professional-quality work, but their services may cost only half as much as those of established doctors. And since they are often still honing their bedside manner, you can give them some helpful suggestions on how to be more sensitive to patients' needs.

The Doctor Is Out

❖ If you want to shave a few dollars off your annual visit to the gynecologist, think about seeing a nurse instead of the doctor. Most gynecologists employ specially trained nurses who can perform annual exams and Pap tests, write prescriptions, and offer advice at a much lower rate. And it's much easier to schedule an appointment with them than it is with the doctor. Of course, if you have a problem, ask to see the doctor.

The 25-Cent Appointment

❖ When you need a quick consultation on your medication or a condition that confuses you, it's okay to pick up the phone and call the doctor rather than trying to schedule an appointment. Doctors aren't like lawyers; they do give free advice over the phone, especially those who work at teaching hospitals. Use this service to enhance your care without emptying your wallet.

❖ Many cities have services, listed in the phone book, that offer free advice to people who have questions about health care. They can tell you whether you need to see a doctor and can even recommend one. More important, they can tell you when you *don't* need to see a doctor—when a little rest, better personal care, and maybe some patience will get you through. One such service is called Ask a Nurse. Others like it are listed in the Yellow Pages under Physicians' and Surgeons' Information Bureaus.

Put Off the Inevitable

❖ The doctor has given you a prescription with a set number of refills. It's tempting to think that you have to make an appointment to get another prescription. That's not true. If you need to, you can often call and get a new prescription over the phone without going in and paying the doctor's fee.

Get a Substitute

❖ If you need a very simple procedure, such as a shot, consider whether the doctor is the best person to administer it. Most doctors rush from one appointment to the next. They also set a minimum fee for each appointment, even if it's just a walk through the examination room with a short pause to administer an injection. It's much easier and cheaper to schedule an appointment with the office nurse. Nurses know more than anyone else about giving injections, and they don't charge $100 a pop.

The Change Won't Do You Good

❖ You will never pay more for a single doctor's visit than you do the first time

---

WORLD-CLASS FRUGALITY

Humility Is a Home Remedy

President Calvin Coolidge (1923–1929) never liked salesmen much. So when his wife gave in to a sales pitch on an outrageously expensive textbook of medical remedies, she knew better than to tell Cal. She realized it was worthless, and since there was plenty of medical advice to be had in the White House, she tucked the book away in the parlor. Days later, she was paging through it, looking for some redeeming value, when she noticed her husband's handwriting inside the opening page. He had written, "This work suggests no cure for a sucker."

you see a new doctor. It takes time to gather your medical history, something the doctor usually does himself in an extended interview. Although it might feel good to have the doctor's undivided attention for so long, you'll pay for every minute. One way to cut down on this charge is to find a doctor you like and stick with her for as long as possible. If that's not an option, call your previous doctor and ask him to forward your records to your new doctor. That will cut down on the time and expense of your first visit.

Get a Letter of Introduction

❖ If you have to see a specialist, your first thought might be to worry about the expense. It's true that doctors who specialize charge more for their time than general practitioners. But you can cut this cost with your own doctor's help. Ask your doctor to write a letter to the specialist explaining your situation and your case history in detail and to send copies of any tests that have already been run. Before you go to the specialist's office, call to confirm that

---

IT TAKES MORE THAN AN APPLE A DAY

Every winter, when the cold season arrives, you'll catch what's going around if you're not careful. If a cold seems to be making the rounds in your office, here are a few things you can do.

1. Keep your office window cracked to allow fresh air in. You might think that cold air causes a cold, but stale air is a much greater incubator for airborne viruses. If you can't open your window, try to get out of the office once or twice a day.

2. Wash your hands several times a day. Most people don't catch colds from airborne viruses but rather through casual contact.

3. Take your vitamins. Keeping healthy levels of zinc and vitamins C and B will help keep bugs at bay.

4. Get some sleep. Colds and flu get you when you're down because of high stress levels and lack of sleep.

5. Throw away your toothbrush. Toothbrushes are a favorite hiding place for bacteria. Change your toothbrush at least every 3 to 4 months to keep from catching a cold.

---

the tests and the letter have arrived. If you see a specialist and she doesn't know your history, you'll waste valuable time and money giving this information again. More important, if you're sitting in a doctor's examination room and the x-rays and test results aren't in front of the doctor, she will probably order new tests and charge you for them.

The Other Club Med

❖ If you have a specific condition or illness and you want to keep informed of new research, the best way to do this may not be through frequent doctor's visits. No one is suggesting that you don't see the doctor, but no single health care provider can offer all the information you need. Many illnesses and rare conditions have support organizations that send out newsletters describing new research, new medications, and innovative ways to get the most out of your health care provider. If you suffer from any of these conditions, from diabetes to autoimmune disorders, you can join one of these organizations and get help and advice that your primary care doctor may not have or would charge for. Just ask your doctor about these organizations or search the Internet for their Web sites.

Free Clinics

❖ One way to save money on doctor's visits is to find another way to diagnose illnesses before they require medical attention. Most hospitals offer free screenings for everything from high blood pressure to depression. Large city hospitals hold several screenings per month. Call your local hospital to see whether you can get on its mailing list for newsletters that detail these free services.

❖ Many hospitals also offer free shots to prevent common ailments such as the flu. Some give free shots to prevent more serious conditions such as pneumonia. These preventive measures can save more than doctor bills. Older family members who have limited means and sparse health care plans often benefit the most from free health care.

CHAPTER 25

PERSONAL CARE FOR PENNIES

The trouble with trying to look good while saving money is that cosmetics and toiletries are sold by people who believe that consumers will spend any amount of money to look and feel better. These days, the people standing behind the department store cosmetics counters wear laboratory coats, as though their products have some secret scientific ingredients that make them work better. Modern fitness centers have enormous rooms full of shiny equipment and staffs of perky but pricey personal trainers. Infomercials try to sell you the most ridiculous gadgets to help you get in shape, while day spas offer elaborate facials and massages at "treat yourself" prices.

As a frugal consumer, you're probably skeptical about all these gimmicks. You may be thinking that you have a whole pantry full of products that can help you look and feel your best. And you're right. That mayonnaise in the economy-size jar could double as your cold cream. Those tomato cans could become your free weights. An old jump rope could be getting your heart pumping. A rolling pin could help you massage your feet. In fact, you could probably give yourself a complete facial right now without making a single trip to the grocery store, never mind a skin care center.

What's more, the yogurt, lemon juice, and club soda in your kitchen are all hypoallergenic and fragrance-free. Tell that to the cosmetics salesperson when she suggests that you buy a $60 firming mask.

SAVING MONEY ON COSMETICS

Fill 'Er Up

❖ You've probably noticed that even the tiniest eyeliners tend to come in big packages. It's as though the company has to make up for the high price with elaborate plastic packaging. Be good to the environment—and your pocketbook—by keeping an eye out for refillable cosmetics containers. More and more companies are providing everything from shampoo to lotion to lipstick in containers that you can bring back to the store and use again. They realize that ecological awareness and lower prices can equal brand loyalty.

Blush Detector

❖ When a favorite blush or lipstick runs out, it's tempting to run back to the same high-priced cosmetics counter to buy a replacement. After all, you already know that you like the color. But there's an easy way to hunt for a bargain replacement shade. Just take the last bit of makeup and smear it on a piece of white paper. Make sure you leave room on the paper for several more samples of makeup. Now take the paper to the drugstore and use the samples there to find a shade similar to the one you're using. It's almost impossible to test shades of makeup on your skin, but the paper will never lie.

Makeup Mop

❖ Beauty experts will fall faint if you mention that you remove makeup with a washcloth. They'll tell you that it's far too harsh for your skin. Then they'll try to sell you expensive gauzes or packages of cotton pads to do the same job. Actually, the softest and best way to remove makeup at the end of the day is with a homemade facecloth. Simply grab an old cotton T-shirt and cut the body into several 6-inch squares. Each square will work well as a facecloth. You can wring it out easily, it will dry quickly, and you can toss it in the washing machine when it gets dirty.

SAVING MONEY ON TOILETRIES

Elbow Grease

❖ If you have patches of dry skin on your heels and elbows, it's tempting to invest in an extra-strength moisturizer. But the truth is that good old-fashioned vegetable shortening will work just as well. Massage solid vegetable shortening into damaged or cracked skin. It will smooth, moisturize, and protect the skin just as well as lotion.

Putting Your Feet First

❖ The skin on your feet gets abused all day long. Yet it's difficult to moisturize them, especially if you're on them all day. The best way to soften the skin is right before bed with a generous amount of good old (and cheap) petroleum jelly and some cotton socks. As you sit in bed, apply the jelly to your feet, then put on the socks. Leave the socks on overnight. In the morning, your skin will be unbelievably soft because the petroleum jelly will trap the moisture in your skin.

❖ Turn this procedure into a soothing spalike treatment by having a heating pad handy. Drape the pad over your feet after you put on your socks. As you do your nighttime reading, the heat will help your skin absorb the petroleum

FRUGAL FORMULAS
HOMEMADE AROMATHERAPY

One of the best ways to relax is to find a scent you like and enjoy it. Most discount stores sell inexpensive scented candles that can fill a room with rose, lavender, or vanilla. You can also make your own scents by boiling some water on the stove and adding the scent you prefer. Add a cinnamon stick, some vanilla extract, a lemon wedge, or a couple of pinches of your favorite potpourri. The hot water will fill the room with the scent and lift your mood.

jelly and will relax you to boot. Be sure to turn the heating pad off before you go to sleep.

❖ For extra moisturizing, heat the petroleum jelly slightly by putting it the microwave for a few seconds or warming it in the top of a double boiler until it is runny but not hot. Not only will your skin absorb it faster, but it will feel wonderful. Warm petroleum jelly will soothe sunburn or any patch of raw, dry skin. It's the only intensive moisturizer you need.

MAKING COSMETICS AND TOILETRIES LAST

Frugal Foundation

❖ The problem with foundation is that it disappears so quickly. One way to use less is to add a bit of water to the foundation before you put it on. Pour half as much as you would normally use into your palm and add the same amount of water. Mix and apply. The foundation will go on more smoothly, and the bottle will last twice as long.

❖ This is also an excellent way to get the last bit of foundation out of the bottle. Put ½ teaspoon water in the bottle, replace the cap, and shake it up. The water will stretch your makeup for at least another day.

❖ If your foundation is oil-based, you can cut it with your favorite face lotion instead of water.

Lost Lipstick

❖ Your favorite shade of lipstick has been used down to the nub, but you still want to get a few more weeks out of it. The answer is to take a small makeup brush and scoop out the last little streaks of color. You'll actually be able to paint your lips with much more precision and get your money's worth.

Watching the Stars

My sister and I always had a lot of things in common. Shortly after we both married, we each had three kids, all of them boys. In those days, we took turns watching the kids to give each other a night out.

When it was my turn, we would go to the local science museum. I could get all the boys in on our family pass rather than having to buy seven tickets to a ball game or movie. I let the boys tear through the exhibits until their energy ran low, then I took them to the planetarium—not because *they* liked it but because I did.

We sat in the dark theater and watched the stars march over the horizon. During the half-hour show, we saw how the stars looked in the spring and the fall. The exhibit director told the stories behind the names of the constellations and showed us how the sky looked over Egypt and Paris. I'm sure the kids thought it was boring; sometimes they fell asleep. But I felt as though I'd traveled around the world. For me, it was the calmest time of the day, a minivacation from the mundane battles of motherhood.

—**Ellen Bean**
Somerville, Massachusetts

Black Mascara Blues

❖ The trouble with mascara is that it usually dries up and gets clumpy long before you've used it up. No problem. Use a few drops of very hot water to dissolve the clumps.

❖ A drop of baby oil in the tube will do the trick, too.

Paint Thinner

❖ The same thing always happens to your favorite nail polish. The more you use it, the more it dries out, getting thick and unwieldy. That last little bit invariably clumps up until it's unusable. Salvage it by adding a few drops of nail polish remover to the bottle. Like paint thinner, it will loosen up the clumps and allow you to get the most out of that bottle of polish.

❖ You can also store your nail polish in the refrigerator to keep it fresh.

Just Add Water

❖ If you want to get the last bit of lotion out of the bottle or you just want your lotion to last longer, add a few tablespoons of water to it. Most lotion is difficult to handle because it's too thick. Adding water will make it easier to apply and less greasy, too. Most times, your skin doesn't need moisturizer as much as it needs moisture. A little water added to the lotion will provide some moisture along with the lubricant that will seal it in.

LOOKING GOOD
WITH HOMEMADE TOILETRIES

Don't Hold the Mayo

❖ You'll never run out of cold cream if you buy mayonnaise in the jumbo-size jar. It's a terrific skin conditioner—better than lotion—because the egg helps firm the skin, the vinegar balances the pH level, and the oil adds moisture. It's chemical-free; it will remove makeup; and when you're done, you can use the extra in your tuna salad.

Don't Sow Your Oats; Wash with Them

❖ You've seen the oatmeal cleansing masks in the store. Make your own by combining equal parts oatmeal and plain yogurt. Apply the mixture to your face and leave it on for 10 minutes, then rinse it off. Oatmeal is a soft abrasive that will scrub away dirt and soak up oil.

❖ Yogurt will firm your skin with its natural acidity. If you use low-fat rather than nonfat yogurt, you'll be adding a bit of moisture to your skin, too, but either will work fine.

Corn-Fed Cleanser

❖ Instead of buying fancy abrasive cleansers, mix up one of your own. Take a tablespoon of cornmeal, dampen it with enough water to make a coarse paste, and add a few drops of liquid hand soap. This will make a gentle facial scrub that will cleanse your pores with a touch of lather but not scratch your skin.

Put These Bags over Your Eyes

❖ Get rid of puffiness under your eyes by using yesterday's tea bags. Black tea bags that are cool but still moist can reduce swelling. Just put one bag over each eye and leave them in place for 10 to 15 minutes.

❖ You can also use slices of cucumber to reduce swelling and cool the skin.

Dandruff Stuff

❖ You can battle dandruff without specialized shampoos if you have a little fennel in your spice rack. Steep 1 heaping tablespoon fennel seeds in boiling water and let sit until the water is at room temperature. Then strain out the seeds and pour the "tea" over your hair after you shampoo. There's no need to rinse it out.

It's Not Easy Being Green

❖ One danger of swimming in a chlorinated pool is that after a while, the chlorine tends to turn blond hair green. To keep your hair from turning green, wash it before the chemicals have time to dry in your hair. If you don't have any shampoo handy, use club soda to wash out the chlorine and the other chemicals that affect hair color.

Lose the Mustache

❖ To bleach the hair over your upper lip, don't run to the store and pay good money for a premade concoction. Rather, use ¼ cup hydrogen peroxide (6 percent) mixed with 1 teaspoon ammonia. Dab it on the hair and let it sit for 30 minutes before washing it off. It will lighten the hair without damaging the skin.

DO-IT-YOURSELF SPA TREATMENTS

A Facial Steam Bath

❖ You know that steam is good for your face. It melts the dirt in your pores and feeds your skin with moisture. What you might not realize is that you can steam clean your face without going to a spa. Boil some water, pour it into a shallow bowl, and lean over the bowl so that your face is directly over the rising steam but 6 to 8 inches above the surface of the water. Then drape a towel over your head to make a tent that will capture the steam. You can even add a few crushed rosemary sprigs, a few drops of mint extract, or some lemon juice to perfume the water and refresh your mood. After 10 minutes of this, your skin will be soft and clean. Pat your face dry, and you're ready to put your best face forward.

Beta-Carrot(ene)

❖ Many moisturizers feature beta-carotene extract, which is supposed to soothe the faint lines and wrinkles in your face. But most of those lotions don't have enough beta-carotene in them to do much good. You can do those store-bought lotions one better by using fresh carrot juice (available at most health food stores). Dab some on the corners of your eyes and let it sit for 10 minutes before

EIGHT STRESS BUSTERS THAT WON'T BREAK YOUR BUDGET

Finding the time and money to get away on vacation isn't always possible, but there are lots of easy ways to relax and get away from it all without spending too much money. Here are a few.

I. Take a bath. Mood lighting and scented candles can make this experience seem exotic.

2. Take a walk. Pick a particularly picturesque setting in a park, on a beach, or in a nifty shopping district with interesting boutiques.

3. Take a coffee break. Spending 15 minutes with some coffee or sweet-smelling herbal tea, a cookie, and some soothing music will fill all your senses.

4. Visit a museum. Looking at beautiful artworks in utter silence is inspirational and calming.

5. Start a journal. Spending 10 to 15 minutes everyday recording your thoughts will get them off your mind.

6. Try time travel. Look at some old pictures from childhood or visit the grocery store to buy your favorite soda or chewing gum to bring back simpler times.

7. Volunteer. A few hours a week working in a food bank or animal shelter will give you a new perspective on everyday stresses.

8. Laugh. Rent your favorite funny movie or go to the library and check out some old episodes of the Three Stooges, the Marx Brothers, or classic sitcoms. Laughter is the ultimate stress buster.

wiping it off. Then drink the rest of the juice. After all, the best way to nourish your skin is from the inside.

Make a Beeline for Healthy Skin

❖ If you have oily skin, you may think that you have to go to a skin care center to get a special face mask that will feed your skin without adding oil. Not true. You can make your own mask by combining ½ cup plain yogurt with ¼ cup honey. The acidic yogurt will nourish your skin without adding oil, and the honey will tighten the pores. Leave the mask on for 10 to 15 minutes, then rinse it off with warm water.

❖ To revive your skin after you rinse off the mask, splash on a little club soda.

Make-at-Home Mud Bath

❖ There's no need to pay for a mud bath, especially when you can make your own at home with powdered milk and potting soil. Pour 3 to 4 cups powdered milk into a bucket. Add enough water to give the mixture the consistency of

THE YANKEE MISER RECOMMENDS . . .
School Days

If you want to get a haircut, manicure, facial, or massage but don't want to pay the high prices charged by spas and beauty parlors, consider looking through the Yellow Pages for a salon operated by a trade school. Even hairstylists and manicurists have to go to school. Once students have completed their studies, they have to practice on someone. That's why the salons operated by schools are so inexpensive. In fact, they often charge less than half the cost of professionals running their own shops. These school studios are manned by students who have lots of training and not much experience. What they have instead is a fresh outlook and lots of enthusiasm—those things are sometimes hard to find out in the real world. (Don't worry, there's always plenty of supervision by instructors.)

glue. Then add sterilized potting soil 1 cup at a time. (This is available at most garden centers, or you can sterilize your own potting soil by spreading it on a cookie sheet and baking it at 180°F for 30 minutes—long enough to kill any bacteria.) Stir in the soil, adding enough water to keep the mixture at the consistency you desire. Continue to add soil and water until you have a muddy paste that will cover your body. Use the mud to cover any or all of the body parts that you want to condition. Leave it on for 15 to 20 minutes, then rinse it off in the shower.

Roll Out Sore Muscles

❖ The toughest part of giving a massage is using enough pressure to really work the muscles. The next time you give a massage, get out the rolling pin. You can roll out the kinks in anyone's back (or have them roll out the kinks in yours) the same way you roll out dough. Just remember not to roll over the vertebrae or other bones, because it'll smart like heck. You can even use the rolling pin on your own calf and neck muscles. Or put it on the floor and massage the bottoms of your feet. Make sure to wash the rolling pin thoroughly after any of these uses.

A Marble-ous Foot Massage

❖ Another way to massage your feet is to line the bottom of a shallow baking dish with a dish towel, then pour in some glass marbles. Put some weight on your feet and roll them over the marbles to massage them gently. You can also put the marbles in a resealable plastic bag and use that to massage your feet.

GETTING FIT ON A SHOESTRING

Use the Buddy System

❖ You don't need a personal trainer if you have a friend who wants to get in shape, too. You're less likely to break workout dates if someone is waiting for you at the gym.

Jump into Shape

❖ You're looking for a good alternative to walking or running outdoors in the winter, but you know that most people who buy exercise bikes end up using them to dry laundry. What do you do? Borrow a jump rope from your kids. Jumping for just 15 minutes a day will increase your aerobic capacity and burn the same amount of calories as a long walk. What's more, an inexpensive jump rope costs less than a paperback book and takes up less space than a single

THE YANKEE MISER RECOMMENDS . . .
Using Those Freebies

Every time you come home from a business trip or vacation, you bring along a collection of half-used hotel toiletries such as soap, conditioner, shampoo, lotion, and bath gel. They collect in a bin because you can't bear to throw them out, but you never use them. Here's how to take advantage of those freebies.

1. Put the soaps in a clean knee-high nylon stocking, or cut the foot off a fishnet stocking. Tie a knot in the stocking to hold the soaps inside. Now you have a homemade scrub brush for the shower.

2. Take all those tiny bottles of lotion and use them to fill one full-size bottle. Pour them into the larger bottle, then put a teaspoon of water into each small bottle to flush out the last bit of lotion. Watering down lotion doesn't ruin it. In fact, it makes the lotion easier to apply and less filmy on your skin.

3. Take each half-empty bottle of shampoo, fill it to the top with water, and gently shake it. You can get at least two more uses out of the bottle. Shampoo is just as effective at half the strength—though you may get only half the suds.

4. Take those used bottles of conditioner and fill them up with olive or peanut oil or whatever else you have on hand. Then, as you draw your next bath, drop the container into the bathwater, or heat it up in the microwave for a few seconds to make a hot-oil treatment for your hair. Use the free shower cap you got at the hotel to keep the hot oil on your hair for 10 to 15 minutes while you bathe. Then wash it out. You've just treated your hair to a special conditioner.

free weight. Of course, if you're not already in pretty good shape, you won't want to start at 15 minutes, because you'll be asking for shinsplints. Start with just a minute or two a day and work your way up from there.

Pumping Paste

❖ Instead of lifting artificially manufactured weights, try lifting the weights in your pantry. Tomato cans come in all sizes, from 1 to 3 pounds. These are excellent to use if you want to start weight lifting, especially if you're following along with a televised aerobic routine. Afterward, you can use them to make dinner.

Insure Your Good Health

❖ If you want to join a gym, check with your health insurer first. Some health plans will give you a break if you belong to a gym because they know that people stay healthier longer if they stay in shape.

❖ Some companies also pay part of their employees' memberships to gyms or fitness centers for the same reason. Check with the human resources department to see if your company supports good health among its employees. If it doesn't, you might suggest such a plan. It will help the gym by bringing in new members, and it will help you by cutting your monthly fee.

FINDING A PERSONAL TRAINER FOR LESS

On-the-Job Fitness Training

❖ If you want to attend an exercise class but don't want to pay the high fee, consider starting a class with your coworkers. If you can get 15 to 20 people together, you can put up flyers at area gyms looking for an instructor. Most exercise instructors are looking for extra classes to teach. You and your classmates can split the instructor's fee and end up paying only a few dollars for each class—much less than a studio or gym would charge. The added benefit is that you won't have to find exercise after work; it will come right to you.

Exchange Rate

❖ If you know someone who's an exercise fanatic, you may have found a personal trainer. Barter with someone who is willing to design an exercise program for you or teach you some specialized aerobic routine in exchange for learning a specialized skill of yours, such as cooking or home repair.

❖ Put up a flyer at a local college that has a physical therapy program. A college student may be willing to help you get in shape in exchange for using you as a reference when he starts looking for a full-time job.

WORLD-CLASS FRUGALITY
Jogging with the President

Theodore Roosevelt was fanatical about fitness, probably because he was so sickly as a child. Even when he was in the White House, with a schedule packed with important meetings, he exercised every day. He did not set aside time for exercise, as many busy people do today. Instead, he exercised all day long, during even the most important diplomatic negotiations. Visiting dignitaries were often amazed to find that they were expected to exercise with him, participating in vigorous games and trailing behind him on hikes.

Not only was Roosevelt inexhaustible, but he was surly, too, and he took no pity on those who couldn't keep up. Once the aging French ambassador Jean Jules Jusserand was summoned to the White House for a meeting and found himself playing two sets of tennis with the president, followed by a brisk jog and a workout with a medicine ball. Then Roosevelt turned to the panting Jusserand and asked, "What would you like to do next?" Jusserand replied dryly, "Lie down and die."

CHAPTER 26

FRUGAL WAYS TO DEAL WITH FINANCIAL EMERGENCIES

*W*e frugal folks respond to phrases such as "Let's go on vacation" with "How much will it cost?" followed immediately by "How can I pay less for it?"

But even the tightest of tightwads can get thrown for a loop when she hits what we euphemistically call bumps in the road. Those are the occasions when life tosses us a curve: the death of a loved one, a divorce, or some kind of legal wrangle. Not only are these situations devastating in themselves, but they also can cost a fortune.

Believe it or not, though, there are many frugal ways to deal with these sometimes unexpected jolts. All it takes is some planning and the ability to keep your wits about you in the midst of a little chaos. When a loved one dies, for instance, you're probably not in any shape to worry about saving money on funeral costs. But if you do some of the planning now, you'll be in a better position to save money then. Did you know that you can shop around for the best funeral prices? Or that funeral homes aren't the only businesses that sell caskets? There's more, too. Just keep reading, because life (and death) is hard enough—there's no reason to pay extra.

PAYING LESS DURING A DIVORCE

Time to Split

❖ Divorce is costly for many reasons, but primarily because it involves two lawyers. Not everyone getting divorced wants to go to war with his or her ex, however. In fact, many divorcing couples are simply looking to go their separate ways. If both parties are clear about what they want, they can lower the legal fees by hiring a mediator. Unlike a lawyer, who works only for one client, a mediator works for both parties. In a divorce, a mediator might help parents design a parenting agreement that works in the best interests of the children, whereas a lawyer would usually work to get the best arrangement for his client. A lawyer may still be needed to advise on complex issues such as alimony and division of property, but mediation can reduce the amount

FOUR THINGS YOU SHOULD KNOW ABOUT CREDIT AND DIVORCE

In the emotional throes of a separation or divorce, it's all too easy to let payments slide or not really notice what your soon-to-be ex is doing regarding various financial matters. To protect yourself, examine how the following issues might affect your situation and consult your attorney or your financial advisor.

1. If you maintain joint accounts, both you and your spouse are responsible for paying the balance, and both of your credit records will suffer if one doesn't keep up with the financial commitments. This is true regardless of what the separation agreement states about who will pay the bills. So if your ex isn't paying as agreed, consider securing payment through legal means.

2. If you divorce, you should probably consider closing any joint accounts or accounts in your name that allowed your spouse to act as an authorized user.

3. By law, a creditor cannot close a joint account just because your marital status has changed, but either spouse can request the change.

4. You can ask a creditor to change a joint account to an individual account, but the creditor isn't required to. The creditor could require you to reapply, and if you are the lower-earning spouse or do not work outside the home, you may have trouble. This is another issue you should address as you divide up your assets or if you are requesting spousal or child support.

of consultation time and, therefore, the cost. You can find a mediator by looking in the Yellow Pages under Mediation Services.

PAYING LESS FOR FUNERAL COSTS

It Was Good Enough for Grandma . . .

❖ Whatever else you may think about the funeral trade, the bottom line is that it's still a business. And that means the folks who run the funeral home will negotiate and work with you because (a) no matter how much they shave off the price, they're still making an enormous profit and (b) they want to keep you (and eventually all your loved ones) in the store. The hallmark of a good funeral home is customer service, and the best measure of its success is when someone says, "My family has always used Smith and Sons."

Nothing Is Set in Stone

❖ We hope that you're not reading this now in an effort to figure out what to do with Grandma's earthly remains. But even if you are, that doesn't mean you can't shop around for the best price. In most states, funeral homes are required to provide a price list on demand, in person or over the phone—with no questions asked and no obligation. So don't feel awkward about making inquiries.

Save for the Grave

❖ Are those ads that claim you'll "burden your loved ones" if you don't prepay for a burial site getting to you? Save money for your funeral and grave site, but put it in a savings vehicle your heirs can tap—don't actually prepay for a specific site. Typically, the amount you save by prepaying is nowhere near as much as you could earn in a savings vehicle for a few years. And the odds are just too great that you'll relocate or your family situation will change before your funeral, and your heirs may be stuck trying to resell a grave site, which isn't easy. Specify in your will which funds should go to pay for your burial. For the very well-off, there are some exceptions to this advice. Check with your tax advisor or estate planner to make sure willing cash won't cause your heirs grief with taxes.

Let Clearer Heads Prevail

❖ When making a trip to a funeral home during a time of need, bring along a friend—preferably someone who knows you and the departed well but who is emotionally removed enough to be able to assist with the questions

THE YANKEE MISER RECOMMENDS . . .
Don't Buy; Rent

One of the more expensive aspects of a funeral is the cost of the casket. A tour through a funeral home's showroom will start with its top-of-the-line models and end with the economy versions. By the time you see the cheapest, fabric-covered casket, it will look just that—cheap, compared to the sumptuous mahogany or cherry boxes. And that's how the funeral director will sell you.

A frugal Yankee knows that no matter how expensive the casket is, after it's seen by the relatives, it's going in the ground or a mausoleum. So why pay the premium price?

One way to save is to not buy a casket at all. All states have minimum requirements for caskets. The most minimal is a pressboard box called an alternate container. It's not fancy; in fact, it's what's used for cremations.

But even the most tightfisted miser may not want to be waked in something resembling a packing crate. So many funeral homes provide what they call a ceremonial casket. That's a mid-priced wooden casket designed to hold an alternate container for viewing during a funeral service. When the funeral is over, the alternate container is removed for burial or cremation. A fee is charged for the use of this casket, but the combined cost of it and the alternate container can be much less than the purchase of a mid-range casket. If the rental price seems exorbitant, negotiate. You can always take your business elsewhere.

the funeral director will ask. We're not suggesting that the people involved in the funeral business are out to take advantage of you, but when you're grieving, you may draw a blank on your loved one's middle name, Social Security number, or whether she wanted to be buried in her favorite bowling shirt. Of course, not everyone needs help. There's the story of the grieving widow who was too distraught to go to the funeral home herself but who sent her adult children to make the arrangements with this bit of advice: "Don't let them sell you the most expensive casket!"

Pay as You Go

❖ When a loved one dies, the first thing you need to do is have his remains removed from the hospital or home where he passed away as soon as possible. However, that doesn't mean you don't have time to shop around for a good price. Go ahead and call several local funeral establishments. It's perfectly acceptable to call one funeral home to take care of the removal and embalming, then have your loved one transferred to another funeral home for everything else. You are under no obligation to purchase any other services from the first funeral home, and you will still have a reasonable amount of time to compare prices. But if that funeral home knows you're shopping around, it should go out of its way to give you a competitive price.

All in the Family

❖ Find out whether the funeral home you're dealing with is family-owned or part of a major corporation. Why should this matter? Family-owned businesses' fees are usually considerably lower than their corporate counterparts'. You need to ask because you won't know by the funeral home's name. No matter who owns the business, the awning will probably say "Jones and Son" (or something like that). But that doesn't tell the whole story. With a little research, you may find that "mom and pop" are working for a conglomerate.

I Can Get It for You at Wholesale

❖ You need to shop for a casket, and your only option is to buy it from a funeral home, right? Wrong. Discount casket companies, listed in the Yellow Pages under Caskets, are the newest thing in the funeral industry. That's bad news for funeral homes but good news for you. Casket vendors are just that, vendors. They're not funeral directors, and they don't sell any other services. Since all they do is operate a showroom and directly represent the casket manufacturer, the cost for you can be as much as 40 to 50 percent less than what funeral homes charge. In most states, funeral homes are obligated to take delivery from a discount casket company and can't charge a handling fee. The funeral home may, however, try to discourage you from making an outside purchase by requiring you to be on hand to accept shipment and by not taking responsibility for the quality or condition of the merchandise.

A Final Gift from Uncle Sam

❖ Keep in mind that wherever you end up, buying a burial plot is essentially a real estate purchase. As cemetery prop-

WHAT TO DO IF YOU GET SUED, PART I

Oops. Your fence fell over and squashed the not-so-friendly neighbor's prize pumpkin patch. Face it, these days you might get sued. As common as lawsuits might be, there are few words that scare us more than "I'll see you in court." Even if you win the case, you know it's going to cost you. Don't just give in. Here are a few suggestions on how to survive the experience with a few dollars left in your pocket.

1. First, make sure you are being sued. If so, you've received a summons. If you're lucky, you may have received only a subpoena. A subpoena is an order to appear in court either to testify or to deliver certain documents. The actual case may not involve you in any other capacity. You may not need to hire a lawyer if you are not being sued. Get in touch with the clerk of the court for some free advice on how to proceed.

erty becomes scarce, the price goes up. However, if you've served your country in a branch of the military, including the U.S. Coast Guard or the National Guard, you're entitled to free burial in a national cemetery near where you live. That benefit is also provided to the spouse of a veteran, provided the vet is already interred there or plans to be. To find out more about the government's benefits for veterans, contact the Department of Veterans Affairs. You'll find the number in the government listings of the White Pages.

❖ Veterans are also entitled to a free headstone, no matter where they are buried. Contact the Department of Veterans Affairs to find out about this benefit.

Ashes to Ashes

❖ It's time for Grandpa to go to his final resting place. Burial expenses include a casket, a plot or mausoleum space, a grave-opening fee (to dig the hole), a burial vault (required in some places), and a grave marker. And none of this is cheap. Isn't there some way to do his thrifty memory proud? An alternative to burial and all it entails is cremation. A direct cremation (no embalming or viewing) is the least expensive funeral service, saving you as much as 90 percent off the cost of a full funeral. If a viewing is required, a body must be embalmed, but many funeral homes will provide a casket shell that is rented only for the duration of the service. The body is actually held in an inexpensive pressboard casket called an alternate container, which fits inside the shell and is used for the cremation. After the cremation, the "cremains," as they are referred to in the trade, are returned to the family for final disposition.

That's No Ashtray, That's My Auntie

❖ Unlike the myriad rules and regulations that each state has regarding what constitutes a proper burial container for human remains, most states have no requirements when it comes to the storage of cremains, the cremated remains of the dearly departed. So don't be coaxed into buying an expensive urn or other container by a funeral director. Rely instead on your sense of decorum and respect for your loved one's wishes.

❖ The burial of cremains is another story. There are a lot of laws regarding this. Check with your state's department of health. You can find the number in the government listings of your White Pages.

The Gift That Keeps On Giving

❖ Want to make a contribution to medical science and save money at the same time? The catch is that you'll have to die first. While you're still alive, donate your body to a medical school. When you die, the medical school will pay for transportation of your body and the final disposition of your cremated remains. Although most donations are arranged with a specific institution while the donor is alive, some schools will accept donation of the deceased with written permission of the next of kin. Medical institutions are not allowed to purchase a body for research or instruction, so don't expect a check. But there's little or no expense to the survivors. Arrangements can be made with any medical school that accepts donations. If there isn't one near you, you can get more information by contacting the National Anatomical Service. You can find its toll-free number by calling (800) 555-1212.

HIRING AND USING A LAWYER

It Pays to Specialize

❖ You wouldn't go to a cardiologist for a foot injury, right? Likewise, when you have a legal problem, don't think that just any lawyer can help you. For instance, if you're getting divorced, you shouldn't consult a criminal lawyer. Although many lawyers are capable of dealing with a broad range of legal issues, it's usually a better idea to see someone who specializes in the particular field you need. As with doctors, specialists may charge more for their services, but they are experts in their field and are less likely to run across a situation they can't handle. This will save you time and money in the long run.

You'd Better Shop Around

❖ Most legal procedures are finite events—and thank goodness, what with lawyers charging by the hour and all. Like paying for any other service, you can save money when hiring a lawyer by shopping around. Schedule appoint-

WHAT TO DO IF YOU GET SUED, PART II

2. Don't hit the panic button. If you've been served with a summons, think clearly about what you need to do next. Depending on where you live, you have 20 to 30 days to reply to it. The time limit will be stated clearly, as will the name and phone number of the suing party's attorney. Also, don't be thrown by the fact that the summons, in addition to telling you whom you're being sued by and what the complaint is, will state the compensation sought. That number will probably seem way out of proportion, which is a typical scare tactic used by attorneys. Generally, this amount will be a lot higher than what would actually be awarded.

3. Meet them halfway. If you are on speaking terms with the suing party—and even if you're not—ask whether they would consider media-

tion as opposed to going to court. Remind them that you would be sharing the cost of the mediator's services; that might help.

4. Time flies, so use it wisely. If you don't already have a lawyer in mind, shop around for one who's familiar with cases similar to yours. If you plan to fight, now's the time to get whatever paperwork or evidence you need to help your lawyer do his job.

5. Pay attention. If you ignore a summons entirely, you are admitting everything the summons alleges, and a default judgment will be awarded against you.

6. Maybe it is the principle of the thing, but don't cut off your nose to spite your face. Think about settling, especially if you'll need to pay more in legal fees than the cost of the settlement.

ments with at least three lawyers. Many lawyers will not hold an initial consultation without being paid for it, regardless of whether you end up hiring them or not, but it doesn't hurt to ask.

Get an Estimate

❖ Hire a lawyer only if she explains how you'll be charged for her services. Ask for a best-case and worst-case scenario and an estimated range for the time and cost of your case. If the lawyer can't do that for you, she probably doesn't have much experience with your type of case. That means you need to keep shopping.

What's the Good Word?

❖ One thing lawyers are especially good at is talking, so you already know that the one you're using sounds good in his own words. But how do you know that he isn't inflating his worth a tad? By asking for references. As anyone who's watched Perry Mason knows, the attorney-client relationship is privileged; however, most lawyers have clients who are willing to talk about their experiences. Ask the clients these questions: Did the attorney consult with them about their wishes and return calls promptly? Were the fees charged close to the initial estimate? Did the case proceed as predicted? Were there any unpleasant surprises? Were they kept up-to-date on the progress or setbacks of the case? If you like what you hear from the lawyer's former clients, you've made a good choice.

Stay Out of the Bargain Basement

❖ Lawyers often base their fees on their experience. A rookie attorney whose fee sounds like a bargain may not have enough experience to deal with unexpected situations and could end up taking more time to handle your case. By contrast, a wily veteran might charge more per hour but be able to handle your case more efficiently, saving you money in the long run. It never hurts to ask how long a lawyer has been in business.

Call (800) RIP-OFFS

❖ We've all seen the advertisements for lawyers who say they'll take your case and get paid only if you win. This is known as working on a contingency basis, and it may not be the best deal for you. Think of it this way: Many cases are fairly cut-and-dried affairs. If you were seriously injured or your property extensively damaged and someone else, fully covered by insurance, was clearly at fault, a competent attorney could easily and speedily handle your case for an hourly fee. Those who charge on a contingency basis will take a large proportion—at least a third—of the settlement.

Help Yourself

❖ One way to cut down on an attorney's billable hours is to do some of the work yourself. For instance, you can help with the paperwork by gathering documents, lining up witnesses, or writing the first draft of a contract. Make the best use of your lawyer's time by doing these and other routine tasks. Always ask your lawyer what you can do to help.

Put Me In, Coach

❖ There's an old saying that a lawyer who represents herself has a fool for a client, and that is doubly true when an amateur tries to represent herself. There's no substitute for professional legal advice, if that's what the situation calls for. In some cases, however, it is possible to represent yourself and still have a lawyer as a backup. Ask your attorney if she would be interested in

WORLD-CLASS FRUGALITY
Nothing to Steal

The French writer Honoré de Balzac lived in poverty for many years before his work caught the eye of publishers. For a long time, he lived in an unfurnished and unheated one-room garret, eating only bread and water. To amuse himself, he carved words in the walls. One wall read, "Rosewood paneling with commode." On another he wrote, "Picture by Raphael."

Balzac was still poor when he achieved some degree of fame, and he lived in a simply furnished one-room apartment. One night a thief broke in and was attempting to pick the lock on Balzac's desk. A laugh came from the bed across the room. Annoyed, the thief turned to Balzac and said, "I'm robbing you."

Balzac laughed even harder and said, "What risks you take to find money by night in a desk where the legal owner can never find any by day." Then he rolled over to go back to sleep.

acting as your legal coach: You'll do all the legwork, but you'll pay her for any consultation time. If you can't afford to hire a lawyer full-time, this may be a viable option.

Reach a Happy Medium

❖ If you have a legal dispute involving contracts, leases, small business matters, employment, or divorce, you may not need to go to court. Most civil (noncriminal) cases can be decided by a mediator. In fact, many small-claims courts are encouraging—and in some cases requiring—people to

---

NINE QUESTIONS TO ASK BEFORE YOU SUE

You may have a good case, but before you go to court, think about what the ultimate costs will be.

The thought of a large settlement may be tempting, but a lawsuit can be expensive and time-consuming. It's often better to settle disputes out of court. One way to do this is through the services of a mediator.

Negotiating or demanding payment, especially when backed up by the threat of going to court, can be productive and cost-effective. But if you're set on going to court, ask yourself these questions (which a good lawyer also will ask).

I. What's the suit all about? If it's not clear to you, it won't be clear in court.

2. What are your objectives in suing? Are you looking for fair compensation? Big bucks? Respect?

Revenge? Are you being reasonable?

3. Do you have credible evidence? Is it going to be difficult or expensive to come by?

4. You may be angry now, but are you in it for the long haul, if that's what it takes?

5. Who is your adversary? Are his pockets deeper than yours?

6. What does your adversary have on you? Will you lose business or suffer some other way, directly or indirectly, because of this suit?

7. If you're successful, will you be able to collect?

8. Will the settlement cover the costs of the suit?

9. Win or lose, can you cover the costs of your case, including your lawyer's fees, court costs, and expert witness fees?

---

settle disputes through mediation. If you are suing or being sued, ask whether the court sponsors or makes referrals to a mediation program. If not, look up a mediator in the Yellow Pages under Mediation Services. Mediators charge a fee for their services, but that fee is shared by both parties, and in most cases mediation is far less expensive than hiring two lawyers.

Get Out of Jail Free?

❖ You may think you're poor and therefore eligible for free legal representation. But if you have a job or own property and have to make an appearance in court, the judge probably won't agree. Every jurisdiction has its own rules as to who is eligible for free legal assistance, but most courts are very strict and require that the defendant be indigent. The seriousness of the charge also may affect the court's decision about whether a defendant qualifies for a free lawyer. A judge may determine that an employed defendant can afford the cost of representation for a minor charge but can't for a more complicated, potentially lengthy trial.

LEGAL SERVICES FOR LESS

No, No Notary

❖ Making your own will? Then save yourself a buck or two: Wills don't need to be notarized. However, you may want your witnesses to sign a short document called a self-proving affidavit before a notary public. Doing so makes the probate process easier. Your witnesses will not have to come to court after your death to swear that the will is valid.

And No, No Court

❖ A will doesn't need to be filed with any court or government agency, so don't pay your good money to anyone who says otherwise. A will does, however, need to be kept where your executor can find it easily when the time comes.

PART IV

Thriving Frugally

LIVING THE GOOD LIFE FOR LESS

ONE OF THE MAIN REASONS we're frugal is to have more money to spend at special times, so that we can decorate for the holidays, entertain friends and family, take a much-needed vacation, or buy presents for those we love. But in this section, we're going to extend the idea of saving *for* the "times of our lives" to include saving *during* those special occasions. In the following pages, you'll find oodles of ideas for cutting down on the good times expenses.

First, we'll look at the ways you can travel smarter. Of course, we're going to remind you that there's almost never a reason to pay full airfare and that nothing is set in stone when it comes to any travel prices. But did you know that you probably shouldn't rent a car at the airport, eat every dinner out, or travel alone when you can help it? Read on to find out why.

We also intend to help you see that going the whole hog on the holidays does not require you to empty your piggy bank. Why should you, when you can use fresh ingredients and materials you have around the house to create even the most sophisticated holiday fare? Let us introduce you to a new definition of Easter grass, show you how to use autumn leaves to make decorations, and give you a surefire way to mimic the expensive look of floating candles using a large glass bowl.

As for the gift list that invariably accompanies any special occasion, how would you like to stay on budget for once? Page through this chapter to get ideas for gifts that are perfect, not overpriced. In fact, many are perfectly free, and we trust that you haven't heard of them all. For example, ever thought about driving the newlyweds to the airport instead of anteing up for yet another useless gadget?

Speaking of tips that are out of the ordinary, do you know how to make edible centerpieces, natural candleholders, or a homemade horse race for a kids' party? All these ideas will make your gatherings more fun and affordable, and you'll probably start looking for other reasons to have people over. May we suggest a "clean out your freezer" party?

CHAPTER 27

FRUGAL FUN

*D*oes your tight budget seem determined to keep you from having fun? Don't despair. You can have plenty of first-class fun—dining out, attending the theater, cheering on sports teams—without draining your bank account.

The key to frugal entertainment is to use your resources wisely and to be flexible. Your best resources are the local newspaper and chamber of commerce. The paper lists most free and low-cost events and activities open to the public, and it may also contain coupons or sweepstakes for restaurant meals, movies, concerts, and so forth. The chamber of commerce can inform you of upcoming events and activities even farther in advance, as well as give you tips about lesser-known (and lower-cost) museums, gardens, and historic homes or sites. Just by keeping in touch with these two resources, you'll know about the all-you-can-eat ice cream festival in the park, the nearby garden tour, and the free concert on the boardwalk.

You can have plenty of fun for less money if you're willing to be flexible. For instance, have lunch instead of dinner at your favorite restaurant; you'll enjoy the same food for less. Head to the minor league field for a great game of baseball at a fraction of the cost of major league tickets. Attend a free showing by local painters or visit an art gallery instead of paying for transportation, parking, and admission to a major museum.

Don't want to go out? Stay home and share video rentals with friends, splitting the cost. Have a family game night. Organize a video or compact disc lending library with neighbors. Hold an annual neighborhood parade, with all the kids decorating their bicycles. (Award prizes to every entrant.)

As you can see, once you get your imagination rolling, there's no limit to how much fun you can have—or how little money you need to spend having it.

GOING OUT: PAINTING THE TOWN RED FOR LESS

This Is Child's Pay

❖ Eating out now and then is a treat, but with the kids in tow, the bill can climb pretty high. Call a few restaurants and find out which ones have kids' nights—one or two nights a week on which children eat free or at a significant discount. Then pack up the family and enjoy your meal out.

Make It a Special Occasion

❖ Does the bill for a nice dinner out make you choke? Call your favorite restaurant and ask about early-bird specials—dinners that cost less if you are seated by a certain hour, say 5:30 P.M. The bonus? Not only will your dinner tab be reduced, but you'll probably have better, more attentive service as well, because the waitstaff and kitchen will be less rushed than during the height of the dinner hour.

Take a Course

❖ Culinary school students love to cook for guests and often serve full-course meals at their own on-site restaurants for considerably less than their professional counterparts. So put their skills to the test. To find one of these schools, call your chamber of commerce or check the Yellow Pages under Schools or Schools—Universities and Colleges (Academic). Your palate—and your pocketbook—will be satisfied.

❖ Don't overlook vocational schools, which often offer cooking or restaurant training to teenage students. These students may serve lunch once or more a week to the public or may run an on-site coffeehouse after school. The next time you want to go out for lunch or a light snack, give the school a try. To get the name of a school near you, call your chamber of commerce or check the Yellow Pages under Schools or Schools—Technical.

Let's Do Lunch

❖ You love that special restaurant, but the dinner prices are sky-high. Try it for lunch instead. Chances are you'll be served the same food at lower prices.

Break an Egg

❖ Dinner at a restaurant can cost a pretty penny, so treat yourself to break-fast instead. You'll get good food and good service, and someone else will do the dishes for you—which is, after all, part of what eating out is all about.

What Goes Around Comes Around

❖ You and your friends like to dine out regularly, but the tab can be a bit daunting. So organize a gourmet dinner club. Each month, one person (or couple) cooks and hosts a dinner for the others. This is a great opportunity for cooks and guests alike to sample new dishes and menus, complete from soup to nuts. You can spice things up by trying ethnic or seasonal themes. Don't forget to add a little ambience to the dinner—an attractive table setting,

FRUGAL MEMORIES

What a Hoot!

Quite a few years ago, my husband and his brother, who came from a musical family, decided that instead of spending a lot of money to go out to hear music, they'd put on their own concert at home. So they invited several friends and their families to gather at our home to play music—folk, country, blues, whatever. We had so much fun at this first hootenanny that we organized another, then another.

Pretty soon, the "hoots" had grown in size and frequency. More friends came with their spouses and children, and all our children joined in as well. Since the hoots tended to last through an afternoon and into the evening, people began to bring food, so we ate and played for hours.

My husband has since passed away, but the music man's baton has been passed on to my son, who now gathers in our living room all his friends, their spouses and children, and my generation. I love seeing this tradition passed along, and I love dancing with my grandchildren. And through all these years, our hoots haven't cost us a single cent.

—**Madelyn Gray**
Amesbury, Massachusetts

good music, and appropriate attire. You'll have a wonderful time sharing a delicious meal with friends, and no one will go home broke.

Join the Progressive Party

❖ Dining out is fun—but one meal can blow your entertainment budget for the month. Instead, get together with some neighbors for a progressive dinner party. Start out at one person's home or apartment for appetizers, walk to the next one for your main course, and then walk to the third one for dessert and coffee. Everyone shares the cost of the meal, which is considerably less than a restaurant dinner. And as a bonus, everyone gets a little exercise between courses. You can even make this a regular event—once a month or several times a year.

WHAT'S THE BEST MONEY SAVER?
Buy the Book?

You're bombarded with coupons, special promotions, and discount offers by the restaurant industry, all claiming to take the bite out of the high cost of dining. Each of these offers applies to a single restaurant visit. Then there are those dining coupon books that offer discounts or free entrées at a variety of restaurants. Which is the best buy?

A. A single coupon

B. A dining coupon book

The dining coupon book sounds great, but if you chose (A) a single coupon, you're correct. First, you must buy the coupon book (which can cost up to $50), whereas conventional coupons are free for the clipping. To recoup the cost of the book, you must eat out a certain number of times. Second, if you don't already eat out often, the coupon book will encourage you to do so—and therefore spend more money than you normally would. (Don't forget to factor in transportation, parking, and babysitting costs.) If you do eat out often, you're still probably better off clipping a few coupons from the newspaper or taking advantage of special discount nights at your favorite restaurant.

Make a Concession

❖ As if movie ticket prices aren't high enough, when you get there the concession stand hits you with outrageous prices for popcorn, candy, and drinks. So beat the system: Have your snacks and treats at home before you leave. That way, you won't be hungry when you get there, and once the movie starts, you won't be tempted to leave. You'll save plenty on Good & Plenty.

Read It and Eat

❖ Got a special place you want to try, but don't want to pay full freight? Check your local newspaper, which may run weekly or monthly sweepstakes in which readers win dinner coupons, tickets to a movie or the theater, and the like. In most cases, you just fill out an entry form with your name, address, and phone number and send it in to the paper. Few people enter on a regular basis, so your chances of winning at some point are pretty good. The cost of your night out? The price of a first-class postage stamp.

Be in the News

❖ You know those free advertiser newspapers you see floating around town? Sure, they're filled with ads—but also with coupons for free or discounted dinners at restaurants, admissions to museums and sports parks, and the like. So pick one up. You may be surprised at how much you can save the next time you want to go out.

Go Minor League

❖ Don't want to pay the multimillion-dollar salaries of professional baseball players? No problem. Head to the minor league field nearest you. Ticket prices, parking, and food are all a fraction of major league costs, and the baseball game is usually just as good. If you're not sure whether there's a team near you, check a newspaper that publishes sports team standings; minor league game results will be listed. Call the sports department of the paper to find out where the team plays.

Enjoy the Sporting Life

❖ You love sports (and love to take your kids), but you just can't justify the cost of tickets, parking, and food. Head to your local high school gym, football field, or Little League field, where the games are free. If the game is outdoors, pack a picnic. Chances are you'll run into friends, and you can all cheer your lungs out for your favorite team.

Horse Around

❖ For a sporting event with a touch of class—and without a high price tag—go to a horse show. Most horse shows, in which competitors ride or exhibit their horses in different classes or events, welcome spectators. And many of them, including some of the larger ones, are free. Check with local newspapers, equestrian associations, or 4-H clubs for listings.

Form Your Own Team

❖ If you love sporting events but hate the prices, organize your own. Get several families together in a local park for a softball game, soccer game, footraces, or Frisbee-throwing or kite-flying contests. Take a picnic and enjoy dining outdoors as well.

Go Along for the Ride

❖ Is there a museum or special destination you're dying to visit but just can't spare a dime right now? Find out whether your child's class is going to visit the site sometime during the school year, then volunteer to go along as a chaperone. That way, you'll most likely get to enjoy the trip at a discount or for free.

Talk to the Animals

❖ Zoos and art museums are terrific places to visit, but they can eat a big hole in your wallet. So call ahead to find out whether they have any free admittance times or free special events. Most of these places have family nights, senior citizen days, and the like.

Do Rush It

❖ Professional ballet, theater, and symphony performances are wonderful, but they can put a pretty big dent in your pocketbook. So don't buy tickets ahead of time. Instead, call the day of the performance to find out approximately how many seats are available. If the odds look good, arrive at the theater in time to buy "rush" tickets—usually sold 15 minutes before the performance—at a fraction of the full price. The savings will be music to your ears. Remember, though, that not all theaters sell rush tickets, so call before you leave home.

Greet Performances

❖ Okay, so you're addicted to the theater or the symphony. But every time you indulge, your purse cries for mercy. Call around to a few theaters to ask if you may volunteer as an usher or ticket taker. That way, you can see as many performances as you want—for free.

Practice Makes Perfect

❖ Many professional performance groups hold open dress rehearsals for the public at a discounted rate. If you like a little culture in your life but don't want pay top dollar for tickets, call the box office to find out when you can attend a rehearsal performance.

YOUR MEMBERSHIP(S) COULD SAVE YOU MONEY

Check your wallet—not for money but for membership cards. Do you belong to the local public television station? Did you join the American Automobile Association (AAA) for car-towing insurance? If so, look back through your donation or application paperwork (or call the organization) for a list of entertainment discounts to which you're entitled. You may be surprised at the discounts for museums, zoos, aquariums, cultural events, and even stores that came with your membership.

More Is Less

❖ If you want to see a music or theater performance but don't want to pay full price, call the box office and ask whether there's a discount for groups and how many people constitute a group. If you can get a discount, gather a bunch of friends and head to the theater.

Play Peak-aboo

❖ At the theater and symphony, all performances are not equal—some are cheaper than others. Call to find out when the less expensive, off-peak performances are, such as matinees or certain weeknight shows. Then grab your opera glass and go.

Listen for Less

❖ College or university orchestras, chamber groups, and jazz bands are often quite good, and admission to their con-

FOUR GREAT PLACES TO SAVE ON DISCS AND CASSETTES

The retail price of compact discs (CDs) and cassettes can be a little steep. But if you shop around, you won't have to pay those high prices. Here are four places to get the music you want for less.

I. Pick through the trash. Spend a weekend visiting yard sales and flea markets for used CDs and cassettes. You'll pay pennies instead of dollars.

2. Buy preowned. Shop music stores that sell used CDs and cassettes. Some of these stores even offer trade-in credit for your old CDs

and cassettes, which you can use toward future music purchases.

3. Approach your friends. Offer to buy used CDs or cassettes from friends.

4. Take that special deal. Try one of the mail-order offers that appear in your mailbox. Often these involve "buy one, get one free" opportunities or the like. But be sure to read the fine print to determine whether you're really getting a bargain and to make sure you're not agreeing to any unwanted contractual obligations.

certs is usually nominal or free. So the next time you get the urge to attend a live music performance, visit the nearest ivory tower for a concert. You and your wallet may be pleasantly surprised.

Go Back to School

❖ If you love the theater but find the ticket prices too dramatic, head to a nearby college for a performance. Tickets will cost considerably less than for a professional show, and the students will appreciate your support.

❖ Alternatively, head to a local high school theater performance, which will cost a couple of bucks at most. The singing and acting won't be professional, but it will be enthusiastic. The students will appreciate your presence, and you're guaranteed a great time.

Park It

❖ Outdoor music or theater performances are one of the joys of summer, and many of them are free in public parks. Check your local newspaper or chamber of commerce to find out whether there are any free shows in your area.

❖ Alternatively, check your paper for exhibits by local or regional artists. Many artists organize group exhibits in public buildings (such as libraries or town halls). They're free, close by, and fun.

Be Crafty

❖ Got a hobby? Turn it into group entertainment. If you like to quilt, sew, craft, play the guitar, read poetry, make scrapbooks, or do any other hobby, get together with a group of like-minded friends on a regular basis—say, once a month. Meet at a different group member's home each time to enjoy your activity together and share tips or memories. The host could be responsible for simple beverages and snacks (or dessert), or the host could ask each person to bring something.

Be a Groupie

❖ If you have a special interest—anything from bird-watching or hiking to knitting or playing a musical instrument—join an organized group. Most likely, your group will be able to take special trips and attend special events or performances at a discount rate. You'll have fun doing something that you love and make new friends, all without breaking the bank.

Take a Walk

❖ Many towns and cities offer free walking tours. Just visit your town hall or call the chamber of commerce to get a map. Then set out to see the sites on your own. You'll see a lot more on foot than you would from a car or bus, and you'll burn calories instead of cash.

STAYING IN: SPENDING LESS ON HOME ENTERTAINMENT

Speak Categorically

❖ Watch your favorite music stores for "category" sales—for instance, an annual spring classical music sale or an annual fall jazz sale. Many stores hold these sales regularly, and you'll save quite a bit on your favorite music.

Set a Sales Record

❖ Save significant change on compact discs and tapes at your favorite music store by asking whether the store offers a frequent-buyer program in which customers buy a certain number of items and get the next one free or at a discount. Just be careful to avoid buying more than you normally would.

Cut It Out!

❖ Browse through your favorite music store for cutout bins—boxes that contain compact discs (CDs) or tapes from several years ago or early works of certain artists at a reduced price. Originally, cutout referred to albums with their corners cut off to indicate they were on sale. These days, holes are drilled in the plastic CD covers.

Off the Record

❖ If a musical artist you like is playing in town and you don't want to pay top dollar for concert tickets, head to your local music store, where the artist's compact discs and tapes may be featured as a special sales promotion. That way, you'll get to hear the music you love for less—and more than once!

Play the Game

❖ To heck with those expensive arcade games. Stay home and have a family game night instead. Get out the board games—Monopoly, checkers, whatever you and your crew like—and settle in for a night of fun together. Add some snacks, and you'll have a better (and cheaper) time staying in than you would going out.

❖ Alternatively, grab a deck (or two) of cards and gather the family for your favorite card games.

THE YANKEE MISER RECOMMENDS . . .

Calling the Station

I love my favorite music, but the prices for compact discs and tapes these days are octaves higher than they used to be. One day I got a terrific idea from a fellow music lover. I called my favorite classical music station (you can call any specialty radio station—jazz, opera, classical) and asked whether it had a preferred customer program or special listener's discount card. Sure enough, it did. The station sent me a discount card (free of charge, just for being a loyal listener) that's good not only at several music stores but also at coffee shops, restaurants, and other stores. I love using my card and listening to my favorite music—all for less!

Hunt for Game

❖ You have a trunk full of board games that you'd love to play, but some of the pieces are missing, and you don't want to shell out the shillings for entirely new games. You can put those games back into action by shopping at yard sales. Buy the same game (or one that uses similar pieces) for a few cents, then pluck out the pieces you need and add them to your own game. Store the yard sale game for future "parts."

Hit the Deck(s)

❖ You'd love to get together with family or friends for a good card game, but you aren't playing with a full deck. When you look through your drawer of cards, you realize that you have several decks that are missing a few cards each. Don't rush out to the hobby shop for a new deck. Just combine a couple of the ones you already have and lay out a game of memory. All the cards are placed facedown, and each player takes a turn flipping two cards over, attempting to make a match—say, two queens or two aces. Don't worry if there are odd numbers of certain cards in your new

THE YANKEE MISER RECOMMENDS . . .
Eating Religiously

I love to eat out, but I hate paying restaurant prices. If you're like me, however, having a good meal out is no problem. Check your local paper for listings of church suppers and breakfasts. These are usually held regularly—once a week or once a month at any given church—and they cost only a couple of bucks. You don't have to be a church member to go. You just have to enjoy good food and good conversation. These are fun meals for children, too.

Alternatively, call the town hall to find out whether the local firehouse holds pancake breakfasts or spaghetti suppers that are open to the public. Just like the church meals, these are cheap and hearty—and buckets of fun.

deck—you can use the extras as wild cards or decoys, depending on how tough you want to make the game. This is a great game for all ages.

Solve the Puzzle

❖ A night out on the town might be more than your purse can bear, so have fun at home instead. Get your spouse, family, or friends together for a puzzle night. Set up one large puzzle for everyone to work on. Or get competitive and set up two or more comparable puzzles and divide your group into teams. The first team to complete its puzzle wins.

Hit the Books

❖ Okay, so you've combed the yard sales, flea markets, and secondhand bookstores for some juicy novels for summer reading. But you can't find the titles you want, and the prices are still a bit more than you want to pay. So what's your alternative? Call a couple of public libraries and ask whether they have annual or semiannual book sales. Most libraries regularly sell off books donated by the public at pennies apiece. The best part is that when you're finished reading, you can donate the books back to the library for the next sale—and take a tax deduction (for the price you paid) for your charitable donation.

Try Pedal Pushers

❖ Want some low-cost entertainment with friends right outside your door? Organize a neighborhood bicycle parade. Announce a date and invite neighborhood kids to decorate their bikes (or skateboards or wagons). Ask a few parents to act as judges, evaluating each participant either at the start or finish line. Have the kids parade their entries around the neighborhood, then award a prize to each entrant (make up categories such as Most Original, Most Realistic, and Funniest. You can find little prize items (pencils, pads of paper, squirt guns) at a dollar store. Everyone will have a ball, and the event won't cost more than a few bucks.

CHAPTER 28

CELEBRATING ON A BUDGET

*J*ust because you're on a budget doesn't mean you can't entertain spectacularly. Sure, you may have to forgo the Dom Perignon and the beluga caviar, but who really eats that stuff anyway? Believe us, there are lots of ways to throw a shindig, to make your table look beautiful, to impress your friends and family, and to celebrate a joyous occasion without emptying your bank account.

First things first. Figure out how many people you're planning to invite. The number of guests often dictates the type of party you are going to throw—an intimate gathering for 5 of your closest friends or a family reunion for 50. In other words, you wouldn't book a hall and a caterer for a handful of guests, and you wouldn't invite every branch of your family tree to share their memories and your famous noodle casserole in your dining room (unless it can hold them all). Planning, and often ingenuity, helps keep the cost of throwing a party to a minimum.

Next, use your imagination and apply the frugal skills you've learned in other areas of your life to the party. Scout out money-saving ideas to get your party started and within budget. Look for those after-holiday sales, where you can pick up many holiday decorations and serving pieces for a song. Also around the holidays, check out the food or lifestyle section of your hometown newspaper, which usually offers many recipe ideas and fun party ideas to get you started.

Putting together a party on a shoestring can be a challenge, but it can also be a lot of fun. Ask guests to search their closets for tie-dyed shirts and bell-bottoms and throw a 1960s party. Or serve drinks in hollowed-out pineapples and coconuts for a Hawaiian luau party. And if guests ask whether they can bring anything to the festivities, let them. It will give them a sense of contributing, and it will give you one less thing to worry about.

The following ideas will help you throw the party of the year without having to pay for it into next year.

INEXPENSIVE PARTY IDEAS

Seconds, Anyone?

❖ Have you looked in the freezer lately? If you have more leftovers than freezer space, invite your friends over for a "clean out your freezer" party. It's a great way to entertain friends without breaking the bank.

HAVE A HEART

Want to wow your sweetie with a homemade cake in the shape of a heart? You don't have to buy one of those costly heart-shaped pans to make this masterpiece. All you need is two 8-inch baking pans, one round and one square. To make this project even easier, use a boxed mix (he won't know the difference, and some taste better than cakes made from scratch).

Bake the cake according to the package directions and let it cool. Cut the round cake in half. Place the halves, rounded edges facing out, on two adjacent edges of the square cake. Frost the entire cake with vanilla frosting (you can even tint the frosting pink with a few drops of red food coloring). Decorate the top with those little candy hearts that have sweet sayings on them (Love Me, Be Mine, and so forth). After your honey takes a look at this glorious cake, his heart will definitely be yours.

A heart-shaped cake looks special but is easy to make.

And the Winner Is . . .

❖ Award shows are the best excuse for a party. But unlike the stars, you won't have to spend a lot of money to throw an award-winning party. Create a menu to go with the theme of the show, whether it's Box Office Burgers with Best Supporting Fries or Chart-Topping Guacamole with chips. For party favors, put together a tape of the nominated songs and make enough copies to give to all your guests. (Many blank cassettes come in inexpensive bulk packs, which will add to your savings.) To add to the fun, put together your own ballot of the nominees and hand them to guests as they arrive. The person who guesses the most winners will get his own award: your award-winning "Rocky" Road Pudding.

Do You Remember When?

❖ Nostalgic for those football pep rallies and school dances? Many people live far away from where they grew up, and getting back home can be expensive. To keep your friends from getting homesick, why not plan a high school "reunion"? Invite guests to dress in the style that was popular when they were skipping homeroom, and spin some tunes that were at the top of the charts way back when. For inexpensive decorations, hang up old school banners, 45 rpm records, or posters. To help keep entertainment costs to a minimum, have your guests bring their high school yearbooks and any mementos from their school days. Imagine how much fun you'll have strolling down each person's memory lane.

Pass the Pasta, Please

❖ Do all your friends claim to have the best recipe for pasta primavera or fettuccine Alfredo? Let them earn their bragging rights at a pasta potluck dinner. Ask each guest to bring a different type of pasta dish (macaroni salad, tuna noodle casserole, baked ziti, and so on), along with the coveted recipe written on index cards to give out to the other guests. And to make sure you aren't swamped with too many leftovers, ask guests to bring along food storage containers to take home some of their favorites. They'll thank you when they don't have to cook the next night—and possibly the night after that.

INVITATION IDEAS

Through the Years

❖ Who doesn't love to look at old baby pictures? For a unique wedding invitation, gather up old photos of the bride and groom and create a collage. Draw a border ½ inch from the edge of an 8½-by 11-inch piece of paper. Arrange the baby pictures within the border and attach them with glue or tape. Next, head to the copy store or library to photocopy your collage. Use a black-and-white machine to add to the nostalgia of the photos (plus, black-and-white copies usually cost less than color copies—only about three to five cents each). Fold the copies in half, with the photos facing out, and write the information for the wedding inside. Your guests will appreciate the personal touch, and the homemade invitations will help you stay within your budget.

Birthday Surprise

❖ Looking for an inexpensive idea to spruce up your birthday invitations? Just before you seal the envelope, add some confetti to the inside of the card. When your friends open the invitations, they

FRUGAL MEMORIES

Off to the Races

When I was growing up, birthday parties weren't as elaborate as they are today. We didn't hire magicians or people dressed as our favorite cartoon characters. Many parties consisted of eating several large pizzas and playing some party games in the comfort of our living room. One of my favorite party games was a horse race my father made with his own two hands.

He taped several sheets of strong poster board together and used a marker to draw the lanes and mark the start and finish lines. For the horses, he drew several horse heads on heavy-duty construction paper, cut them out, attached them to sticks, and inserted them into cardboard boxes. With a roll of the dice, my friends and I were at the races. We'd move the number of spaces indicated by the dice, and the first one to cross the finish line was the winner.

Our game became so renowned that other parents asked to use it. And if horses weren't too popular, they'd use miniature cars and transform the race into the Indy 500.

—**Lynn Naliboff**
Stamford, Connecticut

will love the festive theme and the special touch. Don't want to spend your hard-earned dough on store-bought confetti? No problem. Use your hole punch and some scrap construction paper or wrapping paper to make your own.

Picture Perfect

❖ How do you thank your guests for attending your party? Sometimes it's not easy to express in words how glad you were that your friends and family could celebrate with you. But you know what they say: A picture is worth a thousand words. Many photo shops offer a second set of prints for a nominal amount, if not free. Next time you develop the film from an event, order a second set of prints. When you send your thank-you notes, enclose photos of the corresponding guests to remind them of how much fun they had at your party. They'll think they're very special to receive such a thoughtful note—and they may even want the negative of that picture of your cousin with the lamp shade on his head.

Tickets, Please

❖ The next time you plan to throw a Super Bowl or World Series party, send out invitations that look like tickets. This will give guests the impression they are going to a main event without paying a main event price. Cut some construction paper into strips and include all the necessary information, such as what the event is, the date and time, the person's seat number, and a disclaimer at the bottom of the "ticket" that informs them not to forget the chips. When guests arrive, stand at the door and take their tickets—but make sure they get their ticket stubs.

These invitations are just the ticket for your next party.

Scenic Postcards

❖ Here's a way to save on postage when sending out invitations: Use postcards. The postage is less than for a stamped envelope. Choose an array of postcards—scenic mountain views or something that matches the theme of your party—and write the who, what, where, and when on the flip side. You can usually find postcards for a nominal fee at card stores, or why not raid the stash you've collected from past vacations. For an invitation-turned-decoration, have guests bring their postcard invitations and use them to create a collage to hang on the wall.

ELEGANT SERVING IDEAS

Bowl 'Em Over

❖ For a cool and inexpensive serving idea for cold shrimp or fruit salad, create a freestanding decorative ice bowl. You will need two stainless steel bowls, one larger than the other. Place the larger bowl in the sink and fill it with water. Now place the smaller bowl inside it so that the water fills up the space between the two bowls and so that there's at least a 1-inch space between them. (Make sure the water doesn't spill over the sides.) Secure the bowls with electrical tape or some other waterproof tape. Give your ice bowl some color by sprinkling edible flowers, fresh herbs, or citrus peel strips in the water. Place the bowls in the freezer and leave them overnight. The next day, take the bowls out of the freezer and let them sit on the counter for 10 to 20 minutes to melt a bit. That will loosen the bowls. (Do not run them under hot water, which will melt too much of the ice.) Remove your ice bowl and return it to the freezer until you're ready to use it.

Serve vegetable skewers in half a grapefruit for a festive look.

Veggie Tree

❖ Are you still serving vegetables and dip in that same old serving tray Aunt Edna gave you for your wedding 20 years ago? If buying a new serving tray is not within your budget, try this innovative idea. Plant a tree—an appetizer tree, that is. Arrange cut vegetables on wooden skewers or kebab sticks. Cut a grapefruit in half and squeeze out the juice. Place one half cut side down on a paper towel–lined plate. Insert the skewered vegetables into the rind. Remove all the pulp from the other grapefruit half and fill it with dip. You can serve this dramatic-looking appetizer on Aunt Edna's platter, but it will never look the same.

Bell of the Ball

❖ Many foods can do double duty as serving pieces, but bell peppers are among the best. Most varieties are inexpensive, and you can easily core, seed, and fill them with any number of prepared foods. Appetizers such as dips and salsa and main dishes such as ground beef and rice and

NOT JUST FOR COOKIES ANYMORE

For quick and easy garnishes or food presentations, look through the cookie cutters you've accumulated through the years. It's easy to turn a plain, frosted cake or simple sandwiches into fun and fabulous fare that will delight your guests.

1. Simple stencils. Place cookie cutters on top of frosted cakes for a simple stencil idea. Dust the inside of the cutters with colored sugar for a decorative look.

2. Sandwich cutouts. Use large cookie cutters, such as flowers and stars, to cut sliced bread into fancy shapes. Spread with your favorite fillings for festive sandwiches that will be the hit of the party.

3. Veggie cutups. For a simple salad garnish, use aspic cutters (which look like tiny cookie cutters)

to cut bell peppers, carrots, cucumbers, and zucchini into fun shapes.

4. Fabulous fruit salad. You can also use aspic cutters to make a fruit salad that will wow your guests. Use them to cut fruit such as watermelon, honeydew, cantaloupe, strawberries, pears, or apples.

5. Shapely pancakes. You don't need a culinary degree to turn ordinary pancakes into a work of art. Grease your metal cookie cutters and place them on a prepared griddle or skillet. Pour the pancake batter into each cutter just until it fills the bottom of the shape. When the top of the pancake forms little bubbles, gently lift the cookie cutter off the pancake. Flip those flapjacks with an offset metal spatula or pancake turner and continue cooking until they're done.

beans are all good choices. With the many colors available—green, orange, yellow, red, and purple, for example—you can use different-colored peppers for an even brighter presentation.

South of the Border

❖ If you plan to make tacos for your next fiesta, use that old chip and dip platter (the one with the separate compartments) to serve your toppings. Not only will it look festive, but it will give you another reason to use the platter, helping you to get your money's worth out of it.

GOURMET GARNISHES

Restaurant-Style

❖ Looking for a way to make that inexpensive dessert look expensive? Make any dessert look as if it came from the finest restaurant with just the flick of your wrist. Dip a fork in chocolate sauce (or any sauce that complements your dessert) and drizzle it on each dessert plate. Place each serving in the center of the plate, being careful not to disturb your masterpiece, and serve. Your guests will think that you hired a gourmet chef.

Lemons with Zest

❖ Before you set out those lemon halves for your guests, wrap them in cheesecloth and tie the ends together with some raffia or kitchen twine for an attractive yet practical garnish. When guests squeeze the lemon halves onto their food, the cheesecloth will catch those unruly seeds and help reduce the random juice that often goes flying into the eye of the person seated next to you.

A Bundle of Vegetables

❖ Use fresh chives or scallion tops to tie up zucchini, carrots, or green beans for veggie bundles. Cut the vegetables into matchsticks and, gathering a few at a time, tie them together with a chive or scallion. Set them around a roasted turkey or pork loin for an impressive and cost-efficient presentation.

Stencil Top

❖ You don't need to go out to the cooking supply store and buy expensive cake stencils to dress up your cakes and desserts. Just use what you have on hand. Paper doilies, craft stencils, and other open-patterned material can do double duty as a cake stencil. Place the stencil on top of an unfrosted cake and dust with confectioners' sugar, cocoa, or colored granulated sugar. Gently lift off the stencil so as not to disturb the design.

CENTERPIECES AND TABLE ACCENTS

All about Herbs

❖ Instead of purchasing an expensive bouquet of flowers, fill a vase with fresh herbs. Choose from fresh rosemary, sage, basil, parsley, and lavender. Coordinate your herbal bouquet with the flavors of your meal. Or create individual bouquets for each place setting by tying a few sprigs of herbs with strips of cheesecloth or kitchen twine.

Floating Candles

❖ Want a dramatic look for your next dinner party? Fill a large glass bowl with water. Place several small candles, such as tea lights or votives, in the water along with some flower petals. Light the candles and enjoy the ambience.

An Edible Centerpiece

❖ Assorted fruit makes a great—and frugal—centerpiece. Arrange the fruit on a decorative platter (a three-tier server works even better). Place larger fruit, such as apples, oranges, and bananas, on the bottom and smaller fruit, such as cranberries, strawberries, and blueberries, on top. And after everyone has admired your centerpiece, serve it for dessert.

Lovely Linens

❖ Searching for a way to use those old bedsheets? Why not use them as tablecloths? Flat sheets are great for larger tables when a regular tablecloth doesn't fit. If they are too plain, use fabric paint and stencils to decorate them, or apply appliqués to dress them up.

Apple of My Eye

❖ When you're setting the table for a dinner party, a small decoration, such as place cards, helps dress it up. For inexpensive homemade place cards, cut out leaf shapes from green construction paper and write your guests' names on

CELEBRATING ON A BUDGET

USE A LITTLE GARNISH A-PEEL

You don't need a fancy and expensive gadget to create beautiful garnishes. Search through those overstuffed kitchen drawers, and you may find the one item that can handle all your garnish needs: the beloved vegetable peeler. This old standby can launch a thousand garnishing ideas. Here are just a few to get you started.

1. Squash ribbons. Use these ribbons to make edible knots to accent a summer squash medley, or just blanch them and arrange them around your favorite chicken dinner. Wash and dry an unpeeled squash and slice it in half lengthwise. Lightly drag the vegetable peeler over the squash, creating thin ribbons.

2. Striped cucumbers. For delicious filled cucumbers with thin stripes, drag the tip end of the vegetable peeler down the length of an unpeeled cucumber. Create wide stripes with the blade, peeling ¼-inch strips from the cucumber. To fill these striped delicacies, cut them into thick slices and use a melon baller or grapefruit spoon to scoop out the seeded area—taking care not to go all the way through. Then just spoon your favorite filling into the center.

3. Chocolate accents. Use your vegetable peeler on a block of chocolate to make chocolate shavings. Arrange them on top of a cake or press them against the sides.

4. Citrus strips. You don't need a zester. Instead, use a vegetable peeler to create those strips of zest to garnish everything from lemon pound cake to orange sherbet.

them with a gold marker. Attach each leaf to an apple stem, then set an apple at each place setting for a simple yet elegant decoration.

FRUGAL FAVORS

You're on a Roll

❖ Save those cardboard paper towel, plastic wrap, and aluminum foil rolls. You can easily convert them into fun party favors. Fill the rolls (cut the long ones in half to make two) with assorted candies and trinkets. Wrap them with brightly colored tissue paper, then cinch the ends with ribbon to make English-style party crackers.

Seeds of Love

❖ For an inexpensive bridal shower favor, offer the guests flower seed packets in small flowerpots. Many seed companies and garden stores offer seed packets in bulk for a low price, and some flowerpots can be had for under a dollar. Your guests will appreciate the long-lasting reminder of your shower as they stop and smell the roses.

Garden Bouquet

❖ Gather a small bunch of fresh herbs and tie them together with a ribbon for an herb bouquet. Attach a card with some cooking ideas for these herbs, then place one bouquet at each table setting.

Practical Favors

❖ Many times when we go to parties, we receive favors that sit in our junk drawers for many years to come. (Remember that miniature lace umbrella you received from your cousin Nancy's bridal shower?) Next time you're deciding on favors, choose something your guests can use, such as a fun refrigerator magnet, a small picture frame, or a wacky key chain. Many party stores sell such favors in large quantities at a reasonable price.

CHAPTER 29

HOLIDAYS AND GIFT GIVING ON A BUDGET

*M*ost folks love the holidays: a little bit of glitz and glamour, the warm comfort of friends and family, the thrill of finding the perfect gift. But let's face it, the holidays also generate their share of stress, whether it's setting the perfect Thanksgiving table, decorating the ultimate Christmas tree, or tracking down a unique gift for Uncle Harry, who has everything. To top it off, between decorating and gift giving, the holidays are expensive.

Relax. We're here to help you celebrate the Yankee way, which means creatively and on a budget. As one Yankee advice giver says, presentation is everything. In other words, with some personal touches and attention to details, you can produce an elegant holiday decorating effect or come up with a lovely gift for any occasion without spending a lot of your hard-earned money. Think personal: Put together a scrapbook of photos and mementos from a trip that you took with a friend and give it to the friend as a birthday present. Think small (that is, details): Add sparkle to your Christmas tree with costume jewelry draped over the boughs.

The great thing about today's holiday decorating and gift-giving trends is that unique and homemade are in. You don't have to sacrifice an ounce of style even if you do shave off a few dollars here and there. Make your own Easter basket from an old straw hat decorated with bits of fabric, ribbon, lace, and such. Put together a recipe box with handwritten recipes from family and friends for a newlywed couple. As you can see from these suggestions, you don't need to own a box of tools or craft supplies to make these ideas come to life, nor do you need loads of time and artistic talent.

Finally, gifts do not necessarily have to be things; they can be gifts of your time. Cook a simple, homemade meal for a couple with a newborn baby. Offer to clean an elderly friend's house once a month for a year. Volunteer to paint a room in someone's home. This is just the beginning. We'll show you lots of ways to jazz up your home for the holidays and make your loved ones feel special by using your ingenuity instead of your income.

CHRISTMAS

Go for Faux

❖ Spruce up the hallway (or wherever you hang winter coats and hats) for the holidays by sticking a few branches of those inexpensive faux greens in the pockets of coats you don't wear every day. You can usually buy faux greens for less at discount craft stores than at garden centers. Don't use real greens, which can leak sap onto your garments.

Go Nuts

❖ Get a head start on your holiday decorating by walking the woods during autumn. Collect pinecones, acorns, walnuts, chestnuts, and the like. Wipe them clean with a paper towel or soft rag and keep them in a dry place. When you're ready to decorate, paint them with gold or silver spray paint (available at craft and hardware stores). Do this outdoors or in a well-ventilated area, protecting any nearby surfaces with newspaper or paper towels. When your practically price-less gilded treasures are dry, arrange them in a pretty bowl—crystal, silver, ceramic, or wood. Add a rustic touch to your decoration with twigs or evergreen boughs arranged around the base of the bowl.

Play Pickup Sticks

❖ Make a free and easy decoration from your backyard and do one of those weekend lawn chores at the same time. Walk around your yard picking up long twigs. Spray-paint the twigs red, white, silver, or gold (or any combination of these) while you're outdoors or in a well-ventilated area. Then stand the twigs in a tall container, such as an umbrella stand, in the front hallway or living room. For an added touch, tie them together with holiday ribbon. Your picked-up sticks arrangement will make a rustic and dramatic holiday statement.

IT WORKED FOR ME
Create a Chain of Command

I love getting Christmas cards from friends and family, but I can't bear to throw them away. I also like to stay on a budget when it comes to decorations, so I figured out a way to turn each card into a decoration using a technique I learned in kindergarten. At the end of the holiday season, I collect my cards and stash them in a box. The following November, I get them out and begin cutting. I cut off the fronts, then further snip each front into three long strips. I bend the first strip in half (but don't crease it), gently curling it around my fingers, and staple the ends together to create a loop. Then I fold the next strip, slip it through the loop created by the first one, and staple it to form a chain. I've done this for many years now, hooking each new holiday chain onto the chain from the previous year and draping it over the mantel, up the banister, and across doorjambs. Now that my two daughters are old enough to help me, it's even more fun. I store the chain in a heavy cardboard box so that the links don't get crushed.

—**Debi Wheeler-Bean**
Exeter, New Hampshire

Turn old Christmas cards into decorative chains.

'Tis the Season

❖ For creative ornaments and decorations that are light on the wallet, make them yourself. All you need is flour, salt, and water to make a dough that can be molded, baked, and decorated. Combine 1 cup salt, 2 cups all-purpose flour, and 1 cup water in a medium bowl and stir until the mixture forms a dough. Knead until it is elastic and smooth. You can tint the dough with food coloring and cut out shapes using cookie cutters, or you can create shapes by hand. Bake at 250°F until the ornaments are hard and dry, about 2 hours. Let them cool completely, then paint them with food coloring, watercolors, or acrylic paint.

Winter Wonderland

❖ You can make a spectacular "scent"erpiece for a holiday bash with evergreen boughs, pinecones, and fresh cranberries. Start your masterpiece by arranging the boughs in a ring on a cake stand or serving platter. Place the pinecones in the center of the ring, then sprinkle cranberries over all. Want a little sparkle? Add some silver icicles to your creation.

WHAT'S THE BEST MONEY SAVER?
The Best Wrap

You have a gift to wrap, and you can't decide what type of paper to buy. Which would you choose?
A. A roll of wrapping paper
B. A package with two sheets of wrapping paper
C. A gift bag

If you're thinking like a Yankee, you'll select (A). Why? The roll of wrapping paper will give you the most flexibility. You can wrap several gifts of all sizes, resulting in the least amount of wasted paper. And, of course, you can decorate the empty roll to look like a giant candy cane when the paper's gone. The package has two precut sheets, which may result in more wasted paper. A single gift bag often costs the same as a roll or package of wrapping paper, and after one use it's gone.

Switch Places

❖ Add holiday color to lighting switch plates throughout your house. Buy several cheap ones and cover them with festive wrapping paper. Lay the switch plate on the paper, on a flat surface. Cut the paper so that it is large enough to cover the front of the switch plate and wrap around the back about ⅛ to ¼ inch. Cut a hole in the center for the switch. Then glue the paper to the plate with any type of all-surface glue, polyurethane, or decoupage material. Add gloss to the outside surface with a coat of polyurethane or decoupage. Then screw the plate back on and flick on the lights. After the holidays, simply put your fancy switch plates in storage and replace them with your everyday ones.

Add a Little Salt and Pepper

❖ Don't have fancy holiday candleholders? No problem. Instead of buying designer holders, buff up an old pair of crystal or silver salt and pepper shakers—the kind with the screw-on tops. Then insert your decorative candles into the shakers. If necessary, use softened paraffin or florist's wax to adjust the fit of the candle in the shaker.

These Babies Are Old Enough to Vot(iv)e

❖ You love the look of votive candles flickering around your home during the holidays but don't relish the thought of buying them at the downtown boutique. Just gather up those old glass baby food jars, or any other small glass jars you have around the house, remove the labels, and scrub the jars clean. Place a votive candle in each, leaving the lid off the jar, then arrange the candles as you like.

❖ For a stained-glass effect, apply colored tissue paper to the outside of each jar with decoupage material or polyurethane (both are available at craft and hardware stores).

❖ If you're feeling really crafty, sketch a design on the outside of the jar with a permanent marker and paint it with acrylic paint. The paint will produce an even more authentic stained-glass effect.

Don't Break Out of the Mold

❖ Add a country look to your home by placing votive candles in empty copper or tin gelatin or ice cream molds that you already own. (If you don't own any, you can pick these up at a yard sale.) When the holidays are over, the molds can go back in the kitchen cupboard or hang on the wall as decorative accents.

SIX TERRIFIC THEMES FOR GIFT BASKETS

Gift baskets are wonderful for many occasions. The best (and most frugal) is one you fill yourself—and you can save even more if you think like a Yankee. First, set a budget and stick to it. Second, buy an inexpensive but attractive basket at a discount store or use one you've saved from a flower arrangement. Third, decide on a theme. Hunt for your treasures at the supermarket, discount shops, even flea markets and yard sales. Here are six great ideas for basket themes.

1. A champagne celebration. For newlyweds or an anniversary couple, line a small basket with linen napkins or dish towels, two champagne flutes, and a bottle of wine or champagne.

2. Baby needs. Supply new parents with the basics in a large but inexpensive basket: washcloths, baby wipes, juice or milk bottles, bibs, and so forth. They can use the basket as a wastebasket or toy basket in the baby's room.

3. Entertaining necessities. For a hostess, fill a basket with paper goods (coordinating plates, napkins, and so on) purchased on sale at party outlets and discount stores.

4. Gardening supplies. For the gardener, pack a basket with gardening tools, seeds, even a few bulbs or annuals for planting.

5. Kitchen basics. For a newlywed couple or recent graduate, fill a basket with basic kitchen utensils such as a spatula, tongs, and wooden spoons.

6. Fun and games. Need a gift for a small child? Cram a basket with beach toys or coloring and craft supplies such as crayons, paper, glue, and tape.

Join the Bucket Brigade

❖ For a dramatic lighting effect during the holidays, fill a crystal bowl, a galvanized bucket, or any other unusual container you have around the house with water that you've colored with red or green food coloring. Float votive candles on the water (use votives that are only about 1 inch tall). Nestle the container among greens on the dining table or sideboard, or forget the greens and let the natural beauty of your container shine through.

A Bowlful of Memories

❖ Don't toss out those old glass ball ornaments that admittedly have seen better days. Even if their finish is mottled or crazed and you don't want to hang them on the tree, you can still use them to decorate. Gather your ornaments and arrange them in a pretty bowl, then place the bowl on your dining table, a side table, a mantel, or even a shelf. Not only will they serve their original festive purpose, but they'll remind you of Christmases past.

❖ Another reason to hold on to those glass ornaments? Many are now considered highly collectible.

Branch Out

❖ Get more from your Christmas tree dollar by visiting a tree farm, where you can cut your own tree. A tree from a farm may be less expensive because you're doing the chopping. More savings come when you trim the lower branches around the trunk before putting it in the stand. You can use those extra greens to decorate the mantel or dining table. Buying these greens at the garden shop or nursery will cost you extra during an expensive time of year.

Have Yourself a Merry Little Christmas

❖ Why not get two Christmas trees for the price of one? Make a miniature tree from the boughs you cut off your big tree. Arrange several of these trimmings and hang miniature ornaments from them.

Let It Snow

❖ If you love a soft touch of snow on your Christmas tree branches or among your decorative greens, you can have it without buying a can of that fake spray stuff. Just save the dried baby's breath from flower arrangements you (or your friends and neighbors) get throughout the year, and nestle little sprays of it among your tree branches and boughs. It's cheaper than the canned version and cleaner.

You're Invited

❖ For a creative and cost-efficient holiday invitation, raid your herb and spice collection. Pull out that dried sage and those bay leaves and build yourself a Christmas tree—on paper, that is. On a blank card or sturdy piece of construction paper folded in half, draw an outline of a Christmas tree. Use craft glue to attach the leaves to the card. For an extra-special touch, attach whole cloves to the leaves for

PACK IT IN: HOW TO PACK FOOD GIFTS FOR SAFE SHIPPING

You've spent time and energy baking those special cookies to send to your loved ones for the holidays, so you don't want them to arrive at their destination crushed and broken. But you also don't want to spend extra holiday dollars to have one of those shipping places pack them for you. No problem. You can pack your goodies yourself to arrive safe and sound.

Once you put your treats in a cookie tin or gift box, choose a sturdy cardboard box for shipping. Line several inches of the box with crumpled-up plastic grocery bags, recycled packing peanuts, or air-popped popcorn (no salt or butter, please). Then nestle your gift into the packing material and pour more peanuts or popcorn (or arrange more bags) around it and on top. Tape up your box and head to the post office.

If your cookies are especially fragile, pack them in pairs. Wrap the cookies in twos, bottoms together, with colored cellophane or foil before you put them in the tin. The wrapping will keep them from knocking together and breaking.

ornaments. Whoever receives your card will be impressed with your common "scents."

Such a Card

❖ Many Christmas cards are just too beautiful to throw away. To enjoy their beauty next season, cut each card in half at the fold and use it as an ornament or other decoration. To turn a card into a simple ornament, trim the card or leave it as is, and punch a hole through the top. Thread ribbon through the hole and form a loop. For a festive centerpiece, tape several Christmas cards to an empty coffee can and fill the can with flowers.

The Great Cookie Exchange

❖ If you like to have a variety of fine cookies around the holidays but can't find the time to bake all the kinds you like, host a cookie swap. Here's what you need to do. Contact 6 to 12 friends and ask each to pick one favorite cookie recipe. Then each participant should make as many dozen cookies as there are participants. For instance, if 10 people (including yourself) will attend your swap, each baker should arrive with 10 dozen of her favorite kind of cookie. (It costs less to bake one kind of cookie because you can buy large quantities of ingredients.) It's fun seeing your friends, and everyone will go home with 10 dozen different cookies. You can freeze them, give them as gifts, or just fill up those cookie jars.

Be Progressive

❖ It's very easy to spend too much money when you're putting together a Christmas party. To save some cash without sacrificing the fun, suggest that your friends and family share the expenses and throw a progressive Christmas party. Draw a map that includes all the houses involved and shows what each host will be serving. One house might be serving appetizers, another the main course, and a third desserts, for example. To top off the evening, take a walking tour of the neighborhood and admire the lights and decorations. Or if it's too cold or stormy, gather around the fireplace and sing Christmas carols.

NEW YEAR'S EVE

Lasting Memories

❖ Invite friends and family to a time capsule party on New Year's Eve. Have guests bring an item that best represents what the past year has meant to them. Place all the items in a box and seal it with tape or string. When it's time to celebrate the end of the following year, break out that box and see how things differ from year to year. Your guests will love being involved with the festivities, and it won't take you until next year to pay for the party.

FIVE GIFTS FOR HOUSEBOUND FRIENDS

Instead of asking someone who is recuperating from an illness or living in a nursing home, "What can I do to help?" try these cost-free suggestions for ways to brighten someone's day:

1. Help with the chores. If your friend is confined to a nursing home, collect her laundry and toss it in your own washing machine and dryer, or stop by her home and do a little dusting while she's gone.

2. Reach out and touch someone. Get a list of telephone calls your friend just can't get to. Then make them either from your phone or from your friend's phone, with her permission.

3. Tell her a story. Visit your friend and read out loud to her from the daily newspaper, a magazine, or a book of her choice.

4. Go for a stroll. Take your friend for a walk, even if it's just up and down the hallways of a nursing home. Often patients who are confined or recuperating are encouraged to walk but need assistance. Make sure to check with the doctor or nurse first, though.

5. Prepare a little home cooking. Make a simple meal, then clean up. If your friend is confined to a nursing home or rehabilitation center, check with the staff to see if you can cook a little something there.

VALENTINE'S DAY

Funny Valentine

❖ To show friends and loved ones how much you care, plan a Valentine's Day "cocktail" party without the alcohol. Use cocktail glasses to serve finger foods and snacks. Fill martini glasses with olives and cheese cubes on colorful toothpicks. Serve refreshing fruit cocktail in whiskey sour glasses. And as a bubbly finale, toast the ones you love with sparkling gelatin served in champagne glasses.

The Way to His Heart . . .

❖ Why spend money on a card and a gift when everyone knows that the way to a man's heart is through his stomach? Bake a batch of heart-shaped cookies and use frosting to pipe on your own valentine messages.

EASTER

Let the Green Grass Grow All Around

❖ Make inexpensive Easter table favors or windowsill and mantel decorations with little terra-cotta flowerpots, which you can buy for around a dollar apiece at many garden centers and craft shops. About 3 weeks before the holiday, fill each pot with potting soil, sprinkle the soil with grass seed, water the seed, and place in the sun. Water regularly as needed to keep the soil moist. When the grass in each pot has grown (it will take a couple of weeks), put a

---

IT WORKED FOR ME
Break an Egg

I love decorating for Easter with my two young girls, but we don't have a big budget. So about 3 weeks before the holiday, we take raw eggs (either dyed or plain white), break off the top at the small end, and remove the white and the yolk. Then we gently fill the egg halfway with some soil, sprinkle a little grass seed over the soil and add more soil on top. We paint a face on the egg, lightly water the seed, and set the egg safely aside.

Next, for each egg, we cut a strip of cardboard about 1 inch wide and 5 inches long and staple the ends together, forming a ring large enough for the egg to stand in. Sometimes we paint the ring or decorate it with markers, stickers, sequins, and the like. Then we set the egg upright in the ring and place it on a table or windowsill. By Easter, the grass has grown into a full head of "hair" atop the face painted on the egg.

—Kathleen O'Rourke
Long Valley, New Jersey

decorated Easter egg in it, then place your little decoration wherever you wish.

Get Egg-cited about Decorating

❖ Add texture and glitter to your Easter eggs (without spending a single jelly bean) with bits of colored tissue paper or paper napkins. After blowing out a raw egg (put a pinhole in each end of the egg and blow the yolk and white out one end, into a bowl), rinse it and let it dry. Squeeze a

WORLD-CLASS FRUGALITY

Grandpa's New Shirts

Grandpa Dutch was never a slave to fashion. He worked as a farmer and an electrician all his life, and his wardrobe consisted of a few pairs of overalls and some plaid shirts. He never wanted to wear anything else. When his wife, Mamo, asked him what he wanted for his birthday or Christmas, he never had an answer. If she bought him shirts that were fancy or unusual, he would thank her, then hang them in the closet and never wear them.

One Christmas, Mamo got frustrated with him. She took a couple of his favorite shirts out of the laundry basket, washed them with starch, and ironed them carefully, so they would be like new. Then she folded each one around a sheet of tissue paper, the way the department stores do, and wrapped them in Christmas paper.

That Christmas morning, Grandpa Dutch opened his present and said he loved the shirts. He put them away and never seemed to notice that they were exactly like two shirts he already had. Mamo was furious. She'd been expecting him to get the joke, but he didn't. Every year afterward, she wrapped up the same two shirts, and every year Grandpa Dutch seemed surprised to get them.

Mamo always insisted that Grandpa was too dense to realize what was happening, but I disagree. I think that pretending surprise was his little joke. Mamo died unexpectedly one fall before she'd had a chance to wrap up his shirts. Grandpa washed them himself, folded them, and put them away in the drawer. He never wore those shirts again.

—**Michelle Seaton**
Medford, Massachusetts

dot of white glue over each hole to prevent the egg from cracking. Then go wild. Decoupage bits of brightly colored tissue paper or napkins to the egg and roll lightly in glitter.

Have a Bunny Good Time

❖ Create tiny Easter basket favors for your guests using some inexpensive filler. First, line the baskets with shredded newspaper or construction paper. Make your own chocolate bunnies by melting chocolate bars or baking chips and pouring them into Easter molds. Finally, bake large bunny cookies and decorate them with icing and mini–jelly beans for a homemade treat.

HALLOWEEN AND THANKSGIVING

Take Out the Trash Bags

❖ Fashion a flock of ghosts from those inexpensive white trash bags (either tall kitchen or trash can size), some string or yarn, and newspaper or balloons. Place a ball of newspaper or an inflated balloon (the newspaper will last longer) in each bag, then tie off the end at the "neck" of your ghost. Tie each ghost to a tree branch, lamppost, or step railing. Its white tail will flutter in the wind.

❖ Alternatively, give your ghosts a dandy look by tying off each neck with an old necktie.

Spin Charlotte's Web

❖ Make a spooky spiderweb for your yard out of items you already own: string, yarn, even bits of rope tied together. (In other words, you don't have to buy the premade type from the party store.) Start your web by tying one end of string or yarn around a tree branch, mailbox post, or what have you. Then thread your way from point

HOLIDAYS AND GIFT GIVING ON A BUDGET

Newspapers, white trash bags, and a few neckties are all you need to make a flock of spooky ghosts.

to point, making a large web. See how many trick-or-treaters you attract.

Paper Lion

❖ Save those paper bags with the handles that you get at the supermarket for a make-your-own trick-or-treat bag. Set out the construction paper and crayons and let the kids (or the kids at heart) decorate the brown bags with ghosts, pumpkins, and witches. It will be a treat for the whole family.

Horn of Plenty

❖ Present your own version of the traditional cornucopia this Thanksgiving. Set a large basket in the center of the table and fill it with the fruits of autumn, such as acorn squash, tiny pumpkins, and apples. After the holiday, use your centerpiece to make a tasty fall lover's casserole or other dish.

Giving Thanks

A turkey-shaped place card makes a handy table favor.

❖ For an inexpensive Thanksgiving decoration, create place cards in the shape of a turkey. Lay your hand on a piece of construction paper, with your fingers spread out. Trace your hand and cut out the shape. Color in the "feathers" (or fingers) with different-colored markers, dot the "eyes," and write the guests' names on the bodies. Place each turkey on a plate—just make sure your guests don't gobble them up.

Without a Buy Your Leave(s)

❖ You don't have to buy fancy place mats to give your Thanksgiving table a festive feeling. Simply make your own with leaves, construction paper, glue, and clear contact paper. Collect a variety of fall leaves from your yard or a park. Arrange several on a piece of white or colored construction paper. When you have the look you want, squeeze a tiny dot of white glue onto the back of each leaf and position it on the paper. Let dry for a minute or two, then laminate your place mat by covering both sides with clear contact paper. Repeat for as many place mats as you need. These mats can be wiped clean for reuse, they cost practically nothing, and they're fun for kids to make.

Keeping the Harvest

❖ Why waste money on expensive candleholders when you can use fresh fruits and vegetables such as miniature pumpkins, acorn squash, and even apples to light up the night instead? Cut a hole the same width as a candle in each fruit or vegetable, then insert the candle in the hole. Arrange your holders on a large platter placed in the center of your table.

Make Some Dough

❖ Try these sweet and nearly cost-free Thanksgiving table favors. Make a batch of old-fashioned salt dough using 2 cups all-purpose flour, 1 cup salt, and 1 cup water. Mix the flour and salt together in a bowl, adding the water a little at a time as you mix it in. Knead the dough well, then break off about a cup and form it into a small shallow bowl, smoothing it with your fingers. Make as many little bowls as you need favors. Preheat the oven to 250°F. Spread aluminum foil on a cookie sheet and place your bowls on it, about an inch apart. Bake for about 2 hours. Remove the bowls when the edges are just beginning to brown. When they are cool, paint them with acrylic paint, covering them with designs in fall colors. When the paint is dry, fill each bowl with a handful of candy corn and place it at a table setting. You can make these as far ahead of Thanksgiving as you wish.

Leaf It Be

❖ Add fall foliage to your windows by gathering leaves from your yard or a park. Lay several leaves on a sheet of clear contact paper, sticky side up. Then lay another sheet of clear contact paper, sticky side down, over the top of the leaves. Smooth the two together, cut out your laminated leaves, and tape them to the windows. Or cut a hole in the top of each leaf and string yarn, thread, or raffia through the hole. Tie each leaf to a window lock or doorknob.

The Great Pumpkin

❖ Make a beautiful, inexpensive autumn vase out of a real pumpkin by cutting off the top of the pumpkin, scooping out the seeds, and arranging freshly cut flowers, leaves, moss, burrs, twigs, pinecones, or anything else you can find inside. Place your pumpkin vase anywhere, from the coffee table to the dining table. You might want to place it on a plate or vinyl place mat to protect any wood surfaces from potential water spots.

❖ Alternatively, use your hollowed-out pumpkin as a flowerpot for hardy mums or other autumn-blooming plants. Pour enough dirt into the pumpkin to cover the plant's roots, just as you would in a regular flowerpot, then water. Set your planter inside on a table or outside on the front steps.

Offer to Toss the Salad

❖ Create a rustic Thanksgiving centerpiece without spending a nickel. Just gather up forest findings—sticks,

THE YANKEE MISER RECOMMENDS . . .
Drive Them Crazy

Here's an idea for a wedding gift some frugal friends of mine came up with a few years back when money was tight.

If you have friends who are getting married but you don't have the bucks for a fancy wedding gift, why not offer to drive the couple to the airport after their wedding and pick them up when they return from their honeymoon? You'll be sparing them the cost and the hassle of a taxi or limo. Be sure to wash and vacuum your car before you make the trip. The drive won't cost you any more than your time and a little gas money, and the newlyweds will appreciate your generosity and ingenuity.

pinecones, acorns, chestnuts, walnuts, moss, leaves from your yard (or offer to clean your neighbor's yard) and mix them up in a wooden salad bowl. (Make sure to give your findings a quick look so that you don't bring any insects into your home.) Place the bowl in the center of your table. Your guests will admire your natural sense of style and ingenuity.

Attend the Changing of the Gourds

❖ Nothing says autumn like a collection of colorful gourds, each with its own design fashioned by nature. You can buy these cheaply at a garden center or even the supermarket and get a full season of use by displaying them creatively. Toss a few in a salad bowl, mixing bowl, galvanized bucket, basket, straw hat, child's wagon, small wheelbarrow, planter, wooden crate, or whatever you find around the house.

Be a Little Fruity

❖ Want a delicious Thanksgiving decoration without paying gourmet prices? Head to your refrigerator and grab several apples and oranges. Slice the fruit, arrange the slices on cookie sheets, and cover them lightly with waxed paper. Leave them on a screened or protected porch for several days (2 to 3 days for apples, a week for oranges) to dry. Or arrange them on cookie sheets and place in the oven set on its lowest temperature for 12 hours. When the fruit has hardened to a golden brown, pierce each piece with a needle and strong thread, stringing a garland of dried fruit to hang in a window, wrap around a banister, or drape along a mantel.

GREAT GIFTS

Don't Scrap This Gift

❖ Preserve great memories for a friend or family member—and still preserve your bank account—by making a scrapbook of photos and mementos from a trip you took together, holidays you spent together, or a special occasion such as a wedding, baby shower, or child's first birthday. The recipient will cherish your book of memories long after other gifts are forgotten.

Guess Who's Coming to Dinner

❖ Want the perfect (but inexpensive) gift for someone who has everything? Give yourself! Wrap up an invitation for dinner at your house. Set a date, then cook your best meal. You can even do this for a group of friends or neighbors. Give the invitations as Christmas gifts, then host the dinner in January or February, when everyone needs a lift.

Be a Poster Child

❖ Got a music lover on your list but don't want to pay the high price of compact discs or tapes? Go to a music shop and ask for some promotional or concert posters featuring the artist your friend likes to listen to. Usually, you can buy them very cheaply; the store manager or owner may even give them to you. Not only will your friend enjoy the posters now, but they may become collectibles and increase in value over the years.

FRUGAL FORMULAS
FRIGHTFULLY FUN

Having a Halloween party? Try these handy ideas. To make an eerie witch's brew, combine orange juice, cranberry juice, and ginger ale to taste. Then give the brew a hand—literally.

You can make an icy impression with a pair of surgical gloves. Turn them inside out, wash them, and let them dry (that removes any powder or other residue inside). Next, fill them with water and tie off the ends. Place the hands in the freezer until they're frozen. Using a pair of scissors, make a small cut in the end of each glove and gently peel it off the frozen hand. Then place the hands in the punch. This bewitching idea will help keep the punch cool and your wallet full.

Find Fine Linen

❖ You know someone who loves the finer things in life (and so do you), but your wallet doesn't seem to keep pace. You can still give a fine gift. Go to flea markets and even some antique shops looking for old linen pieces such as handkerchiefs, doilies, antimacassars, and bureau scarves. Choose a few that appeal to you (say, with lovely embroidery or lace) and are in pretty good condition. They're usually no more than $2 to $3 each, and some are even packaged together. When you get them home, carefully hand-wash them with gentle soap and iron them on a low temperature setting. Then fold them and tie a pretty ribbon around them—and you have a gift of distinction.

Get Boxed In

❖ Everyone needs a place to store little treasures, but sometimes those treasure chests can be mighty expensive. Make one for someone you care about by buying an inexpensive wooden box at a craft or office supply store and decorating it yourself. Use decorative stamps, stencils, free-hand drawings, sponge painting, stickers, or decoupage—whatever strikes your fancy. Add a special touch by painting the interior or lining it with fabric, using fabric glue.

HOUSEWARMING GIFTS

Be Neighborly

❖ Welcome new neighbors on moving day with a bag of groceries containing pasta, a jar of sauce, a premixed salad, a loaf of bread, and a carton of milk or bottle of wine. Also tuck in a roll of toilet paper and a light bulb, along with a small package of disposable utensils and plates (you know, those items they may have forgotten to pack). Write your name and phone number on a slip of paper so your new neighbors can call if necessary to find out where the supermarket, bank, or gas station is. This gift is convenient and economical. You can buy it on a regular trip to the supermarket, and it costs less—and will be more appreciated—than many other housewarming gifts. It's also a terrific way to make new friends.

Plant the Seeds of Friendship

❖ Freshly cut flowers are nice housewarming gifts, but they're usually expensive and last little more than a week. Here's a more lasting (and less costly) way to go. Arrive at the new home owner's doorstep bearing a flat of annuals or perennials or a basket of bulbs, then announce that you'll do the planting. Your friends will appreciate the last part the most.

Have a Breakdown

❖ Want to help friends who have just moved, but don't have a dime to spare? Offer to break down their cardboard boxes for them and return the flattened boxes to the mover or take them to the recycling center. Your friends will heap undying gratitude on you.

Get Coordinated

❖ New home owners usually need bathroom towels, and you can supply them without worrying about cost or colors. Buy several towels in neutral, coordinating (not matching) colors at a discount store or outlet. Combine shades of ivory, gray, and taupe; different shades of green or blue; and the like. Roll the towels up in a basket, or just fold them and tie them up with a big ribbon.

Stay Home

❖ If you're suffering from sticker shock over the price of wedding gifts, here's something you can do. Offer to house-sit for the couple while they're on their honeymoon. You can take care of their pets and water their plants while they're gone. It won't cost you a dime, and it will actually save them money because they won't have to hire someone to do these small jobs. It might also give them peace of mind while they're away.

Snap to It

❖ Surprise a newlywed couple with a framed collage of photos from their wedding reception. Unobtrusively snap a roll of pictures at the reception—of the couple, friends, family, even the cake. Once the prints are developed, cut them into unusual shapes, arrange them on a heavy paper backing cut to match the size of a standard picture frame, and attach them to the paper using a glue stick. Then put your collage in an inexpensive frame. The total cost of this fun and thoughtful gift? A roll of film and a few bucks for the frame.

GIFTS FOR BABY

Take a Seat

❖ Want a baby gift that looks impressive but costs just a few dollars? Find a child-size wooden chair at a yard sale—one that has nicks and dings but doesn't need repair. Take it home, sand it lightly, slap a coat of primer on it, and add a fresh coat of paint. If you're feeling especially rushed or lazy, you can even spray-paint it. If you're feeling especially

PUT DOWN ROOTS

Here's an inexpensive gift that's sure to please the nature lovers in your life. Pick up a couple of old wineglasses or bar glasses at a yard sale, outlet, or discount store (or check your own cupboards for glasses you no longer need). Buy a few bulbs of small flowers (such as narcissus) at the garden center or supermarket. Fill each glass about halfway with crushed white stone or pebbles from your driveway. Nestle one bulb on top of the stone, with the roots pointing down, then pour enough water into the glass so that it just hits the bottom of the bulb. Tie a ribbon around the stem or lip of the glass, and your gift is ready. Tell the recipient to keep the water level consistent so that the bulb does not sit in a puddle. The roots will grow down through the rocks, and the flower will blossom.

creative, add a stencil design or the child's name or initials across the back.

Play Mom (or Dad) for a Day

❖ Give the ultimate gift to new parents: Take the baby's older sibling(s) to the park, to a movie, or even to your house for a play day. This will not only give the parents a much-needed break, but it will also make an older sibling feel special during a time when he is likely to be feeling left out of the action.

GIFT WRAPPING FOR LESS

Throw In the Towel

❖ Wrap a food or kitchen gift—or a small potted plant—in a bright, clean dish towel or new cloth napkin. It won't cost any more than a gift bag or wrapping paper, and it will be much more useful and unusual.

It's Your Bag

❖ Don't spend your gift money on those expensive, decorative gift bags. Make your own from white or brown paper lunch bags. Paint designs on them with acrylic paint, or use markers, stickers, crayons, or colored paper. You can even glue on sequins, feathers, or anything else fun and festive. Add an elegant finishing touch by lining the inside of the bag with colorful tissue paper that's puffed up and peeking out the top.

❖ Alternatively, take your kids' art (with their permission and help), cut out several images, and glue them onto a plain lunch bag.

❖ For a personalized design, find a photo of your friend and cut out a square or other shape in the bag about a quarter of an inch smaller than the photo. Glue the photo to the inside of the bag so that the image faces out.

CONTAIN YOURSELF: 10 CREATIVE GIFT CONTAINERS

Instead of wasting money on expensive gift bags, gift boxes, and gift wrap, get more bang for your buck by putting your present in a functional container. Baskets are popular, but here are 10 other interesting ideas.

1. Terra-cotta flowerpot. Fill it with a sack of bulbs or packets of seeds.

2. Plastic sand bucket. Pile it high with beach toys.

3. Wastebasket. Tuck some housewares or powder room supplies inside.

4. Galvanized metal or plastic water bucket. Fill it with gardening tools.

5. Plastic milk crate. Fill it with small and medium-size toys.

6. Laundry bag or basket. No, not dirty laundry. Fill it with coordinated towels and scented soaps.

7. Plastic storage box with lid. Tuck some craft or sewing supplies inside.

8. Mixing bowl. Place baking mix or a few of your favorite recipes inside.

9. Soup pot. Put some soup mixes or recipes inside with a can of stock.

10. Canvas tote. Fill it with household tools or baby supplies.

Start Boxing

❖ Don't have the money for expensive wrapping paper? You don't need it. Simply decorate the gift box itself—with paint, markers, crayons, sequins, glitter, or whatever you find around the house.

Take Action

❖ Want to give a gift box some punch without paying more? Save accessories such as tiny Barbie shoes and hats that your children or grandchildren leave all over the floor and glue them to the top of the box. This doesn't have to be just for children—adults will enjoy the humor, too.

CHAPTER 30

THRIFTY TRAVEL AND VACATION IDEAS

*J*ust because you've been dutifully frugal all year long, there's no reason to think that you have to spend all the money you've saved just to have a great vacation. Some people might feel that they have to splurge, but you can have a wonderful time, learn a lot, and see the world without plundering your savings account—if you know the secrets.

The first rule about traveling is this: The price you read in the brochure isn't the real price. You probably already know that few people pay full fare for a seat on an airplane. But did you know that the same is also true when it comes to cruises, resorts, packaged tours, and hotels? In this chapter, you'll learn that a little research can cut 20 to 50 percent off the published price of your vacation. That can translate to a lot of souvenirs for the folks back home.

You'll find out how to travel cheaply—by traveling with a companion and how to save big bucks by declining certain types of insurance when you rent a car. You'll also learn that when you're traveling, breakfast really is the most important meal of the day—and the biggest—because it's also potentially the least expensive. You'll know that by relying on your own research rather than the advice of an overworked travel agent, you can find free factory tours, weekend passes to museums and trains all over the world, and walking tours that give you an insider's perspective on any city you choose.

TRAVEL KNOW-HOW

Money-Back Guarantees

❖ If your plans may change at the last minute for reasons beyond your control—business, sudden illness or family emergency—it might be worth your while to get traveler's insurance. This typically costs 1 percent of the total cost of the package but will get you a refund if you have to cancel. (Most travel companies won't refund your money.) The catch is that you shouldn't sign up for this insurance over the phone. See the contract in writing and make sure that sudden business or family emergencies are covered. Some policies pay off only for medical problems.

Double Your Companionship and Savings

❖ If you usually travel alone, you know that some things cost less than if you're traveling with someone else. You probably spend less on food and admissions to events, for example. But some costs go up. If you're booking a cruise or resort stay that offers a per person price, that price is based on double occupancy. If you use an entire cabin or hotel room yourself, you'll be subject to the per person price plus a single-occupancy surcharge. The best way around this is to find a like-minded companion who wants to take the same trip. It will also give you someone to talk to.

AIRFARES

Buy Seats on Sale

❖ You probably already know that most airline fares are cheaper if you stay over a Saturday night, and cheaper still if you book 21 days in advance. You may not know that the cheapest airfares of all may be those booked at the last minute. Airlines hate to take off with empty seats, so they sometimes offer big discounts at the last minute that far exceed those on seats purchases at least 21 days in advance. You might be able to visit relatives or friends on the spur of

the moment for much less than you would with lots of planning.

Broker a Deal

❖ There are great deals on airlines you've probably **never** heard of—carriers that can't advertise in this country because they don't regularly fly here. Still, they fly through on their way to other countries, and they often have **extra seats** at incredibly low prices. How can you find them? Call airline consolidators, companies that specialize in buying these seats in bulk and then selling them one by one. They advertise in the travel sections of large newspapers such as the *New York Times* and the *Boston Globe* and on the Internet.

WATCH YOUR WALLET

You avoided having your pocket picked as you planned your vacation. Now you have to avoid the professional thieves who prey on tourists while you are traveling. Here's how.

I. Watch while you wait. Pickpockets strike most often when tourists are waiting in line to get tickets for tours and shows. Watch for people jostling through the line.

2. Don't carry your passport. It's very valuable to a thief. Leave it in the hotel safe and instead carry copies of your travel documents as proof of your citizenship.

3. Be cash poor. Pickpockets most often strike at the beginning of a weekend or in the days prior to a holiday knowing that tourists carry more money at those times. Bring only the money you'll need for that day's activities to put a cap on how much you'll lose if you get hit.

4. Bury your bucks. Keeping your wallet in your back pocket or carrying it in a purse works fine at home, but in tourist spots thieves carry knives to cut through straps and coat pockets. A better bet is a money belt or an around-the-neck pouch that you can conceal under your clothing.

5. Lock your suitcase. Keep your suitcase locked while you're out of the hotel room. This will keep casual thieves from rifling your room when you're not around.

BUSES AND TRAINS

Weekend Passes

❖ When you travel, you usually take public transportation to get around. Why pay pricey cab fares when you can take the train? To save even more money, buy multiday passes on local buses and trains. You'll be traveling more often than the average commuter, and you'll save yourself the hassle of fumbling for exact change at every station.

CAR RENTALS

Catch a Cab

❖ It may seem to be more convenient to rent a car at the airport, but it's also more expensive. Airports often charge an extra tax, called a conversion fee for car rentals. This fee could add up to 10 to 20 percent of the total cost of your car rental, and it's often not part of the quote that the rental company gives you when you sign the papers. The solution? Some savvy rental agencies offer free shuttles to their rental offices off-site. If your company doesn't do that, take a cab to its nearest rental office. Any cab ride should be far less expensive than the $40 to $100 tax you'll pay for a weekly car rental.

Can You Take a Rain Check?

❖ Car rental companies, like some hotels, will charge you a fee for canceling a reservation the day you are due to arrive. Before you reserve a car, ask whether your rental agency has a policy on last-minute cancellations. That way, you can avoid paying for a car you never had the chance to drive.

Insurance Fees Uncovered

❖ When you rent a car, the rental agency may try to sell you collision and liability insurance, telling you that you need both in case you get in an accident. Actually, you might not need either one. If you carry liability and colli-

sion insurance on your own car, you should be covered when you rent. Ask your insurance agent before you go on vacation. The least expensive insurance is the plan you already have.

❖ In some cases, using a credit card to rent a car gives you automatic insurance if the car is stolen. Call the customer service number on your credit card and ask for details.

ACCOMMODATIONS

Avoid Rate Hikes

❖ In most big cities, hotels make their money on business travelers who arrive on Monday morning and leave on Friday morning. These hotels offer steep discounts to weekend travelers. If your travel plans include a city, know that the hotel rate will go down by as much as 35 percent on Saturday and Sunday nights.

IT WORKED FOR ME
Cat-Sitting at the Beach

I have a friend who owns a beautiful house near the beach on Cape Cod, Massachusetts. She also has two rambunctious cats who demand a lot of attention. One day she told me that she had a great opportunity to travel to Europe with her music group for 2 weeks in August. But the cats were still babies, and putting them in a kennel seemed cruel. What could she do?

I live in the city, where the heat and humidity in August is unbearable. It didn't take me long to suggest a solution. I drove down and spent the 2 weeks at her house, playing with the cats, feeding them, and doing a little litter box duty. In exchange, I got a free oceanside vacation, complete with a hammock and an outdoor grill. And she thought I was doing her a favor!

—Michelle Seaton
Medford, Massachusetts

❖ Country bed-and-breakfasts work on the opposite no-tion. They charge their highest rates on the weekends, when the bulk of the tourists visit. By scheduling your visit around the high-paying crowds, you can tour an entire re-gion without paying a fortune.

Tax Time

❖ If you call a hotel to make a reservation, you'll be quoted the room rate, not the total price including taxes. Remember that cities often tax every room rented, as do most states. In addition, you'll pay a state sales tax. This can add up to 20 percent of the room rate to your bill. Since various states and cities charge different taxes on hotel rooms, find out the real cost of the room before you rent it.

Consolidate Your Savings

❖ What do hotels do when they're afraid they're going to have a bunch of extra rooms? They cut the price and sell them to travel consolidators. If you're looking for a hotel room at the last minute, you might have luck calling one of these travel specialists. Look in the Yellow Pages under Travel Agencies and Bureaus. You might be able to get a room at 30 percent off the regular rate. When you do get a quote, be sure to double-check with the hotel where you're planning to stay. At the very last minute, hotels sometimes run their own discount rates that are better than even a consolidator's price.

Hang Up on Phone Charges

❖ When you check into your hotel, you'll notice a note next to the phone saying that every call will be billed at the highest daytime long-distance rate. It may also mention that you'll pay a $1 fee for going through the hotel switch-board and that you'll pay a "nominal fee" on the total cost of the call. What the notice won't tell you is that this means you could pay up to $10 for a 1-minute call home to check on the babysitter or pick up your e-mail. Not even cell phones cost that much. Get around these outrageous fees

by buying a prepaid phone card before you leave on vacation, then make your calls from a pay phone to bypass the hotel switchboard.

ACTIVITIES

History Buffs Take You Back in Time

❖ If you're new to an area and are trying to get a sense of its history, you could go to the local historical museums. The trouble is that they may be jammed with tourists and staffed by a few harried people who don't have time to talk. Instead, look around for the county museum, which is likely to be a bit off the beaten track and staffed by a local volunteer—a retiree, if you're lucky. That person can give

SAVE MORE THAN MONEY

You're on the road in Europe or Mexico, and you get a cold or the flu. You may find that familiar medicines aren't available. Or you can't figure out what's in them—or not in them. The best solution is to be prepared with your own first-aid kit from home. Here is what your kit should include.

I. Aspirin. Who wants to pay inflated hotel prices?

2. Antacid or upset stomach remedy. Hey, you might eat too much one night.

3. Cold medication. Airplanes are incubators for the common cold, and antihistamines are difficult to come by in some countries.

4. Old Band-Aid tin. Fill it with a few Band-Aids, antibacterial wet wipes, and a small tube of antibiotic ointment.

5. Prescription medicine. Bring along a copy of the prescription, too. And be sure to leave the medicine in the original bottle, with your doctor's name on it, in case you get stopped at customs.

6. Flashlight. It won't take up much space, but it will keep you from stubbing your toe on the way to the bathroom at 3:00 A.M. (Okay. A flashlight technically isn't a first-aid item, but your first-aid kit is a good place to store it.)

you much more detailed information, answer all your questions about how to get around, suggest where to eat and stay, and dish the very best historical gossip.

Read All about It

❖ If you want to avoid the gimmicky, high-priced city tours at your destination, check out the calendar section of the local newspaper. You'll find listings for cultural performances and new museum exhibits that won't be listed in travel brochures. Most towns and cities also have historical associations that offer inexpensive walking tours for members and nonmembers. These tours often focus less on the usual tourist traps and more on the city's architecture, horticulture, or literary history. You also will probably meet lots of city residents who can give you advice on what to see and how to get around.

Travel by Association

❖ If you belong to a professional association and you're traveling abroad, you might contact a similar professional group in the country you plan to visit. Not only will you probably meet a local who can give you an international perspective on your work, but you are sure to get a personal tour of the city and a look at its culture.

UNUSUAL VACATION IDEAS

Sing for Your Supper

❖ If you're planning to go on a whitewater rafting trip, think about doing a little cooking on the side. The people who organize these trips need people to cook, clean, and break camp every day. They usually let people swap their skills for a little free rafting. The job involves a certain amount of hard work, but you can't beat the price. To find a rafting company, call your state's tourism board and request a brochure. The Yellow Pages in towns where rafting is common list rafting companies under Outfitters.

Factory Direct

❖ One way to save money on vacation is to take day trips near home. If you have kids, a good starting point is area factories. Many manufacturers of consumer goods offer tours of their facilities for free or for a very small fee. Kids love to learn how the products are made. Each product—everything from crayons to cars to ice cream—has its own story that teaches history, innovation, and how to turn an idea into a business. Call your local chamber of commerce or tourism board to find out which factories near your home offer tours.

❖ If you're traveling around the country, call ahead to the chambers of commerce in the cities you'll be visiting and ask about factory tours there as well.

SAVING MONEY ON ADMISSIONS

Buy in Bulk

❖ Large cities often have special passes to museums that are good for most or all of the museums in those cities. The passes generally cost much less than individual admission prices. To make sure you're getting a good bargain, check the expiration date on the pass. If it's valid only for one weekend and it would take you several days to see all the museums in the city, you may not be getting a good deal. Also, find out the individual admission prices at the local museums, then figure out how many you'd have to visit to make the pass worthwhile.

Enjoy the Nightlife

❖ Some metropolitan museums offer special night fares. They discount their usual admission fees one night a week in the hopes of attracting locals who may become patrons. On those nights, they also offer free lecture series, demonstration dances, and a cash bar in addition to the usual exhibits.

Give It the Old College Try

❖ Itching to see a play or concert but don't want to pay the high prices? Colleges and universities often have their own small theaters and musical groups or performances. At those performances, you can see actors and soloists who aren't famous—yet. The quality of the entertainment is usually quite high, and the ticket prices tend to be low.

SAVING MONEY ON FOOD

The Most Important Meal of the Day

❖ When you're traveling on a budget, it's tempting to skip breakfast to save money. But that's not always a good idea because by lunchtime you'll be starving. Eat a big breakfast instead. It's far cheaper than eating later in the day. Bring along a resealable plastic bag and order more food than you think you can eat—an extra muffin, perhaps, and a bowl of fruit. Transfer the extra to the bag, and you'll have a snack later in the day, when you would normally be paying for lunch.

Out to Lunch

❖ Going out to dinner seems so festive, but it's also expensive. You might not know that most nice restaurants serve almost the exact same menu at lunchtime. The only difference is the

I was traveling with my daughter and her high school singing group last year. Thirty-five of us were on our way from Chicago to London. Before we boarded the plane, the airline made an announcement saying that the flight had been downgraded to a smaller aircraft. The airline needed 40 volunteers to stay behind, and they would get booked on the next available flight. We didn't have anything to do in London the next day, and so the entire group volunteered to take a chance on the next flight. The airline gave us each a $1,000 voucher to go anywhere in the world, and it was good for one year. Since my daughter and I both had vouchers, we had a combined total of $2,000 in vouchers. When we booked our family vacation this summer, we realized that the round-trip airfare to Zurich for my husband, my daughter, and me added up to just under $2,000. So we all flew for free. All it cost us was a couple of hours at O'Hare International Airport in Chicago.

—Laurie Rumery
Monticello, Illinois

On the Road

I don't recall ever taking a vacation with my folks. During the Depression, we didn't travel much, and if we did, we packed a lunch and took the train.

My wife, Mildred, tells of an aunt and uncle who lived in Wisconsin. They came to Nebraska to visit once a year in their old Nash automobile. It took them 3 days. They had a box on the back of the car where they carried all their food and camping equipment, and they stopped alongside the road to cook or camp.

At that time, it wasn't unheard-of for farmers to take in travelers for the night. They usually didn't charge anything, as the travelers brought news and company. I had a friend who was an expert at saving money. He always arranged his trips according to which acquaintances he knew along the way, and he was careful to arrive at mealtimes. He brought news and company, too, and we were always glad to see him.

—**Ed Jensen**
Hastings, Nebraska

portion size and the price. You can get a huge lunch—with an appetizer, entrée, and dessert—for the same price as a single entrée at dinner. Also, if you take yourself out to lunch, you're less likely to buy expensive drinks. And with all the money you'll save, you can take yourself out to a discount matinee afterward for a total bargain package.

Brown-Bag It

❖ You know enough to pack a sandwich or some trail mix and fruit when you go hiking for the day. Why not do the same thing for other sight-seeing excursions? The biggest expense of the day will be food. In addition, most of the food available at touristy spots is high in calories and fat and not likely to help you feel energetic. Cut down on expense and keep your energy high by thinking ahead. Remember that if you're traveling in the high heat of summer, you'll need to avoid temperature-sensitive foods such as mayonnaise and cold cuts.

❖ Also pack your own beverages. You can often buy a six-pack of soda for what some places charge for a large drink. And bottled water may cost even more.

Home Cooking

❖ Rather than pricey hotels, try to stay in college-style dorm rooms or economy hotel suites with kitchenettes. This will allow you to buy a few groceries, such as muffins and juice for breakfast or sandwiches for lunch, rather than relying on expensive restaurant food for every meal. Be sure to bring or pick up eating utensils, too, since most rooms don't come equipped with them.

SAVING MONEY ON SOUVENIRS

Duty-Free Is Not Free

❖ The duty-free shop at the airport is so seductive while you wait for your flight. The shop doesn't charge all those import taxes that can add up to 20 percent of the cost of an item to your purchase. But often it does include airport taxes of other kinds that can easily add up to the 20 percent you thought you were saving. The best thing to do on vacations abroad is to avoid last-minute purchases. The only duty-free goods that will save you money are the ones that are locally produced. Because the premium for buying them in the United States is so much higher, they're literally worth the tax.

WHAT'S THE BEST MONEY SAVER?
Book Your Own?

You're planning a cruise to the Bahamas, and the travel agent tells you that the flight from Chicago to Miami isn't included. You can:

A. Buy a discounted round-trip ticket from the cruise line

B. Shop around for your own best deal on a flight

Given that airlines are constantly discounting fares, you could undoubtedly find a better deal on your own, right? Probably not. Cruise lines buy thousands of tickets from the airlines every year. They are in a position to get very good deals on flights. Also, if you buy the ticket through the cruise line, it is responsible for finding your luggage if it gets lost and for making sure you get on the boat if your flight is delayed. If you go it alone with the ticket, you go it alone on the troubleshooting, too.

INDEX

Underscored page references indicate boxed text.
Boldface references indicate illustrations.

A

Accidents
  auto, preventing, 204
  minor, home remedies for, 275–76
Acting jobs, for extra income, 86
Adoption, pet, 247–49
Advertising
  for business services, 82–84, **82, 84**
  for garage sales, 84–85
Agents, for actors, 86
Air conditioner
  auto, fuel economy and, 203
  covering, in winter, 183
  power output of, 177
  repair and maintenance on, 173
  saving energy on, 182
Airfare
  with cruises, 371
  discounted, 361–62
  free vouchers for, 369
Air filter, auto, cleaning, 200–201
Air travel
  dehydration from, 276–77
  motion sickness from, 278
Alarm systems, electronic, alternative to,
    108
Antiques, furniture, 115–17
Apartment sales
  attracting customers to, 83, 84–85
  selling tactics for, 85
Aphids, repelling, 143
Appetizer tree, 331–32, **331**
Apple pie, crustless, 166–67

Appliances. *See also specific appliances*
  cleaning, 179–81
  covering, 182–83
  power output of, 177
  repairing, 102–3, 173
  shopping for, 177–79
  unplugging, 181
Aromatherapy, homemade, 286
Art, as charitable donation, 65
Arthritis, home remedies for, 270
Artwork
  from art schools and associations, 132
  from magazines, 132–33
  maps as, 133–34
  medals as, 134
  restoring, 136
  from seed packets, 132
Attaché case, as desk, 190
Attorney. *See* Lawyer(s)
Audio equipment
  organizing wires from, 180
  replacement parts for, 175
Automatic teller machines, avoiding fees
    for, 55, 57–58
Autos. *See* Cars

B

Baby gifts, 357–58
Baby goods, saving money on, 154
Babysitting
  for extra income, 90
  as gift to new parents, 358

saving money on
    with babysitting co-op, <u>258</u>
    with friends' services, 257
    by joining social group, 256
    with mother's helper, 257
Baking
    margarine for, 171
    powdered milk for, 155
Baking pans
    for heart-shaped cake, **327**
    to prevent burning, 170–71
Ballet, saving money on, 319
Balzac, Honoré de, <u>307</u>
Bank, piggy, making, 52
Bank accounts
    direct deposits to, 71
    redirecting money to, 71
    for savings, 53, 72
Banking
    online, advantages of, <u>60</u>
    saving money on, 55–58
Bankruptcy, avoiding, 26–27, 34
Banks, vs. credit unions, <u>57</u>
Baseball bats, maintaining, 245
Baseball games, minor league, 317
Baseball glove, conditioning, <u>245</u>
Basil butter, <u>167</u>
Basketball, buying, 239
Baskets, gift, themes for, <u>342</u>
Bats, baseball, maintaining, 245
Bed, water, heating, 99
Bed-and-breakfasts, saving money on, 365
Beef, browning, 171
Bee stings, home remedies for, 274–75
Berries, storing, <u>154</u>
Bicycle
    buying, 233, 238, 239
    for transportation, 195
Bicycle parade, as low-cost entertainment, 325
Bird clubs, adopting from, 249
Birthday parties
    game for, <u>329</u>
    invitations for, 329–30
Biscuits, cutting shortening into, 166

Bites, insect, home remedies for, 274–75, 277
Blade cover, for saw, <u>148</u>
Bloodstains, on clothing, 231
Blouses
    repairing burns on, 228
    restyling, 225
Blush, bargain replacement for, 285
Board games
    for family game night, 323
    replacement pieces for, 240–41, 324
Boating equipment, buying, 239
Bonuses, saving money from, 76
Books
    as charitable donation, 64
    saving money on, 47–48, 325
    on tape, from library, 259
Boots, polishing, <u>222</u>
Bottles, for window treatments, 134–35
Boxes
    gift, decorating, 359
    moving, breaking down, 356
    treasure, <u>265</u>, 355
Brakes
    protecting, 207
    replacing, 206
Breed rescue groups, for pet adoption, 247
Bridal shower favors, 336
Bridesmaid's dresses, donating, <u>224</u>
Brown sugar, homemade, <u>169</u>
Bruises, home remedy for, 275
Brunches, special touches for, <u>167</u>
Budgeting
    as key to frugality, 11–12
    reasons for, 19
    receipt storage for, 23–24, <u>23</u>, **24**
    by tracking and planning spending, 20–23, <u>21</u>
Bulbs, flower, as gift, <u>357</u>
Bulbs, light
    cleaning, for energy savings, 100–101
    economical choice of, <u>96</u>
Bulk buying
    evaluating savings from, 21
    of foods, 155
Burglaries, preventing, 106–8

scratching post for, 254
toys for, 253–54
CD player, used, buying, 178–79
CDs. *See* Certificates of deposit (CDs);
    Compact discs (CDs)
Ceiling fans, cleaning, <u>178</u>
Centerpieces
    Christmas, 340, 343
    party, 334
    Thanksgiving, 350, 352–53
Cereal, saving money on, 156
Certificates of deposit (CDs), <u>48</u>, 73–74
Chairs
    as baby gifts, 357–58
    upholstered
      buying, 115
      care and maintenance of, 119–20
Change
    converting to cash, 74–75
    saving, <u>51</u>, <u>74</u>
Charitable donations
    expenditures not qualifying as, <u>63</u>
    inherited property, <u>65</u>
    matching, for savings, 46
    noncash, fair market value of, 64–65
    tax savings from, 63–65
Checks, saving money on, 55–57
Chicken soup, homemade, 155
Child care
    as gift to new parents, 358
    saving money on
      with babysitting co-op, <u>258</u>
      with friends' services, 257
      by joining social group, 256
      with mother's helper, 257
Children
    babysitting for, 256–57, <u>258</u>, 358
    birthday party game for, <u>329</u>
    carpools for, 197
    clothing swaps for, 258–59
    college savings for, 78–80
    dining out with, 314
    entertaining, with
      books on tape, 259
      clubhouse, 261
      crafts, <u>257</u>, <u>262</u>, 264, **264**, <u>267</u>

flowers, 259
    games, 260, 261, 262–64, 265–66
    gardening, 264
    indoor picnic, 262
    puppets, 263
    slumber party, 262
    summer activities, <u>260</u>
    toys, 258, 259, 260–61, 266, <u>266</u>, 267,
      <u>267</u>
    treasure box, <u>265</u>
    videos, 259, 266
    food shopping with, 156
    helping with budgeting, 22
    library as resource for, 259, 262, 267
    moneymaking projects for, <u>73</u>
    money saved by, 75
    recycled equipment for, 267
    saving money for, <u>48</u>, 72
    ski equipment for, 237
    sports footwear for, 236
Chimney, insulating gaps around, 100
Chlorine, discoloring hair, 290
Chocolates, hand-dipped, 168
Chores, paying yourself for, <u>52</u>
Christmas cards, decorations made from,
    <u>339</u>, 345
Christmas clubs
    joining, 53
    for paying off financing deals, 41–42
Christmas cookies, cookie swap for, 345
Christmas decorations
    candleholders, 341
    centerpieces, 340, 343
    dough ornaments, 340
    greens, 338
    natural, 338–39
    paper chains, <u>339</u>
    switch plates, 341
    trees (*see* Christmas trees)
    votive candles, 341–43
Christmas gifts
    homemade, avoiding unnecessary
      supplies for, <u>36</u>
    saving money on, 44
    tree ornaments as, <u>38</u>
Christmas invitations, 344–45

E

Earache, after swimming, home remedy for, 275
Early-bird specials, in restaurants, 314
Easter decorations, 347–49, 347
Eggs
    Easter, 347, 348–49
    Mediterranean-style, 167
Egg stains, on clothing, 231
Electricity costs, saving money on, 100–102
Electronics. *See also specific electronic equipment*
    cleaning on/off switch of, 174–75
    shopping for, 177–79
Embroidery thread, organizing, 242
Energy audit, for locating heating and cooling leaks, 100
Entertainment
    at-home
        bicycle parade, 325
        books, 325
        dining, 315–16
        games, 323–25
        music, 315, 322–23, 323
    for children
        books on tape, 259
        clubhouse, 261
        crafts, 257, 262, 264, **264**, 267
        flowers, 259
        games, 260, 261, 262–64, 265–66
        gardening, 264
        indoor picnic, 262
        puppets, 263
        slumber party, 262
        summer activities, 260
        toys, 258, 259, 260–61, 266, 266, 267, 267
        treasure box, 265
        videos, 259, 266
    for college students, 78
    out-of-home
        cultural attractions, 318–21
        dining out, 314–15, 324
        discounts for, 317, 319
        group activities, 321–22
        sporting events, 317–18
        walking tours, 322
    party
        birthday, 329
        centerpieces for, 334
        cooking, 158
        favors for, 336
        garnishes for, 333–34, 335
        Halloween, 354
        invitations for, 329–31
        New Year's Eve, 346
        place cards for, 335–36
        progressive Christmas, 345–46
        serving ideas for, 331–33, **331**
        tablecloth for, 335
        thank-you notes after, 330
        themes for, 327–29
        Valentine's Day, 347
Envelopes, uses for, 70–71, 187, 190–91
Escrow account, for tax payments, 40–41
Exercise, paying yourself for, 49
Expenses, tracking and planning, 20–23, 21
Eyeglasses, saving money on, 279–80
Eye puffiness, reducing, 289

F

Fabrics, high-quality, 233
Facecloth, homemade, 285
Facial
    homemade mask for, 292
    steam bath for, 290–91
Fact checking, for extra income, 90
Factory tours, during vacations, 368
Fans, ceiling, cleaning, 178
Favors
    Easter, 347–48, 349
    party, 336
    Thanksgiving, 351
    wedding, 87–88
Fertilizers, 137, 139–40
Financial advisors, caution about, 33
Financing deals
    avoiding, 40
    saving money for, 41–42
    when to use, 42

Fruit
  as centerpiece, 334
  dried, for Thanksgiving decorations,
    353
  pick-your-own, 151
  saving money on, 157
  storing, 154
Fruit juice stains, on clothing, 230
Fruit vines, supporting, 147–48
Funeral arrangements
  casket selection, 300, 302
  comparing costs of, 299, 301
  cremation, 303–4
  donation to medical science as
    alternative to, 304
  help with, 300–301
  negotiating cost of, 299
  prepaid, 299–300
  selecting funeral home for, 299, 301
  for veterans, 302–3
Funeral home
  selecting, 299, 301
  working for, 85–86
Furnace
  cleaning, 99
  when to turn off, 98–99
Furniture
  antique, buying, 115–17
  budget for, 109
  delivery charge on
    lowering, 113–14
    refunded, 113
  deposit on, 111
  floor sample, 111
  joints of, 113
  layaway plan for, 111
  measuring for, 109, 110
  outdoor, 121
  rent-to-own, avoiding, 111
  secondhand, buying, 115–16, 116
  selecting, 122
  shelves, 114
  upholstered
    buying, 115
    care and maintenance of, 119–20
  warranties on, 112

wood
  coating drawer guides and rails on, 118
  durability of, 112
  heat affecting, 119
  humidity affecting, 117–18
  from lumberyards, 114–15
  moving, 119
  removing blemishes from, 112, 117,
    118
  sunlight bleaching, 118
  table leaves, 119

G

Games
  birthday party, 329
  board
    for family game night, 323
    replacement pieces for, 240–41, 324
  card, 323, 324–25
  for entertaining children, 260, 261,
    262–64, 266
  minor league baseball, 317
  organizing ideas for, 261
Garage sales
  attracting customers to, 83, 84–85
  selling tactics for, 85
Garden(ing)
  for children, 264
  Cooperative Extension Service
    information on, 158
  designing, 138–39
  for extra income, 92
  fertilizing, 139–40
  low-cost plants for, 138
  pest control for, 141–43, 147
  protecting, from dogs, 142
  seedlings for, 146
  soil care for, 139–41
  supporting fruit vines in, 147–48
  vegetable
    color in, 138
    planting straight rows in, 145–46
    supports for, 147
    tomatoes in, 146–47, 148
  watering, 139

Gardening clubs, forming, 139
Garden planner, 138–39
Garden tools
    broken handles on, 146, 147
    care of, 144–45
Garnishes, food, 333–34, *335*
Gasoline
    choosing grade of, 218–19
    saving money on, *195*, 200–204
Gas station stores, avoiding purchases at, 36
Gastrointestinal problems, from travel, 277–78
Ghosts, for Halloween decorations, 349, **349**
Gift bags, homemade, 358
Gift baskets, themes for, *342*
Gift box, decorating, 359
Gifts
    baby, 357–58
    Christmas
        homemade, *36*
        saving money on, 44
        tree ornament as, *38*
    food, packing, for shipping, *344*
    housewarming, 355–57
    miscellaneous
        antique linens, 355
        flower bulbs, *357*
        homemade dinner, 354
        music posters, 354
        photo scrapbooks, 353–54
        treasure boxes, 355
    money, saving, 53
    wedding, *352*, 356–57
Gift wrap
    alternatives to, 358–59, *359*
    economical, *340*
Ginger
    peeling, 168
    for tea, 168
Glasses, saving money on, 279–80
Gloves
    baseball, conditioning, *245*
    hockey, repalming, 243–44

Goals, for long-term savings projects, 69–70, 71–72
Goldfish, as low-cost pet, 246, *250*
Golf equipment
    balls, *239*
    buying, 233, 238
    maintaining, 245
Golf lessons, inexpensive, 240
Gourds, for Thanksgiving decorations, 353
Gourmet dinner clubs, 315–16
Grass, growing, 141
Greeting cards
    saving money on, 49–50
    writing, 91–92
Gretzky, Wayne, *242*
Groceries
    creating space for, 156–57
    excess, cooking party for using, 158
    as housewarming gift, 355–56
    spoilage of, avoiding, 158–59
Grocery list
    eliminating items from, *153*
    preparing, 151
Grocery shopping, saving money on
    by avoiding junk food, 154–55
    by avoiding non-food services, 153
    in baby goods department, 154
    with bulk buying, 155
    by buying in season, 157
    cereal purchases, 156
    with coupons, 159
    in deli department, 154
    at food co-op, *152*
    by making own soup, 155
    with meatless meals, 150
    milk purchases, 155
    with price comparisons, 156
    with recipe substitutions, 150
    setting goal for, 149–50
    with shopping list, 151
    by shopping store perimeter, 152
    when shopping with children, 156
    by stocking sale items, 152, 153, 156–57
    strategies for, *157*
    by verifying price scanner, 153
    with well-stocked pantry, 150

Grooming, pet, 249–50, 251
Gyms. *See* Fitness centers
Gynecologic exam, saving money on, 280

H

Hair
  chlorine discoloring, 290
  lip, bleaching, 290
Hairstyling, for extra income, 85–86
Halloween
  decorations for, 349–50, **349**
  punch for, 354
  recycling costumes for, 263
Halogen lamps, 96
Headaches, home remedies for, 269, 274
Headphones, repairing, 175, **175**
Headstones, for veterans, 303
Health care
  home remedies, for
    arthritis, 270
    burns, 271–74
    colds, 270–71, 282
    corns, 269
    headaches, 269, 274
    hot flashes, 271
    insect bites, 274–75, 277
    menstrual cramps, 269–70
    minor accidents, 275–76
    poison ivy, 276
    stomach upset, 269
    swimmer's ear, 275
    traveler's illnesses, 276–78
    warts, 269
  saving money on
    by college students, 78
    for doctor's visits, 280–83
    for glasses, 279–80
    for medications, 278–79, 281
    by understanding hospital bills, 272
Health clubs. *See* Fitness centers
Heat exhaustion, vinegar for, 277
Heating costs, saving money on, 99–100
Heating leaks, insulation for, 100–101

Herbs
  for centerpiece, 334
  for herbal cheese, 163
  as party favor, 336
Hobbies. *See also* Crafts
  group entertainment from, 321, 322
  high-quality materials for, 233
  inexpensive supplies for, 232, 233–35
  low-cost courses on, 240
Hockey equipment
  gloves, 243–44
  shin guards, 244
  skates
    care of, 243, 243
    for children, 236
  used, buying, 233, 236–37
Home business, tax savings for, 67–68
Home equity loans, when to avoid, 31
Home office
  discounted supplies for, 184–87
  organizing, 185, 190–93
  postage savings for, 187–88
  troubleshooting for, 188–89
Homeopathy, for pets, 250–51
Home remedies
  for treating
    arthritis, 270
    bruises, 275
    burns, 271–74
    colds, 270–71, 282
    corns, 269
    headaches, 269
    hot flashes, 271
    insect bites, 274–75, 277
    menstrual cramps, 269–70
    poison ivy, 276, 277
    sore throat, 270, 277
    sprains, 276, **276**
    stomach upset, 269
    sunburn, 273–74, 277
    swimmer's ear, 275
    traveler's illnesses, 276–78
    warts, 269
  vinegar as, 277

K

Kayak, buying, 239
Kebabs, cooking, 171
Key, spare auto, 219
Keyboard, computer, cleaning, 180–81
Knitting needles
  cleaning, 242–43
  holder for, 235
Knives, buying, 162

L

Lamps, electricity savings from, 100–101
Lamp shade
  decorating with, 135
  re-covering, 131
Landscaping ideas, 138. *See also*
    Garden(ing)
Lasagna noodles, 161
Lawn care, 140, 141
Lawn mower care, 143–44, 148
Lawsuits
  considerations before filing, 308
  handling, 302, 305
Lawyer(s)
  for divorce settlements, 297–98
  fees of, 306–7
  free, 309
  hiring, 304–6
  vs. mediator, 297–99, 308–9
  references for, 306
  self as, 307–8
  specialty, 304–5
Leaks
  heating and cooling, 99–100
  plumbing, 103–5, 103
Leftovers, uses for, 168–69
Lemons, as garnish, 333
Library
  book sales at, 325
  for children's entertainment, 259, 262,
    267
Light bulbs
  cleaning, for electricity savings, 100–101
  economical choice of, 96

Lighting
  decorating with, 123, 135
  recessed, insulating gaps around, 100
Linens, antique, as gift, 355
Linings, clothing, 221
Lip hair, bleaching, 290
Lips, chapped, from dehydration, 276–77
Lipstick
  bargain replacement for, 285
  extending life of, 287
Living within your means, as key to
    frugality, 14–15
Loans
  home equity, when to avoid, 31
  mortgage, reviewing ability to pay, 26
Lotion, extending life of, 288
Lumberyards, wooden furniture from,
    114–15

M

Magazines
  artwork from, 132–33
  holder for, 192, **192**
  subscriptions to, 50
Mailer, padded, making, 188
Mailing lists, removing name from, 37
Malls, avoiding, to curb impulse buying, 38
Maps, as artwork, 133–34
Marble slabs, uses for, 120
Margarine, baking with, 171
Mascara, extending life of, 288
Massage techniques, 293
Mass transit, discounted, 195–96
Meal preparation
  avoiding mistakes in, 169–71
  brunches, 167
  desserts, 166–68
  knives for, 162
  with leftovers, 168–69
  planning, 151
  recipe substitutions for, 150
  shopping for, 150–51
  shortcuts for, 164–66
  slow cooker for, 162–63
  stocking foods for, 150

Meat(s)
   reducing expense of, 150, 152
   stew, browning, 171
Meatballs, with cranberry sauce, 168
Medals, as artwork, 134
Mediator
   for divorce settlements, 297–99
   for legal disputes, 308–9
Medical care. *See* Health care
Medical visits, saving money on
   by collecting research information, 283
   with free health services, 283
   by not changing doctors, 281–82
   with phone consultations, 280–81
   by seeing nurse, 280, 281
   when seeing specialists, 282–83
   by using clinics, 280
Medications, saving money on, 278–79,
   281
Menstrual cramps, home remedies for,
   269–70
Microwave oven, cleaning, 179
Mileage, used for charitable donations, 65
Milk, powdered, for cooking and baking,
   155
Mirrors, decorating with, 135
Model railroad club, in Moscow, 234
Moisturizers, for dry skin, 286–87
Mortgage
   deductible interest on, 67
   reviewing ability to pay, 26
Mosquito bites, home remedy for, 274–75
Motion sickness, from air travel, 278
Mountaineering equipment, buying, 238
Moving sales, buying furniture at, 115–16
Mud bath, homemade, 292–93
Mulch, newspaper as, 140–41
Museums
   county, 366–67
   saving on admissions to, 318, 368
Music, saving money on, 320, 322–23, 323
Musical performances, saving money on,
   315, 319–21, 369
Music posters, as gifts, 354
Mutual funds, combining savings for,
   73–74

N

Nail polish, extending life of, 288
Needlecraft
   holder for, 235
   ironing, 241
   maintaining gear for, 241–43
Needles
   knitting, cleaning, 242–43
   needlecraft, protecting, 241
Newspaper subscriptions, saving money
   from, 50
New Year's Eve party, 346

O

Oatmeal, as cereal alternative, 156
Office, home
   discounted supplies for, 184–87
   organizing, 185, 190–93
   postage savings for, 187–88
   troubleshooting for, 188–89
Office supplies
   saving money on, 184–87
   storing, 186
Omelette, baked, 165–66
Online banking, advantages of, 60
Ornaments, Christmas tree
   for bowl arrangement, 343
   as collectibles, 343
   as gifts, 38
   made from dough, 340
Outdoor furniture, care and maintenance
   of, 121

P

Paint
   acrylic, preventing drying of, 235
   decorating with, 135
   mistinted, 130
Paintbrushes
   cleaning, 233
   homemade, 233, **233**
   preventing paint drying on, 234–35
   storing, 243

Paint stains, on clothing, 230–31
Paint thinner, reusing, 233
Pallbearer, working as, for extra income, 90–91
Pancakes, baked, 164–65
Pans
   baking
      for heart-shaped cake, **327**
      to prevent burning, 170–71
   cleaning, 169–70
Paper clips, substitute for, _190_
Paper dolls, homemade, 260–61
Paper shredder, _189_
Parties
   birthday, 329–30, _329_
   centerpieces for, 334
   cooking, 158
   favors for, 336
   garnishes for, 333–34, _335_
   Halloween, _354_
   invitations for, 329–31
   New Year's Eve, 346
   place cards for, 335–36
   progressive Christmas, 345–46
   serving ideas for, 331–33, **331**
   tablecloth for, 335
   thank-you notes after, 330
   themes for, 327–29
   Valentine's Day, 347
Party planning, for extra income, 88–89
Pasta, cooking large batches of, 164
Pastry, cutting shortening into, 166
Patches, clothing, 225–27
Pen and pencil holders, 191–92, 193
Peppers, serving food in, 332–33
Perennials, winter protection for, 141
Personal trainer, finding, 295–96
Pest control, for garden, 141–43, _147_
Pets. _See also_ Cats; Dogs
   adopting, 247–49
   deodorizing, from skunk spray, 251
   discouraging misbehavior by, 254–55
   feeding, 251–53
   flea repellents for, 249–50
   goldfish as, 246, _250_
   grooming, 249–50, 251

homeopathic care for, 250–51
   insurance for, _248_
   toys for, 253–54
   traveling with, _255_
Phone, hands-free, 163
Phone bills, saving money from, 52
Photo arrangements, as gifts, 353–54, 357
Pickpockets, avoiding, _362_
Picture frames
   decorating, _127_
   discounted custom, 129
   distressing, 130
   for stretched-canvas paintings, 129, **129**
Pie, crustless apple, 166–67
Pie dough, cutting shortening into, 166
Piggy bank, making, 52
Pipe insulation, 97, 99–100
Pipes, locating leaks in, 103–5
Place cards
   for party, 335–36
   for Thanksgiving, 350
Place mats, for Thanksgiving, 350–51
Plants
   as gifts, 356, _357_
   low-cost, 138
   protecting windowsill from, 135–36
Play-Doh, imitation, _267_
Plumbing
   do-it-yourself, 103–5
   insulation around, 99–100
Poison ivy, home remedies for, 276, _277_
Pollen stains, on clothing, 231
Postage. _See also_ Stamps
   saving money on, 187–88, 330–31
Postcards, for invitations, 330–31
Posters, music, as gifts, 354
Pots and pans, cleaning, 169–70
Poultry, reducing expense of, 150
Prescriptions, saving money on, 278–79, 281
Produce, saving money on, 152, 157
Psychology, of saving for large expenses, 69–72
Pudding, caramel, 166
Pumpkin, for Thanksgiving decorations, 352

Punch, Halloween, <u>354</u>
Puppets, homemade, 263
Puzzles, for home entertainment, 325
Pyramid scams, 92

Q

Quiche, rice crust for, 169
Quilts, maintaining, 241–42, <u>241</u>

R

Radio, covering, 182
Rafting trips, discounts for, 367
Rainwater, uses for, 96, <u>139</u>
Rake, broken
  repairing, 148
  uses for, 146
Rebates, vs. discounts, <u>66</u>
Receipts, storing, 23–24, <u>23</u>, **24,** 68, **68**
Receipt spindle, making, <u>23</u>
Recipes, substitute ingredients for, 150,
    165
Refrigerator, increasing efficiency of, 102
Refunds, tax, saving, 50–51
Reimbursements, business, saving, 50
Relaxation, activities for, <u>288</u>, <u>291</u>
Repairs
  air conditioner, <u>173</u>
  auto, 204–7, 215–19
  clothing, 225–27, 228–29
  dishwasher, 102–3
  door, 106
  drawer, <u>107</u>
  paying yourself for, 49
  plumbing, 103–5, <u>103</u>
Research, for extra income, 90
Restaurant dining. *See* Dining out
Retirement funds, IRA. *See* Individual
    retirement accounts (IRAs)
Rewards, for saving money, 71–72
Ribbon, storing, 242
Rice, for quiche crust, 169
Rock-climbing equipment, buying, 238
Roosevelt, Theodore, <u>296</u>
Rope jumping, for fitness, 294–95

Rust stains
  on clothing, 230
  on outdoor furniture, 121

S

Salary, saving money from, 76–77
Salespeople, handling, <u>41</u>
Salons, at trade schools, <u>292</u>
Salsa, homemade, <u>170</u>
Sand, homemade colored, <u>257</u>
Sandwich boards, for advertising, 83–84,
    84, 85
Savings accounts
  closing old ones, 53
  direct deposits to, 71, 72
  redirecting money to, 71, 72
Savings projects, long-term, setting goals
    for, 69–70, 71–72
Saw, blade cover for, <u>148</u>
Scams, pyramid, 92
Scanners, price accuracy of, 153
Schmidt, Milt, <u>244</u>
Scratches, on wooden furniture, 117, <u>118</u>
Scratching post, for cats, 254
Screen door, patching, 106
Seedling containers, 146
Seed packets, as artwork, 132
Seeds
  as party favors, 336
  planting, 147
Seeing Eye dogs, as pets, 247–48
Serving ideas, for parties, 331–33, **331**
Shelves
  decorating, 124, **124**
  making, 124–25
  plywood, <u>114</u>
Shin guards, hockey, <u>244</u>
Shirts, restyling, 225
Shish kebabs, cooking, 171
Shoes, sports
  for children, 236
  from factory outlets, 235–36
Shopping list
  eliminating items from, <u>153</u>
  preparing, 151

Shots, saving money on, 281, 283
Shovel
    broken, repairing, 148
    protecting handle of, 144
Shower, bridal, favors for, 336
Signs, advertising, 82–84, **82, 84**
Skates, hockey
    care of, 243, <u>243</u>
    for children, 236
Ski equipment
    buying, 237–38
    for children, 237
Skin, dry, moisturizing, 286–87
Skin care
    homemade products for, 289, 291–93
    steam bath for, 290–91
Skunk spray, deodorizing, 251
Slipcovers, decorating with, 123
Slow cooker, uses for, 162–63
Sneakers, from factory outlets, 235–36
Socks
    darning, <u>226</u>
    whitening, 230
Sofas, upholstered
    buying, 115
    care and maintenance of, 119–20
Soil
    eggshells for aerating, 141
    newspaper for mulching, 140–41
    sifter for, 146
    testing, 140, <u>158</u>
Sore throat, home remedies for, 270,
    <u>277</u>
Soup, homemade, 155
Souvenirs, saving money on, 371
Spaghetti, leftover, uses for, 169
Spa treatments, do-it-yourself, 290–93
Specialists, medical, saving money on,
    282–83
Spending, tracking and planning, 20–23,
    21
Spiderwebs, for Halloween decorations,
    349–50
Splint, homemade, 276, **276**
Sporting events, saving money on, 317–18
Sports camps, lowering price of, 240

Sports equipment
    baseball, maintaining, 245, <u>245</u>
    basketball, buying, 239
    bicycle, buying, 238, 239
    boating, buying, 239
    camping, maintaining, 244–45
    fishing
        buying, 239
        maintaining, 244
    footwear, buying, 235–36
    golf
        buying, 238
        maintaining, 245
    hockey
        buying, 236–37
        maintaining, 243–44
    mountaineering, buying, 238
    rock-climbing, buying, 238
    skiing, buying, 237–38
Sports lessons, inexpensive, 240
Sprains, splinting, 276, **276**
Stained glass, as window treatment, 134, **134**
Stain removal
    on clothing, 223, 229–31
    on quilts, 241–42
Stamps. *See also* Postage
    dispenser for, 193, **193**
    removing, 188
Steam bath, facial, 290–91
Stereo equipment
    organizing wires from, 180
    replacement parts for, 175
Stings, bee, home remedies for, 274–75
Stomach upset, home remedy for, 269
Storytelling, for extra income, 90
Stress, activities relieving, <u>288</u>, <u>291</u>
Subscriptions, saving money from, 50
Sugar
    brown, homemade, <u>169</u>
    vanilla-flavored, <u>167</u>
Sunburn, home remedies for, 273–74, <u>277</u>
Sun-dried tomatoes, homemade, 164
Supermarkets
    comparing prices at, 156
    grocery shopping at (*see* Grocery
        shopping, saving money on)

W

Walking tours, 322, 367
Wall treatments, for decorating, 130–34
Warranties
    auto, 205, 212
    furniture, 112
Warts, home remedy for, 269
Washing machine, saving money
        operating, 95–96, 97
Water
    rain, uses for, 96, _139_
    used, miscellaneous uses for, _99_, _139_
Water bed, heating, 99
Watercolor brushes, storing, 243
Water costs, saving money on, 95–99
    from dishwasher, 95–96
    with furnace shutoff, 98–99
    with pipe insulation, 97
    from washing machine, 95–96, 97
    from water heater, 97–98
Water heaters
    insulating blanket for, 97–98
    reducing temperature on, 98
Water leaks
    cost of, 103
    locating, 103–5
    in toilet, 103, _103_
Web sites, financial advice on, 33
Wedding dresses, 227
Wedding gifts, _352_, 356–57
Weddings
    favors for, 87–88
    invitations for, 329
    sponsors for, _79_
Wedding services, for extra income, 87–88
Weight lifting, low-cost equipment for,
        295

Weight loss, paying yourself for, 49
Whipped cream, as coffee topping, _167_
Whiteflies, repelling, 143
Whitewater rafting, discounts for, 367
Wills, preparing, 309
Window treatments
    colored bottles as, 134–35
    stained glass, 134, **134**
    Thanksgiving, 351–52
    tiles for, 135–36
Windshield wipers, replacing, 216
Wires, electrical, organizing, 180
Wood blemishes, removing, from
        furniture, _112_, 117, _118_
Worm farming, for extra income, _91_
Wrapping paper
    alternatives to, 358–59, _359_
    economical, _340_
Writing, for greeting card companies,
        91–92

Y

Yard sales
    attracting customers to, _83_, 84–85
    selling tactics for, 85
Yarn
    high-quality, _233_
    storing, 242
Yeast infections, vinegar for, _277_

Z

Zippers
    repairing, 228, **228**
    as sign of clothing quality, 222
Zoo, saving money on, 318